W9-BTK-165

ALL HEART

MY STORY

MICHAEL PINBALL CLEMONS

HarperCollins*PublishersLtd*

ALL HEART
Copyright © 1999, 1998 by Michael Clemons.
All rights reserved. No part of this book may be used
or reproduced in any manner whatsoever without
prior written permission except in the case of brief
quotations embodied in reviews.

First published in hardcover by HarperCollins in 1998
First trade paper edition

HarperCollins books may be purchased for educational,
business, or sales promotional use through our Special
Markets Department.

HarperCollins Publishers Ltd
2 Bloor Street East, 20th Floor
Toronto, Ontario, Canada
M4W 1A8

www.harpercollins.ca

Action photographs of Pinball Clemons by John
Sokolowski, courtesy of the Toronto Argonauts
Football Club.

Queries related to personal appearances by
Michael Pinball Clemons should be directed to:
Pro Image Marketing,
1210 Sheppard Avenue East, Suite 701,
Toronto, Ontario, Canada
M2K 1E3 Tel: 416 491-9333 Fax: 416 494-5552

Canadian Cataloguing in Publication Data

Clemons, Michael, 1965–
All heart: my story

ISBN 0-00-638622-9

1. Clemons, Michael, 1965– .
2. Football players – Canada – Biography
I. Title.

GV939.C53A3 1999   796.335'092
C99-930457-7

TC 9 8 7 6 5 4 3 2

Printed and bound in Canada

To my wife, Diane, and our daughters Rachel and Raven, with love.

To my mother, my true hero.

To my Lord and Redeemer: "Ask where the good way is, and walk in it, and you will find rest for your souls." – Jeremiah 6:16

ACKNOWLEDGEMENTS

I would like to thank my friends Lloyd Exeter and Doran Major of Pro Image Marketing Inc. for planting the seed of this book and seeing it through to its harvest. Thanks also to Shirley Forde for the cookies and brownies. And, lest I forget, the Toronto Argonauts, for giving me a podium to express my God-given talents—for giving me a chance.

1

1965 – 1978

The first thing I remember is the house we lived in, on Palmetto Street in Dunedin, Florida. It was a wooden structure, semi-detached in a rather peculiar way, and falling down around the edges. The family next door to us were the Browns — Mr. George, Miss Claritha, and their eight kids. The three boys — Ernest, Nate, and Dimitri — watched over me like a little brother. Thelma, one of the older sisters, drew baby-sitting duty. She was cute as could be, and my very first crush. But that was later on, after we'd moved to The Projects.

My mother was eighteen years old when I was born. Her maiden name was Anna O'Neal. She was the queen of Pinellas High in Clearwater, the next town down the road. It was a segregated school; in that time and place, blacks sat at the back of the bus and drank from "colored" water fountains. Willy James Clemons, my father, was attending Florida A&M University. He'd arrived at Pinellas High as an assistant teacher during his final semester. Mom was the sweetheart of the prom, attractive and impressionable; he was the oldest young guy around, polished and educated. That's when I was conceived.

They never married, and he was seldom on the scene; he lived in Bradenton, about an hour's drive away from Dunedin. Mom had wanted to be a nurse, but she started working as a receptionist for the City of Dunedin shortly after I was born. She still works for the city, as the superintendent of the utility billings program — the first black ever to rise to an administrative position.

I was born on January 15, 1965, and baptized Michael Lutrell Clemons. My godfather, Hilario Rojas, for reasons known only to himself, declared that Lutrell would be a good first name, but he was outvoted. Hilario was a scout for the Philadelphia Phillies, and had settled in Clearwater (where the team trained) with his wife Bennie Mae, who'd taken Mom under her wing.

People ask me how many brothers and sisters I have, but that's an essay question. My mom would eventually marry when I was four-teen, and my sister Kelli came along a year later. My stepfather had two kids already, and neither he nor mom was planning on any addi-tions. Meanwhile, my dad had married a woman with five kids. They had two more together, a girl and a boy, but in between, he jumped the fence and had another boy, whom I didn't meet until he was eigh-teen. Later he remarried a lady with one child, and they've had yet another son. So there we have it: the modern-day hyper-extended family. I usually say I grew up with one kid sister — Kelli — which is quite true, and helps to speed the story along.

My grandmother had died when Mom was five, and my great-grandmother had passed away before that. But my great-great-grand-mother, Annie Sinclair, was still alive, and came to live with us in that little house. She was then in her late seventies, and blind, so Mom had to look after both of us. She had a very distinctive call, like a bird. She'd call me twice: "Mich-ael? Mich-ael!" — up on the last syllable the first time, then down on the repetition, sharper and clipped. I'd try to ignore her, but there was no escape. Everyone recognized that call, and they'd say, "Go see what your grandmother wants," so I'd have to obey.

I used to have to go to the store for her, to get her supply of chewable laxatives. One day I ate one. It tasted good, but suddenly it began to work as advertised. This was the first of two negative experiences associated with Palmetto Street.

Another time, I'd heard somebody swearing, and I was determined to give it a try. I went out onto the back porch and offered up every curse word you could imagine. Miss Claritha couldn't believe her ears, because I was a pretty mannerable kid. But she spread the news, and when Mom returned, she made me regret swearing like I did. What hurt me the most was that I'd disappointed her. I was no dummy; I knew that what I'd said was wrong. I also knew that Mom was a believer in reprimanding with a backhand.

But I wasn't always getting knocked from pillar to post. Our house was full of love and understanding — just as my days were mostly filled with play. Down at the end of our street was Head Start, a preschool you attended when you were five years old. That was our basketball court of choice, along with the one at the Saturday School, a recreation center. I remember making my first basket — going at it and going at it, trying to get the ball up there until it finally went through the hoop. This was a real red-letter day, a huge victory and a valuable lesson.

At this time, Dunedin was considered very much off the beaten track. Nobody thought of it as a suburb of St. Petersburg. It was just one of several small towns that stretched along the Gulf of Mexico, separated by woods and open fields. You barely knew when you left it and crossed into Clearwater or Largo. The main street turned into Highway 580, and even that was still only two lanes wide. The whole feeling was kind of rural and undeveloped, very much unaffected by the world outside.

Within that small town, we lived inside a sort of reassuring little box — a grid of streets connected by alleyways and unpaved lanes.

Our neighborhood was overwhelmingly black. Any white family tended to be transient. One might stay for a while, but then they'd go away again. Everybody knew each other by name; everything was homey and predictable. Survival wasn't the issue — it wasn't like Chicago, where you feared to set foot out the door. Temptations were few, and didn't affect me at all. We had guys who smoked and sold marijuana, though they never attempted to recruit the younger kids. Besides, I shudder to think what Mom would have done to me if I betrayed her teachings. I sank so low as to shoplift a couple of pieces of one-cent bubble gum, and pilfered oranges from Mr. Charlie Hart's tree, but that was about the extent of my lawlessness.

The most insidious pressure inside this little box was the poverty cycle. This was the biggest hurdle to overcome, because you couldn't envision what lay beyond it. You stayed in place — the place society assigned to you. This was the thinking within our community as well.

Most of our parents hadn't gone very far in school, so their fondest wish was that we'd keep out of trouble, get a Grade Twelve diploma, and settle down to a steady job. ("Just finish up, baby. Just hang in there. That will give you something to go on. Don't be like me.") There wasn't much need to excel in class, even if we had the ability. Many of us did, but we weren't supposed to be smart, so why bother? Some of us might enter the military, but not as a career path. We'd put in our time, and then come back where we'd started from, join a local firm, earn decent money, and get a little pension. This was the most that most of us could look forward to.

My mom had other plans in mind for me. From an early age, I knew that I was supposed to go on to something else. This was the goal, the end that she worked and saved for — even though how I'd get there was unclear for quite a while.

Our lives were rooted in the church — or more accurately, churches. The one Mom attended was part of the Baptist Union. It was large with strict protocols: the preacher spoke, followed by the deacon and the deaconesses. I might get a chance to usher, or to sing on Youth Sunday, but otherwise I didn't open my mouth. Miss Ruthamae Lewis was a lady who commanded all respect; you dared not even whisper within her hearing. There was a pianist, and a choir that could really sing gospel. The service itself was formal and structured, and I found this a little boring, but Mom expected me to accompany her — which I did, diligently — even though I preferred another church, run by Mama Jelly, also known as Mama Sara, last name Matthews. She lived across the street from us; she had a green thumb, a nice garden, and eight kids of her own. Her husband, Mr. Frank, was quite a bit older than she was. He was a man of few words, but they were well chosen. Their youngest son, Oral, was my best friend. He was heavyset — plump, but very strong. Like the Brown boys, he was my protector; he'd never let anyone hit me. Mr. Frank called him by his middle name. If he heard us playing outside, he'd cry, "Wesley! What in the ham fat chicken y'all doin' round there, boy, chuckin' them rocks!" This was his saying, and it seemed to suit every occasion.

Mama Sara's sister was Miss Alfonza Moore, but everybody called her Aunty — not Aunty Anything Else, just Aunty. She was the pastor of their church; she gave the message while Mama Sara acted as musical director. I liked to go there because Sunday School got out early, at eleven o'clock.

The main service was also far more to my taste. The church was too small to have an official designation; you went there to read the Bible and praise God. It filled up rapidly — twenty people made for a capacity crowd, but on many Sundays, twice that number would arrive. The doors would be propped open and the fans going full blast to circulate some air. Often bands would come; there'd be drums and guitars and tambourines — a lively setting. Everybody stood up and participated as they saw fit. People would say, "I'd like to thank God for being here this morning; for life, health, and strength; for taking me safely on the highways and byways of life." I remember these things very clearly. It was all very basic and personal — tiny, cozy, and warm.

Have I given you a picture of these strong black women, holding the neighborhood together? This was true; the ladies took control. They were there for their own kids and everybody else's. They had to be, because father figures were in short supply. This I believe is why so many black guys say, "Hi, Mom," to any older black woman they like and admire. Aunty and Mama Sara made my mom part of their family, and I thought of them in this way.

Aunty in particular was very patient, even-tempered, and genteel. She asked me to read the Bible to her, and I did this for hours on end. We'd talk about life, about what I might choose to do when I grew up. Mom provided the sustenance and drive; while she led by example every step of the way, Aunty gave me extra vision early on. She always told me that I'd leave Dunedin and be successful, that I would do great things. If somebody says that often enough, it starts to make some sort of impression, even if you're too young to know exactly what it means.

Around the time I was about to start Grade One at San Jose Elementary School, we moved two streets over, into The Projects. This seemed like a good idea at the time, because the house was on its last legs.

The Projects sounds uninviting. The houses certainly weren't what you'd call luxurious. The sewage treatment plant was just across the way. Even so, they were still on a human scale; they weren't a series of looming high-rises. We were still in the same old neighborhood — The Projects backed onto Aunty's lawn. There were five single-storey sections, built out of brick and concrete block. Each contained half a dozen units of various sizes. The people next door to us were now the Greens — Miss Flossie and her six kids, no husband and no visible means of support.

This is why I never felt poor, because compared with other folks, we weren't. Money was tight, because my great-great-grandmother was still with us, but in truth I lacked for nothing. Mom accomplished small miracles with her salary. Even in her difficult situation, she never took charity, never accepted a handout. Whenever Christmas baskets came, we'd pass them along to Miss Flossie, whose need was far greater.

When I first started school, Mom would design her day around me. She had her own car, so she'd drop me off each morning, then work through the lunch hour so that she could collect me in the afternoon. Later on, when I was trusted to go home by myself, she'd phone to make sure that I was busy with my assignments, and I'd always answer by the second ring.

School was easy for me; I didn't have to work abundantly hard. Often I'd wind up as the teacher's pet, a little black kid who did better than anticipated, and was polite in the bargain. In fact, I was well-mannered and obedient because I was scared stiff of what Mom would do if she got a call about my bad behavior. The teachers didn't know this, so they wrongly gave me the credit, which I took because I was quick-witted.

Math was my favorite subject. I enjoyed figuring stuff out, making sure it made sense. I was also one of the best spellers around; I could pronounce anything you put in front of me. But my comprehension was sometimes lacking, because my mind was elsewhere. I was far too active to read a lot, and when I did, it was either the Bible or a sports magazine. Still, I was ahead of most kids my age, and I knew it.

This was no big deal. I might have hinted that I was better than somebody else at a sport, but I'd never have felt superior because I was smarter. That's not what you're proud of at that age. We were little boys, and physical in nature; the mental part just happened to be there.

And there were times when I wouldn't hesitate to speak my mind, which got me into trouble. If I thought I was right, I'd argue the point to death — in the proper context, or so I thought. Sometimes matters escalated, but I was prepared. I was small but strong, lucky to have the frame of a gymnast, and I didn't mind fighting over an issue.

San Jose was a large school; kids were bussed in from Clearwater. The majority of kids were white; there weren't all that many kids of Spanish or Cuban descent. Some of them were rednecks pure and simple, and I was a little Robin Hood. I'd fight for someone else if I saw him get picked on. I always wanted to make friends with the guy who wasn't popular, who was sitting off by himself. I think that came from my mom.

By far the greatest number of fights hinged on the word "nigger." Once, when Mom was picking me up after school, a white kid called me "nigger." It made me mad, but I was going to let it pass. I told Mom what had happened, and she said, "Well, go get him." I caught up with him, and did what I thought was necessary.

The second time, a black kid made the same mistake. Although in a few years it became permissible, even cool, for blacks to say to each other, "What's up, my nigger?" and so forth, this kid said it in a mean, arrogant way. He was bigger than I was, but I started to beat him on the playground, and when they broke us up I beat him all the way down the hall to the principal's office.

The third and last time was when somebody had taken another kid's pen. I didn't have it on me, but I was in the wrong; I'd handled it as we passed it around. He urged me to give it back, but chose the wrong word for emphasis. So it was *bang!* One punch and blood was everywhere. After that, I calmed down and became a little less meddlesome. I exerted force only to prove a point, and I never picked fights with people I knew I *could* beat. I didn't go looking for trouble, but I wouldn't back down from a challenge, either.

*   *   *

I started playing football with the Dunedin Golden Eagles in the third grade. I was eight years old. It was my first love, my real passion. I got pretty good at it — the club retired my number when I was just eleven years old. This was the real thing — full pads, full contact. By the way, those pads didn't cost Mom any money. Parents paid a small registration fee, but all the equipment was laid on. That's so much better than it is here during the winter, when hockey gear can bankrupt a family as kids keep growing out of their skates.

In those days, most sports up until Grade Nine were organized outside the schools. Dunedin's youth football teams were known as PAL, the Police Athletic League, because the police sponsored and helped fund them. The great majority of the coaches were officers. Other towns and cities had different arrangements, but the age divisions were the same across the board. Eight-year-olds played on the Taxis, sometimes known as the Flyweights. When you were ten, you went up to the Mighty Mites. At age twelve, you were a Peewee; at thirteen, a Midget. When you turned fourteen, you became a freshman in high school and began to move through that system. Grades Nine and Ten were known as junior varsity, while Grades Eleven and Twelve were varsity. In elementary school, these divisions were only a guideline, because weight superseded age. The idea was to keep kids of the same size together; if you were heavy but young, you had to move up a category.

On Saturdays, the games would start in the early afternoon, and run straight on into the evening. We played in high school stadiums, which were as nice as or nicer than some of the university fields. The fields were real turf, and that smell still brings back memories. After you'd played, you'd take your shoulder pads off but leave the rest of your equipment on.

Sometimes we'd take a break to watch the action, but mostly we kept on going with a game of our own devising. It was called "Kill the Carrier," and was elegant in its simplicity. The ball was thrown up in the air, and somebody caught it. He started to run, heading for one of the end zones. There was nobody blocking for him, nobody else on his team — it was that player against the world. If he scored, he could come back the other way. If he got smeared, we'd throw the ball in the air again and start over. This went on for hours at a time. Some guys never wanted to be the carrier, but I did. It taught me a great deal of agility and toughness. If you were skilled, you could fake everybody out. Otherwise, you got into a lot of nasty pile-ups. Sometimes I got whacked pretty good, but I thrived on the game. I'd play with anybody, no matter what his size; I wasn't shy about contact at all.

On the other hand, I soon developed a certain knack for eluding tacklers. I was always the quickest laterally, though not necessarily in a straight line. I'd lose a foot race, but win on an obstacle course — particularly if the obstacles were other guys who wanted to mow me down. I had good moves; even from the time I was eight years old, some of the best moves I've made have been after I've been in the clutch. Even with someone hanging onto me, I've been able to keep my feet moving and bend my body to break a tackle. This is as important as avoiding a tackle in the first place. The real talent is to stay on your feet and keep moving forward, even after that initial hit.

My first coaches were knowledgeable and passionate about the game, and cared about what they did. They were excited for us and with us; they enjoyed our successes and shared our failures. They taught us the basics: keep your head up, square your shoulders when you tackle, hit below the numbers, take the proper pursuit angle, use your vision, believe in what you see. These things become part of you; they're the fundamentals that help you go on to the next level.

We also learned about fair play — the importance of never taunting the opposition. In one game, I had four touchdowns in five carries. The other team was plainly outmatched. On the fifth carry, I stepped out of bounds because we didn't want to run up the score. Then our coach took me out for the rest of the game. So we had solid individuals at the helm, who taught us about football and about life as well.

When it came to running, I was given free rein. The coaches would say, "I couldn't run that way when I was your age, and I can't now. So follow your instincts; I can't teach you how."

It was apparent to them and everybody else that I had unusual skills even then. Some of us are given a bit more to act upon. So my style was developed through trial and error, not through direct instruction. My most obvious ability was as an escape artist. At the same time, my understanding of football was ahead of my years. I watched it in an analytical way; I knew how to use time-outs; I plotted strategy on the sidelines and when I watched games on TV. I played every position at first, but settled on offence as a running back, and started to hone the skills I had. Everyone says you have to run north–south; the idea is to get down the field. But the whole nature, the very essence, of my game — from playing Kill the Carrier to the present day — is east–west. North–south is where I have to go, but east–west, my lateral movement, is my greatest ally, because there are guys who can catch up with me if I run straight ahead. I have good, though not outstanding, speed — in part because I never ran track. I never liked it, never had wanted to do it. Getting from point A to point B was never of consuming interest to me. If you want to get somewhere fast, take a car. If you want to get there really fast, take a plane. Mechanically and technically, I have no idea how to run. My running style is probably as bad as you can get. Nobody would want to imitate it; I'm all over the place. But it's too late to change now, so I've left well enough alone.

I had favorite players, of course. To me, O.J. was the man, which is why, when I was ten years old, and could choose my own number, I wore Simpson's 32. In every sport, there are players who are ahead of their time, who transcend the game and take it to another level. O.J. had that rare mix of size and skill. He was six feet two, well over two hundred pounds, and he could run the 100 as fast as anybody. Not only was he fast in a straight line, he was shifty in terms of cutting; his cuts were as crisp as those of someone five feet ten. He also redefined the game in terms of the cutback run.

Now, of course, there are lots of guys who possess size, strength and speed, all in one package. When I was growing up, this was rare. Simpson — and Gayle Sayers and Jim Brown before him — weren't content with fitting into a particular mold. Their size didn't limit them; they required the most of themselves, and with their unique physical talents, they transformed the game.

Mind you, I never actually tried to emulate O.J. or anybody else. For one thing, I was so small that there would have been no point. I had to arrive at a style of my own, so I made a virtue of necessity.

My mom supported me absolutely during my early football years and beyond. I think she missed only one game from Grade Three until high school graduation. Unlike a lot of parents, she let me be a field rat. I could hang around and watch until the final games were over, except when I was very young. But she was also a staunch disciplinarian, even while a game was in progress. Once, I was moping around the sidelines because the coach had momentarily taken me out. She came over, grabbed me by the face mask, and told me in no uncertain terms that if I didn't shape up, I'd never play again.

*   *   *

I started playing baseball, too, when I was young. Sometimes I was the only black kid in the entire league; this wasn't our fallback sport of choice. I started off in center field, but there weren't very many nine-year-old power hitters, so I became bored, and moved to second base. This became my natural position, although I subbed for everybody else, including pitcher and catcher. I had a great glove and a good throwing arm. My Achilles heel, though, was my hitting. I was instructed to take a lot of pitches, on the theory that I didn't present much of a strike zone. If I got on base, I was a threat to score. Stealing second became practically automatic; I don't know if I was ever thrown out.

I played on the same team as George and Mike Koutsourais, whose father, Manny, was the mayor of Dunedin. He and his wife used to help my mom out a great deal; they knew she was a single parent. Manny owned a drugstore, which stocked a little bit of everything. One day he took me there, and in his special fatherly way talked to me about my hitting. Then he led me to the area where the sporting goods were sold and gave me a new glove. I remember this as clear as if it were yesterday. I realize now that it was a part of the father–son relationship that I'd never had, a possibility I'd blocked out of my mind. This was my way of dealing with things; I didn't acknowledge them at all. Getting that glove and putting it on, being so proud that Mr. Koutsourais had thought enough of me to provide it, was really significant.

Through baseball, I met another guy named Roger Watt. We hit it off really well, because neither of us tried to be like the other. So many times, a guy from our neighborhood, eager to make friends, would try too hard to be white. Conversely, a white guy coming in would try to be black, talk black, listen to black music, whatever that is. Roger and I were just ourselves, and we found that some of those supposedly black and white things weren't so bad.

Mom was very particular about my spending the night away from home. If she let me sleep over, it was with someone she had a lot of respect for. She'd say, "This is why we have a house, you stay here, there's no need for this." But she was pleased to let me stay at the Watts'. One night, though, I frightened them half to death. At that age, I had a terrible problem, which lingers to some degree to this day. My nose would seize up, and my breathing would sound asthmatic, as if I were about to suffocate. Even today, my nose isn't up to snuff. Big as it is, it's not very practical. But as a kid, I'd breathe through my mouth all night long, which was very intimidating on sleepovers. The first night I stayed with the Watts, they thought something terrible was about to happen. The whole house stayed wide awake, wondering if they should call an ambulance (as I rested peacefully).

Roger's parents were German, and they introduced me to soccer. They took me to see the Tampa Bay Rowdies when the North American Soccer League was in existence. They hoped that it would become the next major sport, which didn't happen, but I began to play, in part because they were so enthusiastic. The games took place in open fields; there were no stands or bleachers. Our parents would pull their cars right up to the sidelines and sit in lawn chairs watching the action. Mrs. Watt always brought sliced oranges for us to eat at halftime.

At first, I outran people, but I couldn't control the ball. After some time, I did improve. The very first article ever written about me concerned my soccer "prowess." This must have been when I was eleven. The headline read: "Foes cringe when Michael Clemons does his thing." Whatever my thing might have been, I must have made some sort of impression.

From then on, soccer was twin-tracked with football, even though I felt it was almost un-American. You know what I mean: Canadians are supposed to play hockey, Americans are born and bred for the gridiron, but it suited my temperament at this time and I appreciated the change of pace. Soccer was laid-back, almost lackadaisical, compared with football. Warming up involved goofing around with the ball. You didn't run extremely hard, you saved that for the game. You didn't need a lot of equipment, so you never felt cumbersome. You didn't have to grunt and shout and get yourself all revved up. There weren't a whole lot of interruptions, which is why you had to be in good shape — you kept on running.

However, you didn't find the same sort of depths that you did in football. You didn't have to reach down and demand as much of yourself. You never felt in imminent danger of taking a hard hit. At worst, you'd be tripped or elbowed. You never got your head ripped off; you didn't get knocked down and then have to get back up and go back to the huddle, only to hear them call your number one more time.

In soccer, your number isn't really called. Things just unfold; the game is spontaneous. There's sort of a carefree, one-with-nature attitude; you're out there freewheeling in the open air. Soccer is less strategic, less regimented. You move rhythmically, rather than exerting all your strength and speed. You have more options; you make plays on the fly.

In contrast, football is much more methodical and intense. When you go, you go. You hit it — *boom!* — using everything you've got, every ounce of energy. Soccer is aerobic; football is anaerobic. Soccer is one long tremor; football is a series of explosions. So both appealed to me, for different reasons, and I kept on with both for many years.

Basketball was another story. My mentors here were Dimitri Brown, one of the many Browns who lived next door, and Bo Bryant, also known as Poppa or Bo-Pop — in our estimation, a far better player than Dr. J. (Julius Irving). We had all sorts of little leagues that came and went, depending on how organized we wanted to be on a given day. I was reasonably proficient, though I didn't know how to shoot. Then, when I learned how, I became a bad shooter. I'd devised my own technique: I'd shoot as if I were throwing a football, or doing the shotput. This worked, because once I scored 50 points in a game. My speed made me a force to be reckoned with. I'd steal the ball and dribble through the opposing team — you couldn't see me coming. Then, in the sixth or seventh grade, the coaches tried to make me change some of the natural ways I shot the ball, and I struggled with that. We always want to do the things that come naturally rather than the stuff we struggle with. Maybe that's why I like basketball today — I can appreciate how skilful the game is, and remember how difficult it was for me.

In Grade Eight, matters came to a head. The coach cut me, on the grounds that I was trying to be a show-off. He took exception to the fact that I was dribbling with my left hand without looking at the ball, which is the whole idea.

Just to jump ahead a bit, I played again in Grade Nine, but in Grade Ten I ran into trouble again. There was some talk about bringing me up to the varsity team because I led the team in most categories. Unfortunately, that included missed shots and turnovers. I'd go in for a lay-up but the ball would hit the backboard and bounce away — I did everything at a hundred miles an hour. During one game, the coach wouldn't start me, for no reason I could see. If he didn't think I was playing well, that would have been okay. But as bad as I was, I was still a good player. I sat out the entire first half, and he said nothing. At halftime, he announced the starters — still not a word. I took my uniform off, got dressed, and watched the rest of the game in street clothes.

This was the first and only time I'd ever quit anything. One of the assistant principals tried to talk me into going back, but I wanted to have fun, not cope with somebody else's mind games. I had to make a choice anyway, because basketball and soccer took place at the same time, so I gave up on the NBA and trained my sights on some far-off World Cup.

*   *   *

Meanwhile, life in The Projects took an unexpected turn. Mom had a new boyfriend — a sharp dresser, very slick, who worked in Clearwater. He was a machinist by trade, but he ran a general store, and operated a lawn-care business on the side. He'd use his income to finance all kinds of questionable ventures, none of which panned out. He was a hard worker, always up at the crack of dawn, but a feckless businessman. He never grasped the idea of a profit margin, never kept track of staff and materials. He'd pay out $2,000 over the course of a month and forget what had happened to it. At month's end, he'd receive $1,900 and think he had it made.

On the side he ran numbers, and I was his henchman. He knew that I could count money, so he'd drive up from Clearwater each evening with a cigar box full of it, along with a notepad on which he'd recorded all the bets. The numbers had to do with the results of the Daily Double at a greyhound racing track in Tampa Bay. My job was to go through the sheet, scratch out the misses, circle the hits, find out what the double was, multiply it by the hits, and put that money aside. Everything else was profit. I got five dollars for this — a whole lot of cash at the time, which went straight into general revenues.

It seems odd that my mom, a committed Christian, would have tolerated organized gambling under her roof. She was still very young then, and in a precarious position. She knew her boyfriend had his faults, but she liked him. He also looked more solid than anybody else on the horizon. It's hard to explain. When we moved to Clearwater, we met another lady, a spiritual mentor named Mama Jones. She was a strong Christian; she'd even witness in "the park," commanding respect from the toughest in the community who spent their days there. One day she said to me, "Boys are for the asking, and girls are for the saying no." But Mom said yes to her boyfriend, which was her decision to make. As for the numbers, there was a cultural acceptance of things that were borderline questionable, but not really bad. A guy who ran numbers and was gainfully employed was a whole lot better than a guy who had no prospects at all.

Mom wasn't worried about the numbers rubbing off, because I was getting plenty of guidance at home and elsewhere. Whenever I went to read the Bible to Aunty, we'd have long talks about the future. She said that sports would take me away, but that I'd become far more than an athlete.

I liked the sound of that, and we started talking about various professions. This was a bit of a reach. I don't believe that we'd ever gone to a black professional. All of the doctors, all of the lawyers were white. Yet the idea appealed to me; it was something to work toward. I clearly remember debating with Aunty the pros and cons of different lines of work. I said I didn't want to be a doctor, for fear of making somebody die because I'd done the wrong thing. Next came law. I decided I wouldn't want to defend people who should go to jail or, through my actions, send anyone there who was innocent. No, I was not suited for the legal arena. In search of something that involved fewer moral dilemmas, I conceived a desire to be a dentist. Michael Lutrell Clemons, DDS — that was the ticket! Nothing ever came of this, for which countless patients ought to be most grateful.

I was aiming high, but I don't think I was overly sober and serious. I was very much a kid, and very selfish in terms of hanging onto my childhood. I didn't want to grow up too fast. I thought growing up was highly overrated, and I still do. A child is drawn to the idea of brotherhood, and my idea of a good time was hanging out with my buddies.

My fondest memories are of talking about nothing for hours on end with Big Tuck and Derrick (Bear) Shaw and Fred Dixon; playing ball with Tim and Jimmy Parks; sitting on the curb with Junior Lewis and Freddie White; watching the easy mastery of the older guys (Iconic figures! Someday we'd be like them.) down at the playground; dreaming of dimly imagined success in the wide and mysterious world of sports; and hoping that there'd always be time for just one more basket, one more touchdown, before it got too dark.

2

1978–1983

When I was thirteen, and in the seventh grade, my great-great-grand-mother passed away. We moved to Clearwater when I was fourteen, into a house that had been inherited by Mom's numbers-running husband. I had petitioned Mom not to marry him because I'd seen the way he treated her. At times I'd get upset, enough on one occasion to go outside and put a dent in his sky-blue Riviera. He confronted me, but I wouldn't speak to him.

The next year, I started Dunedin high school. Even though we lived in Clearwater, our house was zoned for Dunedin. I'd remain at Dunedin right through Grade Twelve. The football team was the Falcons, and the senior varsity team was coached by Delmont Murray, who'd come from Georgia. He turned the program around. All of a sudden, I was up against kids who weighed considerably more than I did. By the end of the first week, I was a starter with the junior varsity team, on defence. (In fact, some people would argue that I'm more effective on this side of the ball.) I played defensive back.

Because of my feet I could run with most anybody. And more than that, I knew who to run with, because I understood the game. I'd predict how far the quarterback could throw, and gauge exactly how much ground I'd have to cover. Soon I was intercepting a lot of passes and making my hits. Toward the middle of the season, I became equally effective on offence, too.

At the end of that year, they brought the top-ranked freshmen and sophomores up to the varsity team, with the eleventh and twelfth graders. This was the first time in living memory that Dunedin had made it to the playoffs. Our most intimidating player was Matt Davis. He liked to knock people around. During games, when he came to the sidelines, he never took his helmet off; he just sat with his eyes popping out of his head and nobody came near him.

Now I was on the same team. In preparation for the game, we launched into Oklahoma drills — three huge defensive linemen and an intense and hard-hitting linebacker (Matt Davis) versus three suddenly puny offensive linemen and a back — me. The objective is to break through the line of scrimmage and avoid the linebacker. So my guys snapped the ball, handed it to me, and I took the ball down the field and into the end zone. The words you never want to hear, especially in full-contact ball, *especially* if you were the one who just got away with murder, are "Do it again." So we lined up and did it again, and I scored one more time. Partly because of this showing, I was able to remain on the varsity squad as a sophomore.

That year, Murray pegged me as what we called a monsterback, a combination of linebacker and defensive back. He felt I was tough enough to compete despite my size, and he laid out a timetable for me. He said he expected me to be an all-county player as a sophomore; an all-state player in my junior year; and an all-American as a senior.

I didn't quite make it. As a sophomore, I was honorable mention for all-county and all-district, which are pretty much the same. As a junior, I made first team all-district and all-county, and honorable mention for all-state. As a senior, I was first team all-state, and most valuable player in the county or district I lived in. I never did become an all-American. If I'd had another year, maybe I could have pulled it off. If so, it would have been in large part thanks to Murray. He was a people builder, a confidence booster. He'd tell you that you could run through a wall — that the ability lay within you, that compared with you the wall didn't exist. He built us up and provided vision; he set a tradition of pride and winning that remained after he left at the end of the season, to be replaced by Coach George Hemond.

Coach Hemond was a very dynamic man, almost eccentric in his ways. Others would recycle the same things year after year; he was more creative. He'd constantly devise variations on themes, subtle changes that made all the difference. His motivational speeches were a thing apart. We were pretty rah-rah already. At that age, because everybody's so emotional, you can take your opponents out of their game, beat them mentally before you get on the field.

Coach Hemond used to say, "They're rough and tough and hard to bluff, but we're fast, got class, and gonna kick their ————." He said we had to execute plays with precision and finesse. He showed us a cartoon of a fencer, who wields his sword so swiftly and delicately that his opponent doesn't know his head has been cut off until it falls to the ground.

Hemond had a ritual at season's end. We'd form a circle, and he'd talk about how far we'd come together and how precious our memories would be. Then he'd take an old shoe and pass it around. We were supposed to think about and then dispose of all the bad things we'd gone through — all the anger and disappointments, the regrets and might-have-beens. They went into this symbolic shoe, which in turn went into a ceremonial bonfire.

Under Coach Hemond, I did duty as a receiver and running back.

We wound up 8 and 2 in sophomore, and 12 and 1 in junior. In junior the team was spearheaded by a guy named Craig Blanks, who gained 1,200 yards rushing. When he was injured, I stepped in, and ripped things up from the defensive back position. I really threw my 150 pounds around; a couple of guys had to be helped off the field. Then, in my senior year, we finished 10 and 0, and won our first playoff game but lost the next. I picked up the pace, and rivaled Blanks with 1,000 yards on 100 carries.

Still, I felt I was being held in reserve. Whenever we played a weaker opponent, which would have given me a chance to pad my statistics, I was pulled early, so other guys could play. I'd run the ball all the way from midfield to the goal line, and somebody bigger and heavier would take it the final three yards for a touchdown. My numbers were good — I wound up as most valuable player in the county and led the district in scoring — but I thought I should have made even more of a splash, to gain attention and have a decent shot at a football scholarship.

By now this was a pressing consideration. There are more soccer scholarships than you might think, and I'd probably have qualified in Florida: I was picked for Florida's super-select team, led the county in scoring, and made the first-team, all-state selection. Clemson University in South Carolina had expressed some interest, through Mr. McLean, Dunedin's soccer coach.

But I'd decided to pin my hopes on football. The trouble with Dunedin was it was out of the mainstream. Scouts didn't flock there as a matter of course — and scouting at the time was hit and miss, a loose network of informal contacts that had been built up between regional coaches and college scouts. The bigger colleges had more sophisticated systems, full-time talent spotters who did their best to cover all the bases. Usually, though, they fell back on schools they'd had good luck with in past years. I had no idea how well connected, if at all, Coach Hemond might be, because he kept his own counsel.

As far as I could gather, a scholarship offer came out of the blue — the almighty letter, which in my case never arrived.

I had no wish list of places I'd like to go, no first-hand referrals from guys who'd gone before me. My father had been at Florida A&M, as I've said. He hadn't played ball, but he had been a trainer. He introduced me to a couple of coaches there, but their best offer was the vague possibility that I too could tape people up — not what I had in mind.

So I sat around, waiting for the skies to open. Certainly this showed a certain lack of initiative. I hadn't applied anywhere, hadn't even taken the mandatory SATs (Standard Admission Tests). My marks were no problem — I had a 3.3 grade-point average on a scale of 4, and four of my five classes were at the honors level. My feeling was that I'd jump at anybody who'd take me in, yet nobody showed signs of doing so.

I wasn't particularly drawn to a college with a religious affiliation, although in retrospect that might seem to have been a natural fit. I think that at this stage of my life, I was far more moral than I was spiritual. I thought that, if anything, I could make a more effective witness at a secular university. I was going through my "I'm expressing my individuality" teenage years. Every day was important, and I liked being around people. I wanted to be out in the world. In the back of my mind, I was sure that God had a plan for me; in the meantime I was making decisions based less on my spiritual growth than on a career path. I wanted to figure out where I was going, where I was supposed to go. No matter where that was, I'd be a Christian. Now it was time to leave home, to try out new things and get some qualifications for myself that would pay off down the line.

Another reason for wanting to get away was more down to earth: Mom's relationship with my stepfather had gone from bad to worse. But what if they stayed close? I started to ponder my options. I told

Mom not to worry, that I'd be successful even if I didn't go to school right away. I worked out a plan for a lawn-care business of my own; visions of franchises danced in my head. Then I thought about the military. I didn't particularly care which branch, as long as it wasn't the navy, since I'm not crazy about water. I'd enlist for a few years, hoping that we didn't have to go to war — in which case I'd have had to get out, because I could never shoot anybody. I'd resume my studies after my time was up. As it turned out, I didn't get to the point of exploring this — for bit by bit, the skies began to show signs of clearing.

The first letter came from Morningside College in Sioux City, Iowa. I had to look it up on a map. The mere fact that somebody somewhere wanted me was encouraging, and helped convince me that football was what I should pursue. I don't think I had time to respond before the letters started coming thick and fast. The next was from Liberty Baptist College in Lynchburg, Virginia, a school founded by Jerry Falwell, the television evangelist. I didn't follow that one up, maybe for a strange reason I guess. Growing up in the south, the most hated word was "nigger," followed closely by "lynch." I just didn't like the sound of the place; I thought it was a bad omen. I figured I could afford to be choosy now; I was a lot more confident that something would turn up.

Next came contacts from Columbia and Harvard. Of course, everybody urged me to go after one or the other, but I wasn't so sure. Both were a far cry from Clearwater, population 75,000. Columbia was New York City; for me, it was cold and remote. That was fine in the abstract — Broadway Mike! — but I really couldn't imagine making the transition. It was too overwhelmingly different to take seriously. Harvard, for its part, seemed terribly WASP, buttoned-down, and Ivy League — not the most hospitable environment for a kid from The Projects in Florida. There's nothing like the prospect of a dramatic upheaval to make you start counting your shortcomings, real or imagined. Besides, both offers came with strings attached. Ivy League schools don't give sports scholarships as such. Instead, there's a rather laborious and paper-intensive combination of aid and grants. This process seemed long and drawn out, which offered me an excuse to continue doing nothing for a while.

Meanwhile, my decision was being made for me, even though I wasn't aware of it. Don McCauley, the recruiter from the College of William and Mary in Williamsburg, Virginia, turned up in Clearwater on his annual scouting trip through Florida. He worked the entire state; he hadn't come specifically to see me, and in fact didn't know that I existed. It just so happened that someone had published a newspaper article about me that very day. I should find out who wrote it, and send a note of thanks, because McCauley saw it and came to Dunedin High. Coach Hemond called me out of class and introduced us. After a brief conversation, the recruiter headed for his car. He thanked Hemond for his trouble and said, "There's no way. He's just too small." Hemond said, "Before you make up your mind, come and watch some film." McCauley refused; he wasn't interested at all. Then Coach Hemond said, "I'm not asking you, I'm telling you — come and watch the film." After a brief show-and-tell, they were back at the classroom door for a lengthier interview. McCauley's next stop was city hall, where he told my mom that he was prepared to offer me a scholarship without delay — that is, without discussing the matter with William and Mary's head coach. As I remember it, he wanted me on the next plane. I told him I had an important soccer game, which must have made him wonder what planet I'd arrived from.

The game was on a Friday, and on Saturday I flew to Williamsburg, at the college's expense. Things couldn't have gone much worse. In the first place, I hadn't traveled all that much. We'd gone on family vacations to Georgia and North Carolina, and next to nowhere else in the States. This trip was in February, too, and the weather was bleak, cold, and windy. Williamsburg looks exactly like the photographs: perfectly restored streetscapes and miraculously preserved architecture. The college is right downtown, at one end of Duke of Gloucester Street. The football stadium is tucked in behind the Wren Building — an open-air field with natural grass, the game in its elemental state.

I got a guided tour of the campus and a quick overview of the university's history. It's the second-oldest college in the United States. I think Harvard submitted its charter earlier, but this is about as venerable as they come. Thomas Jefferson went here, though he never graduated, so I'm one up on him. Next came a video presentation designed to sell you on the school's prestige and academic standing. Football was sort of tertiary. I was eager to see the video, simply to get into warmer quarters. Then I touched base with the coaching staff, which was and still is headed by Jimmye Laycock. As I understand it, McCauley had rushed back with the film of my high school performances. Even so, Coach Laycock was dubious, and had to be strong-armed by his assistants.

They put me up with a black athlete during the recruiting trip. I'd been told that the student population was about five percent black — low compared with nowadays but more than I'd been used to. I've talked about being all alone on the baseball field; I was also very often the only black in my high-school classes, owing to the effects of general streaming, a high black dropout rate, and the fact that I'd been taking electives and accelerated courses. My host's name was Jeff Sanders, and we were on different wavelengths. He was considerably older, and busy with his studies. He was also a member of a mixed fraternity (the first all-black fraternity was founded a couple of years later on), and took me there after a basketball game. The main event was drinking beer, so I was totally out of the loop. There's a yawning gulf between eighteen and twenty-two at the best of times. I felt small, out of place, and already homesick.

None of which mattered. I'd already decided that this was a good school, my best ticket to the future. I resisted the pressure to sign on the spot, though. I didn't care if I wasn't demonstrating the accustomed deference and eagerness. I was determined to take the papers back and put them on our kitchen table in Clearwater. Mom and I were going to share the moment together.

That was on a Saturday, and William and Mary wanted the papers signed, sealed, and delivered early the following week. Now came a bit of last-minute to-ing and fro-ing on the phone with Harvard, the other hot prospect. The head coach there, with whom I'd kept in touch, was very kind, and said that he understood my situation completely. He also said that I had an out, in case I changed my mind. Since Harvard's offer wasn't a scholarship, I could sign with William and Mary, take the SATs, and switch back to Harvard with no hard feelings if my marks warranted.

One almost-final formality remained. Over the years, Mom had tried to involve my dad in as many major decisions as possible, even though his parenting had been sporadic at best. She thought it proper that he be notified and that he approve the arrangement. We met on neutral ground, at an aunt's house, because he and my stepfather did not relish each other's company. He scanned the papers, and said, "There's no question. Do it." Then he grabbed the application and signed in the space for parent or guardian.

I was absolutely mortified, because I knew what would happen. I took it home and Mom went ballistic. After everything she'd done for all those years, here was Willy Clemons emerging from the woodwork to take unfair credit for his long-neglected son's success — and I'd let him get away with it. She painstakingly erased his signature, even though it was in ink, and signed hers instead, as she had every right to do.

3

FALL, 1983

An American college football scholarship is pretty much standard issue. Both the college and student/player are locked in for the duration. It doesn't matter if you aren't as good as they thought you'd be, or if you're injured and can't play at all — the deal is still on. You can be drummed out only for terrible marks, or behavior that verges on moral turpitude — things like taking drugs or cheating on exams.

The short story is you don't have to pay a dime. You get full tuition, full room and board for four years. All you have to do is what you've been doing all your life, running and jumping and throwing a ball around. In return for this, you receive one of the best educations available. I realized I'd have to work hard to make the grade — harder than I knew at the time. Academically, William and Mary is one of the toughest schools in the nation. Without Ivy League status, nor the setting and size of places like Berkeley and Cal State, it must — and does — challenge students at every turn to maintain its reputation.

I had no idea what to expect. I managed to get off on the wrong foot almost at once. Because we spent orientation week practising, I missed out on a great deal of advice that would have been very useful — especially the need to keep pace in terms of credit hours. In order to graduate, I'd have to complete 40 classes. Each class counts for three credit hours, for a total of 120. A full-time load is five classes per semester. I unwisely elected to take only four at first, and then dropped out of one of them (a writing class, of all things) in midstream. I had to deal with that in the fullness of time — the point is that I started to run a deficit from the very beginning. This continued to snowball through the years, so that I had to keep going back like a boomerang to earn my degree.

So much for academics. What about the football team? William and Mary had formerly been what's known as a 1-A team, and then reclassified as 1-AA when I arrived. Both 1-A and 1-AA teams play in Division One. The extra letter denotes a smaller and less wealthy school. William and Mary's total enrollment was about 6,000. As a result, the athletics programs were rather modest, as were the scholarship funds available. The school couldn't hope to attract as many top-ranked athletes as, say, the University of Florida, Penn State, or other 1-A schools that play in bowl games and compete for national championships. William and Mary was an independent, like Notre Dame, which meant that it didn't belong to a conference or division.

The football team's name was the Tribe. That's not like the Argonauts being called "the Boatmen" — their name really was the Tribe. The mascot was an Indian, which had lately brought no luck. The season before my arrival had ended 3 and 8. William and Mary was the only place that Coach Lou Holtz (who had departed) didn't have a winning record. He attributed this to the fact that there were too many Marys and not enough Williams, but that's the sort of thing that losing coaches always say.

I arrived in Williamsburg in the late summer of 1983, two weeks before the start of the academic year. I came in strictly as a running back; in college you don't play both ways. It was miles past warm now, extremely hot and muggy, with temperatures in the nineties. I got settled in, and was assigned my first roommate, Dirk Gibson, also a freshman and also a running back. I'd been working on my South Florida cockiness; down there we think we have a patent on the game. All those lingering size issues had been banished from my mind; I was as confident as all get-out. A rude awakening! Dirk was five feet ten and weighed 185 pounds. He looked like a linebacker, and could bench press well over 400 pounds. I thought, Well, maybe he can't run, but he was fast as well. This changed my opinion of what college ball would be like, and my assumption about how good I was likely to be. The comforting thing was that Dirk had a Bible on his dresser. We became good friends, and wound up talking until two or three in the morning. Pretty soon I met a few other guys, including Reggie Hodnett, Mike Hackett, and Anthony Lucas — two of them future roommates, all of them eager to get out and prove themselves.

When practices began, I had my work cut out for me. It also became apparent that Coach Laycock had his priorities. We had an introductory chat about my fondness for running sideways. His exact words were, "Clemons, you don't do things your way here, you do them my way. Keep running like that, and I'll send you back to Florida." I thought, Hold on — I can get the job done. Don't tell me how to run. If you could tell me how, you'd be doing it yourself. And so on and so forth. I shared this with some of the guys, but had the sense to keep quiet about it on the field.

And in fact, he was right — I did run east–west far too much. He'd seen a lot more football than I had. He knew a lot, so he was trying to correct me, trying to help me improve. He wouldn't have bothered saying anything to a free-range freshman if he hadn't recognized I had potential. I think that, given what he had in camp, he knew I'd have a chance to play immediately, and he wanted to start sorting me out right away. So I complained to my buddies, not to him. Over time, Coach Laycock got his point across, though I don't suppose I totally absorbed the lesson. At least I acknowledged that there was a problem I had to work on.

A bit of an adjustment period here, to be sure. This was compounded by the fact that I was so much smaller than the seniors, guys three years older and a good deal heavier than I was. Once we started to play, it became evident that I could hold my own. Whether or not I'd be able to translate that into anything special or significant remained to be seen. Could I handle the game physically? Could I take a hit and get back up, then take ten more and still get back up, and do that over the course of the season? Could I adapt mentally to intensive coaching?

Coach Laycock was and remains one of the most respected offensive minds in college ball — which would eventually help me make the transition to the pro level. Our offence was much more complex than the typical college system — a pass-oriented attack, one that required that you read defences. As a running back, this didn't affect me much, but my blocking assignments weren't all that simple, either. Things went well for me in scrimmages — so much so that when the season began, I was one of two freshmen on a squad of fifty-five who traveled to away-from-home games.

In the first two games, I saw limited action. Then in the third we went to North Carolina, who were ranked number three in the nation. This was their homecoming day, and the crowd was pumped. I for one was already whipped before the whistle blew. I went in early, and we scored first, after I'd taken the ball to the eight-yard line. Then the game became a blur, punctuated by scenes of North Carolina walking all over us and putting 31 points on the board to our 14. Later in the game my number was called. I got the ball, saw daylight in front of me, and made a cut with conviction. I was getting ready to turn it on when Micah Moon, an all-American linebacker, hit me right on the chin. I hit the ground instantly. I thought only, Where in the world did he come from? But there was no way I was staying down. As much as my body said, Stay here, have somebody come and get you, something else ordered, Get up. I went back to the huddle, not in complete touch with the world around me. I tried to give no sign that anything was wrong, although I couldn't even focus. Then Coach Laycock called the very same play again. I couldn't believe it. Hadn't he seen me get knocked into next week? I knew where I was supposed to go the second time around, only I wasn't sure I could get there. Luckily, North Carolina jumped offside, a penalty was marked off, and I thought I was saved. Not so. The same play was called again. By now I'd regained my bearings. When I took the handoff, I don't know whether I saw daylight again, or whether I was simply running from Micah Moon. Whatever the case, I went 24 yards for the first touchdown of my college career. As for North Carolina, they went on to score 20 more unanswered points, and we went back home. For my part, I thought if I could do it against them as a freshman in their home stadium, I could do it against anybody.

Micah Moon's hit was one I'd long remember, but the rest of them were all of a similar order. You always think it's going to be tougher than it turns out to be. You just get out there and play; you stay on your feet and keep running. The odd time you can run over someone. They catch you every once in a while, too, and sometimes they can't hang on. I have never been in a situation where I felt totally outmatched — except for the longest game of my life, a ghastly contest against Penn State during my sophomore year.

And so that first season unwound, with mixed results. Dave Scanlon, the starting tailback, usually did well. If so, I sat on the bench. If we needed a boost, in I went. I began to wonder why I was traveling. We roamed the countryside by bus, with little box lunches. We brought books and planned to study, and never got around to it — just talked, played music, and tried to sleep on the return trips. We covered a lot of ground, up and down the eastern seaboard: to Marshall College in West Virginia; Holy Cross; Harvard; Delaware; Lehigh, Pennsylvania; Virginia Military Institute; Virginia Tech; and the University of Richmond, just down the road. We ended the season at 6 and 5, a marked improvement over 1982. And, despite my feeling that I wasn't doing all that much, I was named Freshman of the Year.

Then it was time to get back to the classroom, where I had mixed results as well. For most of the first year, I was in a freshman fog, away from home for the first time, with no family around. The whole idea of university was foreign to me. I hadn't read all the literature I should have. Things were going on around me, yet I was pretty much oblivious to them. I'd put all my stock into football; that's where my comfort zone was. I'd made some buddies and been marginally successful, and now I had to adapt to accommodation in the only all-male freshman dorm, one of the oldest buildings on a very old campus.

When classes started, it didn't take me long to figure out that no one called the roll, that the lecture hall was so large that I would be inconspicuous by my absence, and that there was no such thing as homework. All we were going to do was take notes for two months and sit a midterm exam. At that point, attendance became optional. For years, growing up, I'd never missed a day of school. Suddenly there was something in the air that first year at William and Mary. I sometimes felt that others considered me inferior because I was there to play football, because I wouldn't have been accepted otherwise, because I probably wasn't good enough either to be accepted by, or play football at, another school.

My concentration suffered; I was distracted and kept coming up with excuses for long-delayed assignments. I got through the first semester only because I could retain information long enough to regurgitate it, then never recall it again. Dirk and I spent a lot of time shooting pool, talking about our woes and cares, and debating a transfer to Delaware State, an all-black school. Neither of us was happy with college life in general.

There weren't a lot of things consistent with the culture we'd been used to — to put it bluntly, the experiences of the average black kid. If you've ever been to Williamsburg, you know what I'm talking about. You walk down Duke of Gloucester Street — affectionately referred to as Dog Street — and you notice that all the black people are dressed up in slave costumes. The only blacks we met lived away from college. They weren't teachers; they washed dishes and cleaned the dorms. For the first time in my life, I felt like a member of a visible minority, the only black in the entire freshman hall, let alone the only football player. It was a gloomy scene that first year, made worse by the death of our friend Anthony Lucas. He'd long been diagnosed with Hodgkin's disease, and sudden unexpected complications from a common cold did him in. Reggie took this particularly hard, because they'd been the best of friends. All of us were shaken, and commemorated Anthony in our own way, with a basketball team we dubbed the A.L. Express.

But all was not lost in my first year at college. It's interesting that despite all the ups and downs, I wasn't looking for a place of formal worship. Eventually I found a little Baptist church to attend, though I never really became a part of it as I had with our home church. Dirk and I would go to the Fellowship of Christian Athletes, a circle that convened, sang songs, and shared a few thoughts in informal settings. This was not, however, a period of personal growth for me. Before, I'd gone to church more and read the Bible less. Now, the reverse was true. By constant reading, I came to know that my relationship with Christ was real, because Mom wasn't looking over my shoulder. I'd been in the church long enough to hear almost every chapter and verse; I just hadn't actually read for myself before. So now was the time, and I found my beliefs becoming more and more concrete.

4

The best thing about freshman year is that it only happens once. I returned home for the summer, looking for work at any wage. As I've said, Mom worked for the city. She knew a woman named Mrs. Ely, whose husband Bill was with Honeywell's aerospace division. This was an enormous complex of plants that employed hundreds of people. If you got in the door, it could lead to the classic Good Job — security, better-than-average pay, almost professional status. Honeywell had a long-standing intern program, and with Mr. Ely's help I was accepted. Unless you have an abiding interest in the aerospace industry, you won't much care what I was doing and would continue to do over the years that followed. It had to do with a huge and diverse inventory of bulk products, which had to be tested, inspected, reordered if necessary, shipped, received, and costed. Suffice it to say I was in training as an expeditor or facilitator — speeding a number of interconnected processes along. It paid well,

I liked my co-workers, and I knew that it might develop into something long term.

Toward the end of May, a girl named Kim Mason turned up at my house, wondering when and where a football jamboree was going to take place. She was with another girl named Diane Lee, whom I'd seen, but hadn't met. I came to the door wearing shorts and no shirt, thinking I looked suitably buffed, the nineteen-year-old athlete with stomach muscles on display. I gave them directions, and they went on their way.

A week later, I went with Darren Tate to check out a dance at the National Guard Armory. We arrived stylishly late, and ran straight into Kim and Diane. Now a sort of arm's-length mating ritual took place, concerning how everybody was going to get home. I managed to learn that Diane was a year younger than I was, that she wanted to go to college but was short on funds, that she was saving for her tuition by working at a bank, and that she had her own car. Meanwhile, Darren was deep in conversation with Kim. Diane asked where he was going, and he answered, "Wherever Kim is going." This got him a quick ride to his place. I thought I'd try my luck, and when asked where I was going, I said, "Wherever Diane is going." It worked and I got a one-way drop back home as well.

The next day, I was wandering over to the park, when who should appear but Diane, driving her burgundy Chevette. She whistled at me, shouted, "Nice legs!" and sped off. Was this the same demure bank teller I'd met the night before? I knew I'd better find out. Fortunately, through Kim, I learned that Diane was taking tennis lessons from my buddy Fred Dixon. I'd never held a tennis racquet in my life, but I could run, I could play Ping-Pong, and I was for some unaccountable reason seized with the desire to practice lobs. Diane and I went from the beach (with Kim) to the tennis courts (with Fred) to a pizza parlor. I got to eat the whole thing because she didn't want to look unladylike. I'd never met an eighteen-year-old lady before. The description

ALL HEART

had always followed her around; her friends and nieces and nephews
called her Lady Di. She was utterly feminine, not in any way girlish,
impeccably groomed and dressed, with smooth hands and long,
natural nails. And so began a magical summer.

I was around by her house every night, conducting a very public
courtship. Her parents lived on a busy street corner, so we lacked a
romantic hideaway. We'd sit for hours under a tree, out front. At
eleven o'clock I'd jog home, then jog back half an hour later. Her
bedroom window was on the ground floor, so we could continue
talking in whispers well past midnight. And I'd serenade her as best
I could. She'd ask me a question, and I'd respond with a song lyric.
I had an inexhaustible supply of old songs with a rap sort of beat,
committed to memory in the days when they were playful and innocent. I can't sing a lick, but she seemed to like the way I sang — proof
that love is tone deaf.

The first time I heard her sing was at the St. John Missionary
Baptist Church. For her tiny size she possessed a powerful voice. This
was like falling in love all over again. As far as I could see, she had
only one failing: she had no rhythm at all. The first time we danced,
she demonstrated that her feet had no idea what the beat was doing.
I think that's because her family were devout Seventh-Day
Adventists, who frowned on certain types of music in the house.

How did they view my nightly rumpled appearance on their lawn?
At first, they weren't sold on the idea. Over time, they figured out
that I was gainfully employed and attending a pretty good school.
Plus, although I wasn't of their faith, I had more than a nodding
acquaintance with the Bible. When the shock wore off for them, I
became accepted more and more.

After a very few dates, I'd realized that here was someone I might
eventually marry. Diane was just so beautiful, inwardly as much as
outwardly. So I wasted no time in making my honorable intensions
known. I said I had no interest in premarital sex, and would never

pressure her in that way. I also told her that I didn't want to see anyone else, and wouldn't, when I returned to school that autumn. So that's the way we left matters at summer's end. She wrote me cards and sent me balloons and flowers. I wrote her poetry, and sent flowers in return — one red rose at a time.

*   *   *

Shall I tell you about my sophomore year at William and Mary? Reggie and Dirk lived with me off-campus, which proved to be cheaper than individual rooms in a dorm. We were joined by John Menke, a white guy from Kentucky who spoke in slow motion. Three speedy black running backs would be bouncing off the walls, as one sky-high offensive lineman drawled his way through another day. But one of the running backs stopped bouncing right away. I sprained my ankle in the first game of the season. Then I sprained it six more times. Then I sprained the other ankle four times. Then the season was over.

Perhaps I should explain the difference between pain and injury. I understand it now, when I didn't then. You play with and through pain; that's par for the course. Playing football is not what God intended us to do with our bodies. Everybody hurts from time to time, and pain will eventually go away, without doing you lasting harm. Trying to play with and through injury, on the other hand, will cause further damage. I kept on trying; it was my own bright idea. This sounds as if I had a death wish, or as if the trainers should have been shipped back where they came from. At that age, you think you're immortal, which is the impression you try to convey to the therapist, who can only diagnose what you tell him. If I insisted that I was ready and willing to suit up, that was my responsibility.

At one point, Coach Laycock ordered me to stay out for two weeks. I rested in bed, drank plenty of fluids, and felt much better. The week I came back, I walked straight into another sprain.

Crutches became my boon companions. Can anything good be said about 1985? In my virtual absence, the team's record improved to 7 and 4. I found I had more time to attend to my studies.

That summer, I returned home. Diane was working at another branch of the bank, and had decided that, starting in the fall, she'd take business courses at the Southern College of Seventh-Day Adventists in Chattanooga, Tennessee — a long haul from Williamsburg. We still spent hours in front of her house, but I was feeling guilty about seldom getting to see my old buddies, and guiltier still about my sprain-prone ankles. I was back at Honeywell, and assuming more responsibilities, which meant more overtime. I'd eat on the run or standing up; it was a case of "Hi, Mom," and hit the road.

This was not a happy time for Mom and my stepfather. He worked and drank, sometimes making drinking his job. He was a decent enough guy when sober, but short-fused and abrasive when he'd had a few. I couldn't understand the thought patterns between two consenting adults who couldn't get along. Nor were the arguments always his fault; at times, Mom would egg him on. And who could blame her? She'd had so much junk in her life. Your tolerance of more of it lessens with age. She was getting tired and frustrated; she saw no way out of a dead-end relationship.

Why did she prolong it? Fear plays a part — of living alone, of not having the same quality of life and financial security. Of course, what good is money if you're miserable? They did strange things, mortgaging the house to carry living expenses. I tried to get them on a budget, to no avail. When I was there, things would calm down for a while. I could run interference and be the go-between, so she could get a little peace.

I could see how all this was affecting my little sister, Kelli, and I started taking her away with me as much as possible. We were close, so this was no a hindrance; I liked her company, and I was happy knowing she wasn't at home in the thick of the arguments.

I was fortunate in that my personality was pretty much formed before my stepfather moved into the house. A lot of my foundation came from Mom and others who were around. My dad's absence left a void, but at least I didn't have to witness a battle royal day in and day out. After a while, you start to perceive it as normal, which is why I wanted to give Kelli a break. Oddly, the more I tried to spare her, the more Mom wanted me to be there as a buffer. I found myself being pulled in all directions at once.

That fall, Diane went off to Tennessee, and I headed back for my junior year at William and Mary. By now, I was over the worst of loneliness and disorientation. Dirk, Reggie, and I found a new room-mate, Mike Hackett, who took John's place. I hoped I'd thrown off the sophomore jinx, because I never wanted to sit with my foot in an ice bucket again. I could tolerate that for about ten seconds. I hate the cold; it moves me to tears. This year, the team went to a single-back set, and I was the guy. Dirk wasn't — he'd torn up his knee and missed the entire season. We were committed to throwing the ball, not covering a whole lot of distance running. I was doing exercises to strengthen my ankles, and gladdening the heart of the phone company with long-distance bills to darkest Chattanooga.

The real breakthrough this year was the appearance of a new running coach named Derwyn Cox, the second black coach in William and Mary's history. Growing up, I'd met a number of black people in healthy family situations, though I didn't know them well. This was my first look, at age twenty-one, at a black man who took a genuine interest in what his two kids were doing; who loved and respected his wife, and was there for her every day.

Coach Cox was far more than just a coach to me, throughout that year and the next. He was younger than other people on the staff, a former fraternity man. He related to us culturally. I could talk with him about what was happening back home with my mom, and he understood at once. He used to come to our apartment and get us

up and moving; he knew my habits weren't the best. We'd reciprocate by running errands for him and his wife. On the field, he didn't
try to change or cramp my style. His aim was to make me practise
and keep me rested and fresh. He protected me to a great extent. He
knew I was carrying a lot of load.

More than he knew, he was a role model and mentor. He taught
me that I didn't have to put up Afro signs or march for black power.
I could be a good guy and not be prejudiced. I could like everybody
and still maintain my culture. I didn't have to marry outside my race
to gain status and acceptance. I could be myself and get along with
everybody and have a positive family situation that wouldn't necessarily end in ruin. I didn't have to live with anyone in misery. He
knew the game, yet that wasn't what I needed from him. I knew it,
too, and could get what he could give me in football from someone
else, or from myself. What I needed from him was himself — and
Derwyn Cox delivered, each and every day.

Throughout that junior year, I did what I needed to do to finish.
Maybe Honeywell had made me complacent; I knew I had a place
to go to. By this time, I'd decided to major in economics, with a
minor in sociology. Football turned out well. I caught 70 passes, a
new William and Mary record; gained 700 or 800 yards rushing as
a running back; and was elected co-captain at year's end by my teammates. We'd begun to attract a degree of notice on the national scene,
too, and finished 8 and 3, before we were knocked out of the playoffs by Virginia Military Institute. The idea of a pro career was still
remote. My aim at the time was to get through, get hired, and get
working so I could improve matters on my home front. Some days
I wouldn't acknowledge what I knew was going on there; on others,
I'd try to solve the problems long distance. Even at a distance, I know
they affected me, just as they affected Kelli to an even greater degree,
because she saw them up close.

The summer between my junior and senior years, I headed back to Honeywell again, a young corporate man in the making, with football very much on the back burner. The pendulum began to swing back that fall when Coach Laycock was contacted by Mike Faragalli (who'd later surface with the Argonauts). He had served at William and Mary as an assistant coach, before joining his father Joe in Edmonton. He informed Coach Laycock that Edmonton wasn't interested in me, but that Calgary was — and that they'd put me, sight unseen, on their negotiation list. This meant that they'd have the right to attempt to obtain my services if I went into the National Football League (NFL) draft. There was an exchange of correspondence, and by way of orientation they sent me a poster featuring Ray Alexander, a very graceful receiver from Florida A&M, who'd played with them and had recently retired. This seemed like the long shot to end them all. I put it out of my mind, and buckled down to what proved to be a stellar season for me and for the team, which improved to 9 and 2, though we failed to prosper in the playoffs. I covered 2,000 all-purpose yards, which I think is fifth- or sixth-best in National College Athletic Association (NCAA) history. This included 1,000 yards rushing and 72 receptions, breaking my club record of the previous year.

I was named the Virginia major college player of the year — in other words, the state's foremost offensive player. While I didn't return a lot of punts, I was taking kickoffs, serving as a running back, and catching balls out of the backfield. I owe a lot of that to Coach Laycock, who'd prepared me to learn a diverse process. A lot of players who come out of simple college systems have a hard time adjusting to the professional level. His scheme was wide-open, multi-dimensional, sophisticated by college standards, and very similar to what I'd encounter later on. When it came, as it would, to switching positions on five minutes' notice and doing everything at once, the precedents had been set for me a long time before, back on the grass field at William and Mary.

At season's end, just for a change of pace, I'd sprained my knee in the first-round semifinal against Delaware. This was a bit of a downer. I thought I'd have plenty of opportunity to rest, at least — until I received an invitation to something called the Combine, which took place in Indianapolis, Indiana, in late January 1987. It's sort of a super tryout camp organized by the NFL. The 200 top college seniors go to be tested en masse, preparatory to the annual draft. With my knee healing, and still awkward and painful, this was exactly where I didn't want to be. I was trying to take it in stride, but people spoke in hushed tones about Knee Injuries, which I'd never had before. It felt odd rather than incapacitating. I do remember wondering if it was going to feel like that forever. I hadn't done any running since mid-November. When a plane ticket arrived, I thought I'd go anyway and see what the Combine was all about.

The Combine is a chance for the NFL teams to send their scouts and representatives on a mid-winter junket that's probably of tremendous value to the organizations involved, if not the poor bewildered post-adolescents who are lined up in rows for their inspection. Individuality is the first thing out the window: I, for example, was Running Back Number 24. I felt utterly unprepared and out of place, side by side with people I'd seen play on television — top-rated talent from Nebraska and Oklahoma and Notre Dame, players from every conference and division, most of whom were huge and in far better shape than I was. This was the best of college football, at a glance.

First come two solid days of tests. I couldn't help thinking about the slave trade. You stripped to your shorts and they took mug shots of you, front, back, profile. You waited in lines to be poked and probed by teams of doctors who stared balefully at every inch of your body. You had to confess every injury you'd ever suffered. Then came further tests and X-rays. If you weren't hurt going in, you were when you came out. Then, if you passed the tests, you had to do strenuous exercises — unless, of course, you were already touted as a top draft choice. If so, you could opt out, and stand around looking blasé. The rest of us had to bench press 225 pounds as many times as we could. I think I did it nine times — not bad for a little guy. I was thinking, This is not a good thing for me. It would have been far better for them to hear about me from a distance rather than see me in the flesh, which was getting weaker by the hour. Next came the vertical jump, the shuttle run, and the 40-yard dash. I ran a 4.55, which was .13 seconds slower than usual, because I was favoring my knee. Even so, when all this heave-and-ho was over, I rose above everybody. The guys who were directing the drills set me as an example for those who were fouling up. When it came to playing football, I came out of my shell.

Then everybody went off to party with their agents, and I flew back home again. I'd been approached by several agents, and one or two of the team representatives. I didn't think any interest would amount to anything in the foreseeable future. I'd shown my quickness, and knew my straight-ahead speed was lacking, thanks (or no thanks) to my knee. Coupled with my size, I didn't believe anyone would take me seriously. I'd attended because they'd sent me a ticket, not to win a job or influence people. In retrospect, I know this sounds absolutely crazy. At that point, my heart wasn't in the entire procedure.

All of this seemed a lot less important because of an event that shocked us all. Diane's father was shot and killed near the Lees' home in Clearwater. The killer was well known to him; they'd been acquaintances for many years. Ironically, Mr. Lee had prevented the man from shooting someone else earlier that day. They'd gone off together to talk, but an argument ensued. Diane's father tried to leave, and the other man turned on him and gunned him down. The killer was convicted and sentenced to a prison term.

I ended up going back to William and Mary to deal with the sad state of my disappearing credit hours. At the end of my second semester, I'd still have a way to go. Amazingly, salvation awaited, in the form of Al Albert, William and Mary's soccer coach. He'd had his eye on me for some time. He'd built the college team into one of the top twenty in the nation. Albert suggested that I apply for a separate soccer scholarship, which he'd do his best to help along its way. Then I could come back for a fifth year, work at whittling down my missing classes, and run around after a black and white ball. That sounded fine to me. I could complete my degree on somebody else's tab before proceeding (or so I still believed) to put on a suit and tie with Honeywell. Accordingly, in the spring of 1987, I joined the soccer team, and the seemingly impossible dream of the NFL began to fade more and more into the distance with each passing day.

5

Every agent everywhere, with the notable exception of my friend Gil Scott, promises you the earth on a platter. Not only will he make you a star, he'll make sure you hang on to large portions of the large amounts of money that you, with his expert guidance, will get. When an agent is trying to sell you on himself in preference to someone else, the going gets hot and heavy indeed. Both contenders try to justify themselves by disqualifying the opposition, while you sit in the middle, struggling to keep track of the charges and countercharges.

Two guys were at it hammer and tongs to handle my as-yet-nonexistent professional football career. One was younger, black, and just starting out, so he tried to appeal to our common culture. His line was, "Give a brother a chance. We'll understand each other on a different level. I'm new, but I'll work harder for you because of this. I won't be distracted; I'll offer you personal service." The other guy, who wasn't black, was a William and Mary graduate. He said, "I know what you've done; I've followed you these past four years. You

can check me out — people you know and trust will give me refer-
ences. I'm mature and stable, and I have a track record."

In the end, the Old Boy network prevailed. I wasn't all that
attracted to the idea of agents in the first place. I considered them a
necessary evil. What they could actually accomplish was another
matter. I wasn't banking on instant football stardom; I didn't rush
out and buy NFL logo paraphernalia. Even if I was drafted, I wasn't
about to head out on a shopping spree, because I knew I wasn't going
to command a premium price tag.

So I just quietly bided my time, and went on playing soccer. If
football happened, it happened. The victorious agent said that he had
high hopes for me because of the way I'd performed at the Combine.
By his telling, several teams were prepared to give me a try despite
my size.

Which was fine with me. I was eager for a change of pace. I pinned
no great hopes on the draft; I thought it more likely that I'd wind up
back at Honeywell. Where I didn't want to be any more was William
and Mary. School had become, for lack of a better word, unnecessary.
I wanted it over and done with; I wanted to get on with life. I looked
around me at the people who were delving into their books every
night, and knew that they'd be rewarded with good jobs in the end.
I also knew I wouldn't want any of them anywhere near me, as most
didn't have the common sense of a peanut. They might get an A while
I got a C, but if we were given a project to do, I could get it done ten
times better. The sin of pride! It kept rearing its grisly head that year.

I was bound and determined to finish up. I thought that I could
be of more value to Honeywell if I went there and gained direct experience. None of my courses was remotely related to the aerospace
industry or hands-on business management. The closest I'd come
was theoretical economics, and I didn't need any more theories. I had
a few of my own, and was itching to put them into practice.

This was my frame of mind, and it was to an extent unfair to my classes. Some were fun; I enjoyed learning about practical solutions to social problems. That seemed tangible and useful. If I got the chance, I could implement them, and others would benefit. Mostly, though, I was there under protest, not at all convinced of the relevance and significance of my studies.

The importance of university is twofold, to me. First, it places you in a setting where you have to make good decisions on a daily basis, away from the security of home and structured family life. Can you cope with all the obvious stuff? Budget yourself, pace yourself, get assignments done on time, and in some semblance of order? Second, and much more important, is the intellectual challenge of dealing with thinking people. This was the real opportunity for growth, both in and out of class — the unfamiliar ideas that stretched your mind and broadened your horizons, the exposure to all sorts of different people who planned on taking different paths in life. In college, everyone around you is looking forward. They believe that what they're going through will be in some sense profitable, that it's leading them toward a desired goal. This was for me by far the greatest benefit — learning and hearing things that fueled my optimism and pointed the way to future accomplishments.

I don't mean to denigrate any aspect of the university experience. I could have benefitted from studying more, being able to retain more information. Knowledge really is power; it frees you up, and more knowledge wouldn't have hurt me. But at this point in my life, I just wanted to strike a balance.

In the past few years, there's been a lot of talk about our Emotional Quotients, a measure of our ability to persist and survive. The theory is that this is a far greater determinant of individual success than our I.Q. I think I'd have scored high, if anybody had bothered to conduct the test in the 1980s. The other theory that's currently in vogue is known as the Lower Half Club. It suggests that three out of four U.S. presidents have done poorly in their college classes, as a disproportionate number of successful entrepreneurs have done, many of whom haven't gone to college at all. I'd have taken comfort in this notion then. To me, it wasn't important at which rank I finished. The big thing was to see and get to the end of the road. The degree was vital; all the stuff that revolved around or related to it wasn't going to do a lot for me out in the real world — or so I thought then.

Now, close to the end of my senior year, NFL draft day loomed. This isn't what you'd call a proactive situation; you wait for the phone to ring. Teams make their selections in order, worst to first, depending on their previous year's standing. At the time, there were twelve rounds. My agent felt that I'd be chosen — he didn't know or wouldn't say by whom — in the third, fourth, or fifth. Buoyed by this, I made a deal with my roommates. If I was chosen at all, I swore to drink one — count it, one — draft beer.

We played a pickup football game to while away the hours that day. The draft coincided with our reading week, so we had time on our hands. This was clearly a displacement activity. Until then, the idea of the NFL wasn't real, so I simultaneously tried not to acknowledge it and to brace myself for a fall. That's why I'd put all sorts of safety nets in place — a soccer scholarship and a job at Honeywell. On draft day, however, I realized that what I really wanted to do was play pro ball. I wanted it bad.

Eventually the call came from my agent while we were watching TV that evening. The draft was into the eighth round, and the club was the Kansas City Chiefs. Elated, my buddies broke out the beer. For the first time in my twenty-two years, alcohol passed my lips. I drank it all, and fulfilled my obligation. Still, I didn't want to celebrate too much. All of us weren't being drafted, for one thing. Everybody had the potential, given the right set of circumstances. I was happy, and the guys were happy for me, but we had to keep it all in context.

After the initial surprise, reality began to sink in. I'd never once thought about Kansas City. They hadn't been asking about me; they'd never approached me at the Combine. They were a half-decent club, and had gone to the playoffs for the first time in a while the previous year; I believe their record had been 10 and 6. Their head coach at that time was John Makovic, who was later replaced by his assistant, Frank Ganz. The players believed he had got them where they were. Ganz believed in special teams, which was a good sign — maybe he liked punt returners. I knew all this because I'd followed their fortunes to some degree, mostly out of a fondness for Otis Taylor and Len Dawson. Growing up in Florida before the Tampa Bay Buccaneers went into action, I'd been a man without a team; we spread our loyalties around and latched onto favorite players, wherever they might be. Then, when the Bucs arrived, you still had to have an alternative because you knew they weren't going to do anything substantial as a young team.

Then I started doing the numbers. These were good and bad. That year, there were 28 teams in the NFL. I was an eighth-round pick, the 218th player on anybody's list. Not so hot. On the other hand, there were roughly 500 college teams, and a large school might have as many as 100 players. William and Mary had 80, despite its size. So 218th out of at least 4,000 put me among the favored few.

After my final exams were done, I packed up and headed west — a long way from Clearwater and Chattanooga. The Chiefs' mini-camp started in May. At that stage, their level of commitment was still in doubt; they wanted to take a look at their choices and see who merited being brought back to full training camp in July. A dozen rookies at most would make the cut, and someone five feet six was no lock, by any stretch of the imagination.

I got off on the right foot, ran decent times, and survived the basic drills. When we started to play, I made a good showing right away. I thought everybody would do the here-comes-the-midget routine, but they seemed to feel that if the club had bothered drafting me I had to be able to do something.

Just for the record books, I was, and still am, the smallest person ever to play in the NFL. I think one guy — Gerald McNeal, the Ice Cube — might have weighed less, but he was a fraction of an inch taller. In general, though, they hadn't seen my likes before, nor would they again. Just as at the Combine, I took one look and thought, *These guys are huge — people aren't supposed to be that big and strong and fast.* But, just as at the Combine, try as they might, the linebackers were too bulky to cover me.

I made some good friends right away, many of whom would eventually make the team. My roommate was James Evans, another running back from Southern University in Baton Rouge, Louisiana, one of the largest black schools in the nation. He was the life of any party, with a flair for the dramatic, a resonant voice, and a magnetic personality. Darrel Colbert, a receiver, was from Texas Southern, another all-black college. He was tremendously funny, and thoroughly into the NFL life style. Kittrick Taylor, another receiver, had come from Washington State. He had good hands, a model athlete's body, and the mildest of tempers. The final member of our little clique was Paul Palmer, a running back who'd finished second in the Heisman Trophy voting, and the Chiefs' number-one draft choice. Later on, we'd meet Christian Okoye, the Nigerian Nightmare, who'd grown up playing soccer and had never seen a football until he came to the States on a track scholarship. He was six feet three, weighed 255 pounds, and could run as fast as anybody on the field. He didn't arrive until the full training camp began.

Impressive company. And I figured that I had a good shot at being among them. I was missing Diane, missing home, a bit lonely although happy to be there at all. I was staying at a hotel, the nicest accommodation I'd ever been in. I was relishing it momentarily in the NFL, holding my own against guys who stood a foot taller than I did.

Eventually, I got a $60,000 contract, plus an $18,500 signing bonus. All of this went straight to my mom's credit cards and, for me, a car. I'd been cruising around in a 1978 Monte Carlo with tinted windows and pin striping, everything short of foam dice dangling from the rearview mirror. I wisely traded this in on something better suited to Mr. Pragmatic's new, mature status — a Nissan Maxima. I bought it back in Florida, with not a penny down; I'd learned the almost magical effect of dropping the news that I was in the NFL. To look practical, I'd ordered a stick shift, which I had no idea how to drive. Diane gave me a quick lesson, and I lurched proudly off the dealer's lot. For a kid who was used to working with next to nothing, this was heady stuff. Fortunately, I didn't go overboard, which would prove to be just as well.

When I got back to full training camp, the rookies had to entertain the veterans after a meal. This is traditional. Most people chose to sing. While I couldn't carry a tune, I got up and said, "I can't sing, but I'll do the best I can, and take you back home, back to my little church, and sing the way the deacons used to do." By doing this, I accomplished two aims at once: I figured I made an effective witness, and I made sure they'd never ask me to sing again!

Our first pre-season outing was the Hall of Fame game in Canton, Ohio, against the San Francisco 49ers. Our offence was awful. I had a couple of catches and two not-bad returns. The strange thing about that game was how natural it seemed. I wasn't so much impressed by particular players (Joe Montana in the flesh!) as I was by the realization that here I was, among all these players, part of something that a few months ago had seemed so other-worldly. That was the biggest surprise — after so many years of hoping and dreaming, to be there.

During the second pre-season game, against the Houston Oilers, I had a 51-yard punt return. I split two guys and took the ball inside the 10-yard line. This did much to nail down my place on the team. I'd been patting myself on the back during practice, knowing that

I'd made some decent moves. I was hoping that Ganz would notice, too — my employment status was still in doubt and I knew cuts were yet to come. Then, in a triumph of bad timing, I hurt my ankle. During the next week or so I played sparingly, if at all, which was the club's decision. They wanted to hold me in reserve for punt returns, and give me a shot at being the third-down back. What surprised them was my ability to block, which I proved during the first regular season game against the San Diego Chargers — a sloppy and uneventful contest, which we lost. I went in three times and made my blocking assignments on all three plays. A reporter asked me how I'd done this, and I said something about just sandwiching myself between the rusher and our quarterback and closing my eyes. This showed up on the news the next day, and might or might not have aided my cause when the time came for the final cuts.

Wherever you are, that day of reckoning is always tense and eerie. Guys disappear without a trace, leaving only an empty locker. You're supposed to stroll by nonchalantly, see that your own stuff is still there, and pretend that this is the most normal thing in the world. At the end of the day, my locker was still full, so I jumped in my car and headed for the highway with the stereo cranked as loud as it would go. The song was called "Don't Disturb This Groove," which was truly the way I felt. I didn't want to reveal my elation and relief in front of anyone else, so this was a private celebration, a whole bunch of emotions rolled up into one — among them the knowledge that I'd been incredibly blessed.

Almost immediately, bad news disturbed my groove and everybody else's. A week later, the long-threatened NFL players' strike was upon us. Don't ask me what the issues were, what purpose the strike served, or what the long-term benefits might have been. An eighth-round rookie keeps his mouth shut and stays out of the line of fire. All I know is that we lost four weeks, during which no one was paid. The clubs, which had TV contracts to fulfill, scrambled to find ad hoc replacements. That sounds like an impossible task, but in fact there are tons of guys out there, literally thousands, who were almost good enough, and missed the boat. The saying is, There are all-stars on the street corners of every major city. Maybe that's an exaggeration, but in this case there were certainly enough decent players, ready and willing to go at a moment's notice.

I hung around Kansas City for a bit, until it quickly became apparent that there'd be bad feelings once the replacement team came in. There was a picket line, which they'd have to cross, and I wanted no part of it. Angry words were exchanged, and people lashed out in frustration. There was a shoving match between Jack del Rio and Otis Taylor, and another very odd incident involving Bill Moss and Dino Hackett, who arrived in the back of a pickup truck, brandishing shotguns. They were trying to make light of a bad situation, which was indeed bad, with the potential of getting worse.

I went to Chattanooga and visited Diane, not under the most ideal conditions. I camped out in a small ten-dollar room in a spare dormitory, and kept an eye on her eleven o'clock curfew. Then I thought about continuing on to Florida, or possibly Williamsburg. I decided not to, because the strike could have ended at any moment. After a week or so, with no end in sight, I headed back to Kansas City and began to work out with some of the other guys. We couldn't use the team's facilities, since we couldn't cross the line, and our efforts didn't amount to much, except that I managed to ding my ankle again.

Finally the strike ended, and back we went to what remained of an extremely inconsistent year. One game went into the void, and was never made up over the course of the schedule. As I recall, the Kansas City replacement team lost the three games it played. Ganz tried to pick up the pieces, with only limited success. He would last one more year before he, too, went his way. The strike had thrown everybody off-stride. We used to have hole-in-the-corner meetings that we called stress management sessions, every Monday or Tuesday night, down at the Red Lobster restaurant. Darrel, James, Kittrick, Paul, and I would sit around, rehashing the trials of rookies tangled in a web of losing. We seized the chance, because it was novel for us to be able to eat in restaurants on a regular basis.

Most people dream about getting everything they want. Of course you never do, though you do get bogged down in the frenzy of the chase. The real (and sometimes attainable) dream is freedom of choice. You've got it made if you earn enough money to enjoy yourself in a modest way without undue strain — especially if you can also put enough aside so you can breathe easy, perhaps take a break to decide on and set off in some new direction.

That's the kind of freedom that football had given us. Our salaries weren't exactly magnificent — especially as we'd lost a portion of them because of the strike — but we took simple pleasure in being able to go out for a meal. Most of us hadn't been able to that before. So even as we were wallowing in our many and varied complaints, we realized how truly fortunate we were.

Other than these dining experiences, the season for all of us was up and down, mostly down. It taught me that I could compete at the NFL level, and compete very well, put in the right situation. I had no problem with punt returns, though even there I didn't shine for a rather strange reason. The Chiefs were strong on defense, and put incredible efforts into blocking punts. The year before, they'd successfully blocked more punts than ever before in the team's history. This carried over into 1987. You'll appreciate what happened: If a punt is blocked, the returner just stands around with nothing to do. If it isn't, there's so much happening up at the line of scrimmage that there isn't adequate blocking available for him when he starts to run. Either way, I had very few chances to shine.

Still, I wasn't really making good on the opportunities that did come my way. On Thanksgiving Day, we were playing in Detroit, and the game was on national TV. Toward the end, the coaches put me on the "hands team," the sure-fingered squad a team sends in when the important thing is just to get and keep possession of the ball. Down it came and I dropped it, right in front of an audience of umpteen million viewers, not to mention any coaches who might have been watching for fresh new talent. I recovered, albeit badly, and made five yards. Sometimes a fumble-and-recovery works in your favor; it confuses the coverage team and you can take off. But not that Thanksgiving Day. I forget now whether we won or lost the game. In any case, we weren't going far.

That's almost the end of my Kansas City stardom. I was hurt in the last three games — another freak accident. We were practicing the day before we were about to play the Los Angeles Raiders, which might have been a chance for me to win some last-minute notice. By this time, the playoffs were out of reach; now we were playing for jobs. Tim Cofield (who would join the Argonauts in 1996) came on a blitz and caught me in the thigh with his knee. We weren't wearing full pads, and I got a deep bruise that effectively finished me off for the season.

What an inglorious season it was. The team finished 4 and 12, a far cry from the previous year. I picked up a lot of garbage. I did disciplined things that translated into poor statistics. For example, when the ball is bouncing around, you usually let it bounce. If you get a good bounce, you catch it and go down — a return for no yards. That sort of thing, coupled with the team's zeal for blocking punts, made my average look worse than it was. I missed eight games — four because of the strike, and another four because of injury. This was the primary concern. At five feet six, you can't get hurt or be seen as fragile. The small guy has to be twice as durable just to measure up. If a big guy gets the wind knocked out of him, people think, That must have been a heck of a shot. If I get hit the same way and stay down the same length of time, they think, Well, he's certainly getting bashed around out there. That's why I've had to get up on some of the plays that a big guy would take lying down. Pound for pound, I've got to appear tougher than he is; that's a perception that becomes a fact of life for me.

In the course of the wrap-up meeting, the club had talked about an off-season program, to start at the end of the following March and continue for five or six weeks. The idea was to bring guys up and have them work out under supervision, a sort of maintenance regimen. This wasn't uncommon; most teams do it to some extent, and it's a good idea. The problem is it doesn't pay well, just a per diem that covers room and board. They'd asked me to sign up for it, but I'd explained that I was due back at William and Mary to complete my credit hours. I promised I'd be back in time for the next season's mini-camp. I didn't want to put all my eggs in the NFL basket; finishing school was still my number-one priority.

So that's the way we left it. I knew I could play, and I thought the club knew I could play. The next step would be to take my game to the next level and get me more involved in punch offense. I knew they wanted me in the program, I just didn't know how much — obviously, more than I understood, even though I never got the sense of an ultimatum along the lines of "Be there or else."

Maybe I missed the signals; I was still the naive kid. I thought they'd respect my decision to return to college. In reality, all they wanted to do was win football games, and having me in the program would help them do this. They expected I'd put off school until I was a bit more established on the team. I was sending them a signal of my own: football didn't come first for me. And truth to tell, I'd have benefited from the program. I could have done with some improvement. I was, at best, very okay; my position wasn't at all secure. When you're my height, the negatives crop up and all sorts of doubts emerge. The club thinks, Is he really what we're looking for? Can he stand up to the pain? Can we do better, take less of a chance with someone else? We've got bigger people who can take the shots and do the job.

But none of this worried me at the time. I spent Christmas at home, enjoying the fact that I finally had an income. I seized the chance to play Santa Claus, rather than sit there on the receiving end. I'd deferred $30,000 of my $45,000 salary (down from $60,000 because of the games lost during the strike). All I had to worry about was a car payment, half the rent, and — worse luck — the cost of returning to William and Mary. Besides, Honeywell was waiting in the wings. I contacted Mr. Ely at season's end, to make sure that option stayed open, and let him know that I had a bit of catching up to do at school.

I was still seven classes short of my degree. The original scholarship had expired, and I faced a $4,500 bill for out-of-state tuition. I thought about taking all seven and getting it over with, and decided that was impractical. Five would have to do. I felt confident that I could handle them, as I'd have fewer distractions than before. I couldn't play football, because I was now a pro. I couldn't even play soccer — and there went the idea of a separate soccer scholarship, this now being the spring semester. Soccer took place at the same time as football, so its season was over and done. In fact, I shouldn't have thought about playing anything, in case I might have been injured, which would have been the final straw back in Kansas City. The club wanted me to keep busy lifting weights and building my strength.

Which is what I began to do, for the first time ever. I was putting up 225 to 240 pounds in sets of five on the bench press, the classic gauge of upper-body strength. Along with a leg workout, some endurance exercises, a bit of running, and a little basketball on the sly, this kept me in good shape. Dirk and Reggie were there to cheer me on, since they'd come back as well, in the same missing-classes boat that I was. Only Mike Hackett had graduated and gone his way. The only glitch in the program was around April, when I developed bursitis in my shoulder. I was in constant pain; I couldn't move my right arm, which really cramps your style when you're driving a stick shift. I got my first-ever cortisone shot — no treat, believe me. Then I consulted a chiropractor, who discovered I had the ever-popular pinched nerve. Eventually it mended, and I calmed down on lifting weights and launched into the end-of-April exams. I passed and this left me only two classes short. This was no big deal; I could knock them off in summer sessions or by correspondence.

Meanwhile, I'd missed the first stage of the Kansas City workout program. Round two would be better than nothing. I hustled out and joined in, still under contract. The shoulder was back in working order, and I felt good; I could be in fighting trim within hours. During the first week, we started to play some racquetball to augment what we were doing on field. It's a total change of pace — fun, competitive, and it helps you get in shape because you're moving around a confined area. Almost at once, and for the first time ever, I pulled a hamstring. I didn't know what this was like; I'd seen it happen to other guys, but it sounds so corny until you actually experience it yourself. It isn't corny. It's painful and debilitating, especially when it hits you out of the blue.

By now, the Chiefs were probably thinking, Maybe this kid is more trouble than he's worth. I was the eternal optimist, nonetheless, and I decided to pull myself together in the time remaining until full-scale training camp began. For focus I went to Williamsburg, and lived with Coach Cox and his family for about five weeks. I began to run several miles a day in the heat of a Virginia summer, and dove into a regimen that had worked for me before — 21 pushups followed by 21 situps, then 18 of each, and so on down in increments of three.

So there I was, under the watchful eye of Coach Cox and the kid next door, who obliged by playing basketball with me. He was a high school senior, and full of energy. We were out there every day on the front lawn, and I was toned, in maybe the best shape of my life. The hamstring was healed, which I knew, because I could move around with agility. I felt like Rocky, off in the wilderness doing the mental imagery thing, visualizing being super-successful when I hit Kansas City.

I arrived the day before camp began, and went through my physicals. The next morning, I was heading for the first practice when somebody told me that "Whitey" wanted to see me. This was the player-personnel guy, a gentleman called "Whitey" Duvall, whose full head of snow-white hair gave rise to his monicker. I went to his office.

"Mike," he said, "I was one of the guys who brought you here. I know you've had some injuries, but I know you can play. You're our best punt returner, our best running back in terms of hands. But the club is paying some other guys more money, and they have to figure that into their calculations. It's easier to get you out the door right now, without anybody really noticing. If we delay, and you start to practise, the club's concerned that they won't be able to justify releasing you. We don't want to cut you at the end of camp because you wouldn't have a chance to go anywhere else. You're going to be picked up; there are teams that are interested in you already. I hate that this has happened. It's just part of the game."

This was a shock, to say the least. I tried to look on the positive side. "Whitey" was right — I might still get the chance to go somewhere more appealing. I thought about Romans 8:28 — "And we know that in all things God works for the good of those who love Him, who have been called according to His purpose" — and decided that there was a different direction for me. But all this came as an even greater surprise to the rest of the team. The guys were in seeming disbelief. I say "seeming," because a lot of times, when this sort of thing happens, your teammates are trying to console you. I've been on the other side of that one. But their reaction seemed genuine, as if they felt I had a lot of talent. Several of them remarked that Kansas City was notorious for cutting players who then moved on and did very well — which was something for me to look forward to, after driving all the way from Florida, and never getting a chance to set foot on the field. So I packed up again, which wasn't hard, because I'd barely opened my suitcases, and got back onto the Interstate. I found a lot of peace in the knowledge that God was going to work things out. This was the Friday of a long weekend, and I was in no rush. Nothing was going to happen for a couple of days.

When you're cut by an NFL team, you're put on waivers. First, your name goes out over a network known as the waiver wire. Any other team can pick you up, but, like the draft, the worst choose first. Later on, my agent alleged that quite a few clubs had expressed interest in me. Somehow, Tampa Bay got there ahead of them, by virtue of its rock-bottom standing the previous year.

Tampa Bay had its problems, but it was just up the block from Clearwater. Getting the opportunity to play professional football close to home was a huge blessing, something most people would have jumped at. You know what they say: Be careful what you pray for, because you just might get it.

I lasted with the Buccaneers for a week and a half — among the longest ten days of my entire life. Tampa Bay was a miserable organization. The players weren't very good and thought they were. We struggled in Kansas City, where we had guys who were legitimate players, some of them all-stars. Tampa Bay had nobody of any esteem or acclaim, yet their egos matched their stadium, an architectural nightmare known as the Big Sombrero. I didn't know how bad the place was until I got there. You think, It's the NFL; how awful can it be?

I'd have tried to make the best of it, had I made the team. I wasn't going to walk — to say I'd rather not play than play here. As things turned out, I didn't get the chance. I played in just one pre-season game, and once again committed the Cardinal Flub. I dropped the first punt that came my way. I picked the ball up and made three or four yards, a penalty was called, and they rekicked. Instant redemption! This time I caught the ball and returned it for 18 yards. That's pretty good.

The league-leading average the previous year was 14 or 15 yards; Tampa Bay's guy had been racking up about eight. If you do 18 yards every time, you're an all-pro, so I was looking all right.

When I'd come into camp — midstream, because of the delay involved in getting back from Kansas City — everybody thought I was a receiver because of my hands, the way I caught the ball. I'd made a couple of nice cuts, run a little offence, and managed to open some eyes.

I was feeling my way, trying to find my niche; I thought there was somewhere to go. And so there was. After that first game, I got called into the office by Ray Perkins, the head coach. He told me that he wanted to make some decisions early, and that he'd settled on a couple of "younger backs." This is not what you want to hear when you're twenty-three. I had no idea what he was talking about. Now I believe his plan was to make way for a guy named Goode, whom Perkins had recruited while at Alabama. Goode was very highly touted, but he'd torn up his knee at Alabama. In fact, he'd done well in that first game, but he wasn't a punt returner, which didn't help Perkins very much. The Buccaneers, like the Chiefs, failed to make the grade that season.

So there I was, out in the cold again. In truth, it's doubtful that I would ever have enjoyed playing in Tampa Bay, aside from having my mom close by. The guys in Kansas City had made me feel comfortable from the very first whistle; this was a totally different atmosphere. So much so that when Perkins cut me, it came as almost a relief.

Curiously enough, the thing I remember most about those ten depressing days is an incident that took place after one of the evening meetings. I was at a gas station, and a man came up to me at the pumps. He was quite drunk, obviously living on the street, and he asked for money to get something to eat. I feared that he'd spend it on drink, and asked him to promise that he'd buy food. If he broke his word, I couldn't control that, but I wanted his assurance. He gave it, and I handed him five dollars. He was very grateful, and said, "Are you a Christian?" I said, "Yes, sir, I am." He said, "I used to teach the Bible," and asked me how many books there were in it. That's one of the things you're supposed to know. I didn't, and confessed as much. He said, "Remember this: How many letters are there in the words 'old' and 'testament'? Three and nine — so put them together, and that's 39 books in the Old Testament. The words 'new' and 'testament' have the same number of letters, but this time you multiply them, so that makes 27 books. Add 39 and 27, and you get 66 in all." I've never forgotten that to this day — I myself teach it now to others. The lesson to me was that you can learn something from anybody. Everyone has a story, if you're willing to listen, and you never know who you're convening with, even if they seem down on their luck.

Diane met me on the day of my release, expecting that she'd have to cheer me up. I think she was surprised to see I was fine — happy to be out of a bad situation, and hopeful that, if I went back on the waiver wire, there would still be some interest from another quarter. There wasn't — and I know why. I'd been cut by two different teams, at times when no cuts had to be made. While Kansas City wanted to be fair, and Tampa Bay was weird, to somebody who didn't know the circumstances, I looked like a possible problem. My agent suggested I wait it out. Once the teams had assessed their specific needs, he felt sure they'd come looking for me, by which time I'd be a free agent, and we could start the ball rolling all over again.

Just as a precaution, I went back to Honeywell and met with Mr. Ely. His offer was still on the table. I told him that I'd like to intern from September to December 1988, then go back to William and Mary, finish up my credit hours, and return to the aerospace industry full time, eventually getting my MBA. I'd have to pay for that, and Honeywell would reimburse me as part of their education program. I do believe that God put Mr. Ely in a position to help me out, and he went to bat for me one more time. The intern program is usually offered only during the summer, and it was August by now. Fortunately, he saw me as a valuable asset, and agreed to bend the rules. We decided that if another club picked me up by Labor Day, I'd give the NFL one more shot. If not, I'd report for duty. I had to report for duty somewhere, because by this time, counting taxes, travel, and tuition, the money was running low.

If professional football had ended then and there, I could have accepted it. I'd always assumed that there'd be more work for me outside football than within it. If not, I'd have gone to the off-season camp in Kansas City rather than back to school. Faced with the same choice, most guys would have chosen football; I simply wasn't all wound up in the NFL experience. I'd been very fortunate to play at all, and I looked at it as a one-in-a-million chance. Whatever I managed to accomplish, I'd always be one decision away (on a coach's part) from unemployment. An average football career runs 3.3 years. I knew a lot of guys had played for ten years, which skewed the curve, so the median was probably closer to 2.2. Starting from square one — a rookie salary — you couldn't possibly bank enough to get yourself established in another field when the time came for you to make way for the younger backs. To me, security was the most important consideration, and I thought I could make a living doing and enjoying just about anything. That's the approach to life, whatever setting you're in. A lot of ball players I'd met were very unhappy despite the money they were paid. And they'd have been unhappy with or without money — that wasn't the issue. I didn't feel I'd been cheated or screwed or deprived. Whatever had happened was part of my own maturing process, and part of God's plan. If I never played another down of football, these things had been very important to my growth, to my understanding of where I was and my relationship with God. If my childhood dreams had been taken away, I was able to say, Thank you, Lord, for this opportunity and all the other wonderful things around me. I was ready to be happy and content and ask, Now where do I go? There was some indecision there, no doubt about it, but also a great joy, an excitement about the future.

In fact, this was one of the greatest periods of my life. My little sister was coming of age now, and we were communicating more and on a different level. Diane was back home, helping her mother. Things had been difficult ever since her father was killed, and she felt that she should take some time off from her studies. We'd both been all over the map for so long that four months together was an eternity — a welcome one. We fell into a regular routine for the first time in ages, and with it the opportunity to fall in love again. I was working nine to five, just like a normal person. I didn't brood on football, or madly work out in case a team might suddenly decide to pick me up. I didn't watch the games on Sunday and think, I should be out there instead of those guys. I wasn't the armchair running back; I enjoyed them for what they were worth, having fun as I used to do, as a spectator.

I also became the youth director of our church, which kept me on the run. Every Friday night, I'd pack the kids into a van, and away we'd go, to a football game or an amusement center, singing church songs at the top of our lungs. Often we'd get back late at night, which made even Mom wonder what was going on. Diane, on loan from the Seventh-Day Adventists, at times helped with activities for the girls. The culmination of all this was the Christmas pageant. I wrote a couple of skits and revised the lyrics to the Whitney Houston song "The Greatest Love of All." These things really drove me. I was passionate about them, because I got to see the fruits of my labor, week in and week out.

That's part of the reason why I was reluctant to return to William and Mary in January of 1989. The job at Honeywell was panning out and the church activities were infinitely rewarding. Yet hanging over me like a cloud was the issue of those last-gasp credit hours. So back

I went, with just enough money to cover expenses. In fact, I got a bit of a break, as Coach Laycock signed me up as an assistant in spring football, which meant that I didn't have to look for a job on the side. The old crowd was dispersed by now, with the exception of Reggie, who was trying to nail down a few missing credits of his own. We roomed together, as sort of a last hurrah, the last chance we'd have to spend time with each other, unless for some reason we cross paths in the future.

Around about March, my almost-absent agent phoned me, and resurrected the prospect of playing, but in Canada with the Calgary Stampeders. According to him, they were counting the minutes until they could get me in uniform. This seemed unlikely. To be frank, I didn't much care what he wanted me to do. I felt he hadn't done a lot for me, but I told him to go ahead and research the situation anyway. He did, and told me Calgary would send me a contract by return mail. In early May, I'd walked the aisle at William and Mary, and had my degree in hand — but nothing resembling a contract. Nor had one made its way to Mom's place in Clearwater. In June, Honeywell was expecting a firm declaration of my intent. In my own laissez-faire way, I didn't bother getting in touch with Calgary, or with my agent, who I thought could afford to call me. Weeks passed, and he finally did call to ask whether I'd signed yet. I said no, and around we went some more. Calgary said they'd send the paperwork again, in time for me to make the start of their training camp.

By this time, somewhat against my better judgment, I'd decided that I was going to give football — even the Canadian variety — one more shot. I'd informed Mr. Ely of this, and he understood my feelings. Understandably he stressed that he couldn't promise to hold the job open for me. That was more than fair, and I felt okay about it. The Stampeders weren't talking about a tryout; they wanted me to sign on the line. Meanwhile the paperwork was nowhere in sight.

More time passed, and we were into mid-June — two days, then one day, away from the start of Calgary's camp. Meanwhile, they'd been in touch with me, saying that there'd be a followup call to give me all the details on my flight. That was fine, except I still had no contract or plane ticket. But I wasn't worried or panicked. At best, I'd be coming late to camp, as I had in Tampa Bay. Was Calgary a Tampa Bay-like organization? What did they think they were playing at? If you want somebody, you get them there on time. I tried to pack, but didn't have much in the way of winter clothes, so I gave up the attempt. Was God trying to give me none-too-subtle hints that I should take the job at Honeywell and live corporately ever after?

Finally, on a Sunday, the call came. The story was that the Stampeders didn't want me after all. In fact, they were going to release me from their negotiation list. And that, for about twenty-four hours, was that.

What I didn't know was that getting cut from somebody's negotiation list was roughly the same as being cut from camp. The news goes out on a waiver wire of its own. The good thing about waiver wires is that people listen in.

The next day, Mr. Ralph Sazio, then the president of the Argonauts, was catching up on current events and saw my name. He was a William and Mary alumnus, and his son Gerry was the Argonauts' U.S. scout, based in Virginia Beach. I'd never met or spoken with either of them — when Mr. Sazio himself phoned me just before noon, and asked me how I'd feel about coming to someplace called Toronto.

I said, "Well, I don't know." (In my mind I'm saying, I'm not all that sure about football, I've just had a bad time with Calgary, I have an opportunity here at Honeywell, they haven't hired anybody else yet, I've got my degree from a prestigious university, and I'm a minority, a hard worker, my friend Mr. Ely has bent over backwards for me, and so on and so forth.)

I couldn't make a decision, so I just spun my wheels, mumbling to Mr. Sazio, who finally said, "Excuse me, I don't think you understand. Can you make a three o'clock flight today?"

I said, "Yes, sir, I can do that." And I did.

6

I'm embarrassed to admit how little I knew about Canada in 1989. You wouldn't believe the misconceptions that persist today throughout the southern U.S., even though there's at least a smattering of daily news in print, kids are learning quite a bit more in school, and the Internet has put everything at our fingertips. Back when I was young, I was totally out to lunch. The fact that the Blue Jays held their spring training camp a couple of miles up the road did not breed familiarity. I used to follow them in the standings, but I didn't tune into all that many games. Baseball was too slow-moving for me. Our only real contact with Canadians occurred during spring break. We would think it was freezing cold outside, and they would suddenly arrive and jump merrily into the ocean. This made no earthly sense to us. They seemed bizarre, almost from another world. That's where I thought I was going.

Naturally, I assumed that Toronto would be frigid, even in late June. I was convinced that I was going to live next door to Alaska. I didn't know whether three-quarters of the season would be played in snow. I had no clue how large Toronto was, and landing at the Pearson Airport did nothing to enlighten me. I didn't have a window seat, so I got no impression of urban sprawl as we began our final descent. Besides, I was too edgy to appreciate the view, even if I could have seen it. That morning, I'd been thinking about a return to Honeywell. Eight hours later, I was trying to make sense of Terminal One. I'd heard that Canada had two official languages, and I wasn't sure whether Toronto was French- or English-speaking. Bilingual announcements aboard the plane had left this issue in doubt. Of course, Terminal One was and is among the most multicultural places on earth, and I heard about two dozen languages being spoken all around me, which utterly baffled me. This was my frame of mind when I encountered Canada Customs.

True to form, I'd managed to bring only my driver's license and a birth certificate. I had no passport, no contract or work permit, nothing to prove that I had a job of any description. I put on my very best gab to talk my way through the interviews. I wish I'd had a tape recorder; it would have been fun to review the conversation: "Hello, you don't know me, but I've come to play professional football, the club's president said so, never mind I'm five feet six," and so forth. I just kept smiling and called upon all my William and Mary debating skills, picked up by field experiment in the student lounge. The first officers I met were stoic and strait-laced. Gradually I convinced them that I might by some slim chance be eligible, and my reception became more and more pleasant as I slowly worked my way down the line. I remember hoping that football wouldn't be as tough.

After a bit of floundering around, I found the person who'd been sent to meet me. We hopped into a van, drove to Highway 401 and turned west toward Guelph, where the Argos were in training camp. Nobody had bothered to mention this to me. All I gathered was that we were heading away from Toronto to someplace I'd never heard of. I kept asking the driver what the city was like, and he kept trying to explain. He seemed excited about the new SkyDome, which I hadn't heard of either. (It was brand new that year; its first season was mine.) I wanted to know if football was popular, if the games were broadcast on national TV. By now, I was getting a jumbled picture of what I thought he was trying to tell me — all sorts of wonderful things, none of which I could see, as we drove on and on past acres of open farmland. He told me he'd just dropped someone else off at the airport — another player who'd been cut from the team. On the one hand, there seemed to be a place for me. On the other, I wondered if I might be the next to go. So I was filled with, shall we say, optimistic apprehension. At least the weather was warm, and I was good with that.

We left the 401 and took another highway to Guelph, which didn't square with the driver's description of a thriving metropolis. Nor did the campus of Guelph University. While it's very pretty, it's a ghost town in late spring, the students having decamped for the summer. At this point, I wasn't even sure if the country was inhabited.

After I'd been assigned my room in one of the dormitories, I headed down to the dining hall, jumpy to begin with, because I had a horror of coming late to camp. All the players were there, just finishing their meal. I confess that I'd been expecting a crop of sub-par athletes — this was, after all, the backwoods. But I could see at a glance that these dudes were big and in excellent shape. Because I'd missed the food, I went to get a physical while everyone else was in meetings. The trainers were somewhat amused by how small I was, as were the other guys when they started filtering in for their treatments. There's always some chatter about the new arrival, especially if he's my size. You pretend you're oblivious to it. The trainers ribbed me a bit — but only a bit. They knew that I'd played in the NFL. In fact, Bruce Holmes, who'd also been drafted by Kansas City, was already here. Whether I'd stunk or whether I'd been great, at least I'd been there, which counted for something. The theory was that the club wouldn't have brought me in unless I could deliver.

Well, that remained to be seen. Obviously, this was real football — a major league I'd barely known existed, and filled with unknown quantities. There weren't as many guys as I'd been used to, because NFL teams carry a 25-percent-larger active roster, which means that their camps are larger also. The 50-50 racial split looked familiar, though. The Argos' final regular-season cut would be 21 Canadian and 16 American players. The Canadian talent pool is smaller and more solidified, so most of the new prospects were competing for American positions, and most of the Americans, both veterans and newcomers, were black.

Then I discovered one or two surprises in the mix. I'd heard about a running back named Gill (The Thrill) Fenerty, who turned out to be white. This was a shock. Where I come from, speedy white running backs aren't exactly thick on the ground. Then again, the first-string quarterback, Gilbert Renfroe, proved to be black, which I hadn't expected, either.

After the physical, I went back to my room and called my mom to tell her that I'd arrived safely and that it wasn't going to be a walkover. I was a trifle intimidated, which is always the way. You settle down once you're on the field. The trouble was that in every other camp, I'd shared a room. Here I was alone, with no one to talk to, to ask what things were like. I lay awake, wondering if I was ready for this, whether I was in shape, and, incidentally, where my contract was.

Things looked up the next morning, when I met Ralph Sazio. He told me more about his experiences at William and Mary, and outlined the terms of my contract, a standard year-and-an-option, starting at $50,000. I said I'd have to consult with my agent, who'd done nothing, as usual, but would want his percentage anyway. We went back and forth on the phone for a while, I signed the contract, and got onto the field.

Or, to be precise, I sat on the sidelines and watched a general practice, which utterly confused me. There seemed to be no rules for motion; everyone was taking running starts. Both backs were moving, heading for the line of scrimmage when the ball was snapped. I thought, I'm never going to understand this game. So there was some trepidation there. This was also my first look at the other players in action. More trepidation! Carl Brazley and Doran Major were the defensive backs. I'd assumed that Doran was a linebacker — his arms were huge. Darrell K. Smith, the receiver, stood six feet three and weighed 190. All these guys looked like tight ends — sleek, svelte, and tough, with massive upper bodies. Plus, they were quick — Carl ran, and talked, like the wind. The words tumbled out a mile a minute, so fast that sometimes I couldn't understand him. Doran and Darrell K. were totally wound up, going at it as if they were in the Eastern final. I sat there wondering, Is everybody else this good? This was more intense, and the guys were a whole lot better, than where I'd been lately — and it was only the first practice. It's safe to say I was a bit overwhelmed.

As usual, once I began to play, things leveled out. The first chance I had to practise was a special teams drill. I was busy catching punts; there was no hitting and I had no blockers. All the other guys came swarming down to cover. I'd seen this movie before, and it was called Kill the Carrier. I took two steps in one direction, went back the other way, and faked out the entire team. Eyebrows rose. Bob O'Billovich, the head coach, came over to talk with me. I went on to catch a few more with no problem, which made me feel pretty good. I'd made a nice, smooth move and started people thinking. However, as the practice wore on, it became apparent, at least to me, that I was in the worst shape of my career. The sum total of my exercise lately had been working at Honeywell, directing the church youth group, and sitting with my nose in a book at William and Mary. I'd played no soccer, and only a little basketball. This was the least activity I'd had in a nine-month period all my life, and it was only a matter of time before somebody else noticed that fact.

At least my prospective role on the team was clear. I'd been called up to audition strictly as a return specialist, as heir apparent to the designated import position. The plan was that I'd replace Pernell Moore, a very adept player who'd just been injured. The plan was also that I'd add a needed spark. The previous year, the Argos had finished 14 and 4, their best showing ever, but then had been upset by Winnipeg in the Eastern semifinal, to the dismay of everybody who'd counted their bonus money before it hatched and ordered new cars. That sounded promising enough: I'd be part of a team that almost made it, and could probably go all the way this time around. All I had to do was prove myself.

That same afternoon, during the one-on-one drills, I proved (1) that I could make it in the Canadian Football League, and (2) that I was woefully out of shape. I was running a route, closely guarded by a free safety named Floyd Salazar, who was working out at halfback. I made a slick move and totally lost him, pulling my hamstring in the process. I caught the ball and stayed with the route, but considered this as an evil portent, right off the top. O'Billovich was as excited as he was justifiably concerned. I apologized for not being ready, and asked for a little time. In fact, the hamstring wasn't badly pulled, which I demonstrated a few days later when we had a goal-line scrimmage, and I scored a touchdown. This was a live drill with full-fledged tackling. All the young offensive players formed up into something known as the scout team, whose job was to execute an opposing team's likely strategy for the benefit of our first-string defence.

I got the ball, made contact, ricocheted off, and went all the way around the other end to score. Déjà vu! You'll recall my freshman year in high school, with Coach Murray at the helm. I'd just come up to the varsity team, and scored in almost exactly the same way, whereupon Murray said, "Do it again." Which is exactly what O'Billovich said this time, so I made another move, went the other way, and scored one more time. O'Billovich pointed at me and yelled, "You! Get out of this drill!" — after which I didn't have to run scout team any more.

And that's how I finally got my nickname, after going twenty-four years without one. The media started to pay attention to me from the very first day — on the theory, I suppose, that I was a curiosity; people always want to root for the little guy — the underdog. I was overwhelmed by the number of reporters who wanted to interview me, and I obliged them, as did O'Billovich. During that week, he said, "We've got this new guy who bounces around like a pinball." The press picked this up and ran with it, and it stuck.

But now, despite my assurances to O'Billovich, I pulled my hamstring again. This time it was worse, and I knew I'd have to have it seen to. Rehab and physiotherapy loomed. There's an old saying: "You can't make the club in the tub." I didn't want to be away from the action, sitting in a whirlpool bath; I still wasn't totally confident about making the team, even though O'Billovich had said there'd be a place for me. In effect, I was a rookie all over again. I'd played a year of pro ball, a long time ago and in another country. In the meantime, I was getting positive signals from the other players as well, and I found a couple of buddies early on. Darrell K. Smith took me under his wing the night that I was asked to get up and sing (more déjà vu). I chose another church song, so that was an opportunity to make a stand right away. I asked him if we'd have a chance to go to church, and he hooked me up with Reggie Pleasant, who rode herd on us to Bible studies and chapel.

The hamstring took its own sweet time mending. I sat out the rest of camp, watching the play and trying to fathom the CFL rules. Finally, we boarded a bus for Toronto. Suburbs everywhere are pretty much the same, and it wasn't until we reached the Gardiner

Expressway that I started to get a sense of the city. Down along the lakeshore, people were out bicycling and jogging. The lawns were manicured; there were flowers everywhere. Company advertisements made from colorful floral designs graced the side of the expressway. This was the most beautiful approach to a city I'd ever seen. By this time, the guys had told me more about what to expect, but I still wasn't prepared. Along the way, I was thrilled by the numbers of people on the streets, by how spacious and open everything was. I thought, I'm going to like this place.

Then we got to the SkyDome. Of course that in itself blew me away. This was our first pre-season game, and I watched it from the 500 level. Now I could see the plays as they developed and unfolded; this was a much better vantage point than down on the field itself. Suddenly, the nuances of the game, the rules, the motion — everything made sense to me. I thought, *I can be really good at this game. When I get my chance, I can be special at this game.*

First, we had one or two problems to overcome. I sat out the next game as well, of necessity. The hamstring was still very tender, and I continued with my therapy. O'Billovich had decided to keep me around, even though I wasn't healthy. This meant that I was placed on the practice roster, a squad that does everything the other guys do except play games. The idea here is that you can step into the breach if somebody is hurt; you're ready to go, and you know the system. It's a good place to park promising rookies; it brings younger players along and offers them constant lower-level exposure. The trouble is, it paid only $500 a week. Even in 1989, and although the club picks up hotel expenses when you're on the practice roster, living in Toronto wasn't cheap. Fortunately, the club decided that I was eligible for the Crows Nest.

Mom Crow was then almost seventy and going strong. She'd been housing players (and the occasional coach) for twenty-odd years; she preferred to have two or three lodgers at a time. There were strict qualifications: no party animals needed apply, though if one did, Mom Crow would tame him before he knew what was happening. You stayed with her while your status with the team was being resolved. It was a temporary roost until you found a place of your own. A favored few were allowed to hang around for longer periods, and eventually I'd shatter all the previous records.

Mom Crow was the first person outside the team I met in Toronto, and the single most significant influence on my life during my first four or five years in Canada. She lived in a three-story row house near the Canadian National Exhibition grounds, where the team held practices on natural turf at the old outdoor stadium. Mom was a white lady, married to Pop Crow, who was a couple of years older than she was, a chain cigar-smoker with advanced emphysema. His "seat" was on the porch which had a large window that he'd open when he indulged. This did little good for Mom Crow as she herself was heavily into cigarettes. Coffee and tobacco formed their staple diet. Pop was an extremely opinionated man, but very progressive in his thinking. In the southern States, a seventy-year-old, cigar-smoking Caucasian man would never allow a black man (or black boy, as I'd more likely have been termed) to live in his house, let alone permit that black man to call his wife "Mom." That's when I realized I'd come to a different place. All of a sudden, everything was different.

Imagine, now, my being in this little house, totally out of my element, and semi-allergic to smoke of any kind. My room was up on the top floor, and was, if anything, far too warm in the middle of a humid Toronto summer. Everybody else I knew, everything I'd been familiar with, was miles away. I couldn't even do what I was supposed to do, which was play football, with my hamstring shot. I couldn't talk with anybody else on the team, because they had a road game the next day, which I was going to read about in the newspaper. I knew nothing about this city, even that it was so large, that I'd abruptly been

MICHAEL "PINBALL" CLEMONS

deposited in. So I was feeling sort of alienated again. In fact, I was thinking that, if I was going to be alienated, then I might as well go all the way, and that a hotel would be really nice, because I'd have my own shower. The Crows didn't have one; there was only a tub. I didn't know when or if I should use it — it was Mom and Pop's tub. So there were a lot of issues here. The one thing I did know right off was that Mom Crow was one of the nicest people I'd ever met. I didn't know quite how to take her, and I didn't try to figure it out. I knew I was safe and sound, if not really comfortable yet.

The next morning, things still looked solid. Mom Crow handed me a map and told me to take a streetcar to the Eaton Centre, walk around, and begin to learn about the city. I wasn't certain there was much point to this; I didn't know if I was going to make the team, but I followed her advice anyway.

Once I arrived downtown, I went crazy. People were playing music on the street. This was a storybook; this didn't happen in Clearwater, Florida. It didn't happen in Kansas City, or in Williamsburg, Virginia. By now I was used to the color of the money; just everything else was new. I was totally taken aback. People were very helpful and showed me where the Eaton Centre was. I didn't go inside it until a week or so later, because I didn't realize that there were shops behind the street frontage. That didn't matter. I was amazed, enthralled, engulfed by the whole experience. I called Mom Crow to tell her I was okay; this was about ten-thirty at night, because I'd made a late start that day. I said, "You won't believe this, but stuff is still open! People are everywhere, things are lit up, there's a record store that doesn't close until midnight!" All of which came as no surprise to her. She said, "That's nice, Michael, but you'd better come home now." And from that point, things just kept on getting better. This was obviously a great place even without football. And I hadn't played a down yet.

Then the guys got back to town, and the final cuts were

announced. I was still on the team, or, more exactly, on the practice roster. Now I had to make a decision: to call Honeywell and see whether my job was still available, or to stick it out. After some deliberation, I decided that, since I was here anyway, I might as well go for it. I was settling in at Mom Crow's, I didn't need a whole lot to live on, and I thought I should give it my best shot when and if the time came that I could play.

Now we were practising every day. My hamstring was better and I was flying around the field. But the starting lineups were set, so I sat out the first two games of the season. For the third game, O'Billovich decided to give me an opportunity to add punch to the special teams. That day, an article appeared in the paper that did little good for my nerves. The headline read something along the lines of "Pinball wizard to make debut." As it was, my debut was less than auspicious. In front of 35,000 fans, I took the opening kickoff — the first time I'd touched a ball in the CFL — and returned it 40 or 45 yards. Then I got hit and promptly fumbled. The Eskimos recovered, and I was totally chagrined. All the guys seemed delighted anyway. Darrell K. picked me up, slapped me on the head, and said, "That's okay! Don't worry about it. You're going to be great!" Then Carl and Reggie ran over and did the same.

Later I had a couple more good returns, and was named offensive player of the game, so I'd made a splash and gained instant credibility. In fact, I collected that award in four of my ten appearances — a tie with Gill Fenerty, and ahead of Darrell K., which wasn't bad for the new kid on the block. There was talk of my being up for Rookie of the Year, until they checked the rulebook and found that I was ineligible, having played in the NFL. O'Billovich kept on trying to give me more offensive duties, until I pulled my hamstring a third time. This was the worst; I didn't have the chance to strengthen my hamstring because of the game schedule. It happened during practice, as even there I was going full-speed ahead. That's what I felt I was supposed to do — not to mention what I believed I had to do, to be allowed to stick around.

One other game stands out as something I hoped wouldn't be repeated, but was. We were playing in Winnipeg, on the first day of October. Snow was threatening, or worse, freezing rain. The wind made it seem much colder. In fact, it was the coldest I'd ever been in all my natural life; by comparison, Kansas City was a walk on the beach. I was freezing to death, homesick like crazy, missing my mom, my girlfriend, and my little sister, missing the warmth of Florida, and missing winning, which we hadn't been doing much of. Fenerty was hurt, and Terry Underwood had started in his place. Then he, too, was injured.

I filled in as running back in the second half. I covered about 70 yards rushing, and had my first punt-return touchdown, which was something to behold. The kick went up, came back to the line of scrimmage because the wind was blowing so hard, and started to bounce around. Everybody tried to get out of the way; you had to give the receiver five yards, but no one could figure out who the receiver was going to be. I felt like Moses at the parting of the Red Sea. I picked up the ball and scampered into the end zone unscathed for the easiest touchdown of my career.

From there on, it was all downhill. We somehow managed to finish ahead of Winnipeg, which gave us the dubious honor of hosting the Blue Bombers in the Eastern semifinal. Everything went afoul. O'Billovich had banished Darrell K. Smith to the sidelines, our best receiver and an all-star the previous year, to just sit there. Gilbert Renfroe had flown the coop in mid-season, having feuded with O'Billovich, who eventually said goodbye and good riddance. John Congemi got hurt and Tom (Elvis Is Not Dead) Porras, the Singing Quarterback, had difficulty getting the passing game in tune. By that time, our offence consisted of handing off to Fenerty and hoping for the best, which failed to materialize. Winnipeg put everything and the kitchen sink up on the line of scrimmage. They played with no free safety and went man-to-man against our four receivers. As a result, they beat us handily, 30 to 7, but lost to the Hamilton Tiger-Cats, who in turn lost to the Saskatchewan Roughriders, 43 to 40, in one of the greatest Grey Cup games ever. The frustrating thing was that we had tremendous talent, but we couldn't get it together, couldn't click, despite the fact that there was so much carryover from 1988. Our season ended 7 and 11. I caught the first plane for Florida.

So that was my rookie season — a disappointing one for the fans, and a roller-coaster ride for me. It's worth examining in some detail, because many of the people I'd met would continue to play a part in my life.

First, I'd like to talk about Coach O'Billovich, and take the liberty of calling him "Obie," as almost everyone did. He'd had a great run, and enjoyed great success, until this year, when his luck ran out. You can't argue with winning. Many of his techniques and decisions were perfectly correct. To a large degree, however, longevity depends on the ability to adapt. The game evolved, and he couldn't or wouldn't keep pace. He had both the ability and the desire to change; if you could prove to him that something else would work, he'd try to incorporate it, albeit grudgingly. The difficulty lay in getting his attention and proving your case. He was the classic "If it ain't broke, don't fix it" kind of guy. If something wasn't broke, well and good. If it was, we were in trouble.

Gill Fenerty was a stellar running back, and Obie misused his talents. Our entire offence became predictable to a fault; the opposition knew exactly what we were about to do — put more and more guys up there to block for Gill, all of whom flailed away to no good purpose.

When it became plain that a fix was in order, Obie's first inclination was to switch personnel, not to modify his scheme. If we'd taken a long, hard look at the scheme, instead of shuffling players around, we might have been less snake-bitten. He was like the driver who's faced with a car that's running a little rough. Instead of looking under the hood to see if a wire might be disconnected, he'd rush off in search of a new mechanic. Actually, he'd fly mechanics in by the planeload. Fresh new talent arrived at the drop of a helmet, all through the year. Sometimes these guys lasted only a day or so. Obie would take a look, decide against them, and they'd be gone. Those who stuck around seldom made an impact or stayed more than a single season. Those of us who had to watch these goings-on felt even more dispensable than usual.

All that having been said, Obie was absolutely steadfast — a polite word for "stubborn." In some ways, this had contributed to his success. He'd feel, against all evidence and reason, that he could get the job done. His stubbornness would prevail, and it would be done — for a while. Even while he was parachuting in all these other guys, he remained loyal to his proven regulars, and commanded loyalty in return. His saying was "Better's better." By this, he meant that the best man would get the job, and that was that. He played no favorites, and very few guys could claim that he'd treated them unfairly.

Despite his very structured views, he had a knack for talent that wasn't hidebound in the least. I'm the prime example. His traditional side should have said, Someone who stands five feet six doesn't fit in my scheme. But unlike so many other coaches, with the notable exception of his colleague Don Matthews, Obie stressed special teams. He loved guys who could not only make the big play that would win, or at least put you in a position to win, but could change the very tempo of a game. He took great pride in the players he'd brought up, and was responsible for many guys being here. He put me forward to an almost inappropriate degree; he saw to it that the media heralded my arrival. And, lest we forget, he gave me my nickname, "Pinball."

But, in the end, his traditional side won out. Obie had more desire than Matthews to control you as a total person, not just as a football player. He believed in curfews, and wanted us to dress correctly even on the plane: always a sport coat, if not a tie. He wanted us to carry ourselves in a certain way, which he felt would translate into performance on the field. He had a clearly defined line, and you crossed it at your peril. Obie would bench a player on principle, even when it came down to the wire at playoff time. That is what happened with Darrell K. Smith. Obie had somehow decided that he'd done something detrimental to the team, so he was out, with no reprieve, even though Obie's own livelihood — and ours, come to that — were at stake.

And so much, for the moment, for O'Billovich, whom we'll meet again several years down the road. Moving off the field, I can't say enough about Mom Crow. She was a gem, the best thing that could have happened to me. She's an amazing lady, and taught me so much about the city and the game, about guys who'd played it in the past and the history of the league. This helped me to make a relatively quick and easy transition to understanding Toronto, Canadian culture, and the CFL.

Then there were my new friends on the team. Reggie Pleasant and I grew very close. He is the nicest man in the world, blessed with a boyish humility, a childlike honesty that's often so startling, it's borderline offensive. The truth just spurts out of him; he can't help himself, and he can't believe what he's just said. Nor can he believe all the good things that have happened to him; he feels he's undeserving of them. He'll get excited over a good meal, and with good reason. He was one of fourteen brothers and sisters. Fourteen kids are a lot, by anyone's standards. At the dinner table, his mom and dad used to serve a single chicken, which had to make do for everyone. Dad got the breast, and then the bird went down the table, where the kids were seated in descending order by age. Reg was the second youngest, which meant that sometimes he'd get a neck or a gizzard or nothing at all, and would have to fill up on rice. To this day, he gazes reverently upon chicken; he speaks of it as others might of gold. If you wanted to prove that all black people love chicken and you took Reg as your study group, you'd have to conclude that they do. Twelve of those siblings graduated from college, and the other two went into the military — a wonderful testimony to his parents' fortitude. Reg tells these stories not out of a sense of deprivation, but with deep respect for the sacrifices his parents made to raise the family. It's no surprise that he and his wife, Jessica, themselves have a happy and loving home.

As a player, on the other hand, Reg had his little ways. Both of us were masters of procrastination; we'd bring a Bible with us on the plane but sometimes we wouldn't open it up. He was also superstitious beyond all belief. For example, he wouldn't do anything the day before a game. I'd be out in a shopping mall, or sightseeing, but not him. He even took great pains to stay off his feet. He'd take cabs everywhere; he felt that walking would rob him of the bounce in his step. When we were on the road, he'd make an ice bath in the hotel room — not a little container for his feet but the entire bathtub full. He'd empty the ice machine in the hotel corridor with loud clattering sounds. This took place at least once a week, yet to him twice was better. The night before a game, he'd really hit his stride. He had all sorts of vitamin supplements and natural remedies, things like bee pollen and ginseng. He'd line them up in neat rows and contemplate the miracles that they'd work. I told him there were too many, and they'd just cancel each other out. He'd just smile.

And that's not all. He wouldn't have dinner with an opponent, until the game was over and done. The idea of accidentally bumping into quarterbacks or receivers filled him with dread. He'd plunge into stores to avoid having to say hello to people on the street. He's so nice that you could almost understand this; he thought he'd lose his edge if he talked with them. Over time, his self-imposed seclusion grew more and more embarrassing. People would invite us home to meet their families, and Reg would fabricate increasingly frail excuses to beg off. For eight years, he went nowhere. You couldn't lure him, not even with chicken.

Reggie was part of a group that hung together during my first few seasons. As I've said, he was in the forefront of our Bible studies. So were Carl Brazley and Jeff Boyd (who come into the story soon). Rodney Harding (also known as Cat Daddy), Doran Major, and John Congemi were also part of this circle. None of them was married, and they were maybe a little less committed spiritually. But Rodney led the charge when it came to down-home food. One year he ran something called the Soul Kitchen; he'd cook up a storm at night and bring it in the next day for lunch.

Rodney was instrumental in helping me mature as a professional athlete. He stressed the necessity of going the extra mile to keep my body healthy, of not just sitting around waiting for the trainer. He really got on me, and on everybody else, too. He taught us how to work at our trade. He was the locker-room man with the big "S" on his chest; he could get along with anyone, any race or nationality. He could talk business with you or drink with you (which was more than I could, or was prepared to do), give you sage advice on football or high finance.

A lot of people wonder what place a Bible group has inside a foot-ball stadium. For the uninitiated, here's what happens. Chapel is coordinated through a network called Athletes in Action, a world-wide professional sports ministry that's a branch of Campus Crusade for Christ, which came to the CFL in the mid-1970s. We meet on game day, no matter what city we're in. On the road, we assemble early in the afternoon at our hotel; at the Dome, where we can control the timing, we get together two hours before the whistle, in a separate area behind the locker room. The chaplain is Steve Kearns, a former player. Bible studies tend to vary from team to team. In

Kansas City, they were loosely structured. Some teams try to round everybody up by having dinner at a player's home, often the quarterback's, because he makes the most money and can afford to cater. Ours take place immediately after practice at Exhibition Stadium (and, after we moved, at the Dome), because in Toronto people live in the suburbs, and it can take hours to get back and forth. For the studies, we pick either a particular book in the Bible or, more commonly, a study book that might contain a dozen different lessons.

It's fair to say that our witnessing is more characteristic of American athletes than Canadian. At the risk of generalizing, Canadians are more noncommittal, though more all-embracing of cultural differences and beliefs. The American players find that among Canadian players, there isn't the same degree of interest in witnessing, which possibly stems from the fact that they haven't had the same degree of spiritual experiences. Religion plays a big part in the formative years of many American players. Deep down, it's where they want to be, even if they aren't there yet.

Our groups aren't exclusive; we invite everyone to join in. The trainers can't, since their services are much in demand just before a game. Over the years, we've had several coaches, and they too tend to get overwhelmed by their duties. Adam Rita would often join us when he was an assistant coach; then when he was promoted he had different tugs on his sleeve. As for what we say and do, there's no formal service; the approach is nondenominational. There is a speaker — usually AIA staff or the pastor of a local church — and I suppose they are from a Protestant background. Mind you, the guy who attended chapel most scrupulously was Donnie Moen, a Catholic.

There's always been a generally positive attitude toward what we do, partly because we've been fortunate to have very consistent guys, people of real accomplishment on the field. This helped ensure that we commanded respect as well as acceptance. Over the years, besides Reggie, Carl, and Jeff, we've had Kenny Benson and Chris Gaines, all-star linebackers; Tracy Ham and Mike Kerrigan, all-star quarterbacks; Glen Harper, a kicker; and Brian Warren, a defensive end, who later became a minister. They were very open and honest in terms of communicating their beliefs, but not to the point of applying pressure or being manipulative. That's always the most effective way to go — let others draw a lesson from what you do and say on a daily basis. Of course, there were and are plenty of guys who absolutely avoided chapel and study groups.

That's okay, but we were never oblivious to a degree of disrespect. While a locker room can be rough and ready, we had a secret weapon. Chris Schultz, an offensive lineman, was extremely protective of us. If anyone cursed within earshot, he'd make them apologize. People tended to pay him heed, because Chris stood six feet eight and weighed close to 300 pounds.

I'm sure that some players wonder what we're up to — talking about God, when they're getting ready to go out and take the opposition's heads off. If it could be argued that Bible studies make you want to turn the other cheek on the field, they might have a point. I suppose there'd be a problem if you had chapel-goers who were laid-back, who might have been seen as prima donnas, who weren't physical or tough enough. That's not the case. Among the Argos, some of our most successful performers have also been leaders in chapel. No one would suggest that the likes of Reggie and Carl didn't go all out every minute of every game, so there have been very few negative incidents over the years.

*   *   *

During this off-season, one of the most significant events in my spiritual growth took place. It came about through Steve Kearns, who'd been organizing events in Belleville and Kingston, Ontario, called Pro Weeks. This year, at his urging, I flew back early from Florida and we all trooped off to Kingston.

The basic drill was pretty much the same in every case. A busload of athletes would descend on a school, Bible in one hand and ball in the other. There'd be an assembly in the gym, and we'd stage a relay race, a tug-of-war, a volleyball game, and a situps contest — us against the kids. If you won, you got ten points. If you lost, you got nine. During the intermission, one or two of us would share our personal testimony. The general message was, "If you're a Christian, we're Christians, too. Be encouraged. It's okay to be a Christian; you're not a zombie from nowhere. Christians aren't weirdos — they're people just like you and me. If you haven't thought about it before, maybe you should consider having some sort of spiritual foundation in your life."

Then we'd play basketball, which took over from the cumulative score of all the other events. Sometimes we'd visit three or four schools a day, and we were good and tired at the end, looking forward to a billet, which was arranged with a local family. Occasionally there'd be an evening session, and on Sunday we might speak very briefly in a church. The main idea, though, was to meet the kids on their own turf.

That first week, Steve announced that the following day would be a good time for me to give my testimony. This meant yet another sleepless night for me. I'd spoken in church before, I'd read scripture or said a few words about this or that. At Mama Sara's, I'd gone so far as to give my thanks for the week, but I'd never come out and talked directly about what Christ has done and meant to me in my life. I didn't know what to say, and I knew this wouldn't do. The experience was nerve-racking at first, but rewarding in the end. It forced me to verbalize my beliefs, and made me more accountable.

So this was a very personal and explicit message. We find that we're invited to deliver it most often in places like Kingston and Belleville, areas that may be more traditional, where there's more respect for and belief in family values. Even in the smaller centers, the organizers have to fight for it in the schools. When we arrive, the way has been prepared, but we know and understand the opposition they sometimes face. We've never gone to a school that didn't welcome us, and we're careful not to overstep the bounds. Occasionally the sessions are presented as an option during the lunch period, which is fine with us. There's no sense in the kids having to sit there bound and gagged, listening to guys force-feeding them something they don't want to believe in. On its own level, I think this exposure works. The kids really open up to you afterwards. They share their experiences, and ask a whole lot of questions, not necessarily religious or spiritual ones. "How do you do it when you're so small?" always seems to head the list of queries to me.

*   *   *

In my four scholarship years at William and Mary, I totalled 4,778 all-purpose yards. In 1990, my second season with the Argonauts, I racked up 3,300 — more than any other player had ever done in any league — and I did it in only 16 games. This got me a couple of awards: all-Eastern and all-Canadian all-star on special teams, and the CFL's Most Outstanding Player.

There are many reasons why 1990 was one for the record books. One was Derrick (Bear) Shaw, of Clearwater, Florida. He was a promising football player, but like so many others he'd torn up his knee. He never knew his dad, and his mom had passed away, so he was living with his grandmom and helping support his younger brothers. He came to stay with my mom and me during my senior year at Dunedin High. He was a loyal friend, a tireless worker, and a skilled craftsman. Give him a pile of mismatched parts, and he'd assemble a masterpiece in no time flat. Whether he could do the same for me was the point at issue.

During the off-season, I decided to mend my injury-prone ways. I had no intention of risking another pulled hamstring. The coming year was full of enough imponderables. O'Billovich was gone, having failed to come to terms with Mike McCarthy, the new general manager. The new coach, Don Matthews, fresh from his successes in Edmonton and Vancouver, might not have been overwhelmed by the little he knew about me. The last thing I could afford was an injury, so I vowed to transform myself from Mr. Neverworkout into Instant Iron Man.

Bear was instrumental in keeping me on track. Because of his knee, he couldn't run with me, but he was there for me every day, out at the old high school stadium, making sure I hotfooted it up and down the banks of steps. He'd throw me balls and drag me into the weight room, because he knew I hated, abhorred, detested, and loathed lifting weights. So I did do a lot of anaerobic stuff, which added up to the closest I'd ever come to a proper off-season program.

In fact, all things considered, this was in many ways the ideal off-season. Diane was back in Florida, at hairdressing school. Since the death of her father, the financial situation at home had worsened, and she couldn't afford to go back to Southern College. She was only a semester away from finishing her business degree. Instead of sitting around, she thought she might like to get her cosmetology license; she'd always been very talented in that field. I was back at the Baptist church, not as heavily involved with the youth group as before. For the first time, I didn't have to hold down a day job or run off to William and Mary to pack in a few more classes. So everybody was happy. I was eager to get back to Toronto, prove myself, and play football for as long as I could — in other words, postpone having a real job for as long as I could, if not forever. I sent my best wishes to Mr. Ely but by now, the prospect of a career at Honeywell had pretty much receded.

Then, almost before I could turn around, it was time to head north again. To recap the situation, O'Billovich was out, Matthews was in, and Adam Rita was assistant coach and offensive coordinator. He'd come from the British Columbia Lions, as had Matt Dunigan, the new quarterback. Gill Fenerty had headed south, to the New Orleans Saints. Darrell K. Smith was back, hoping for a better year, as were most of my other friends on the team.

I hadn't started a single game offensively in 1989. I'd played running back once — and only because the backup running back was hurt. I'd returned a few punts and kickoffs for major yardage. Otherwise, I was coming from nowhere — but I might have been the most potent offensive player we had, along with Darrell K. The question was, what was I going to do? I was a designated import, brought in specifically to handle punt and kickoff returns. I couldn't play another offensive position unless another American player vanished from the lineup. Fenerty was an American, and he was gone. Very few people would have picked me to fill his shoes as running back; Don Matthews did.

I met Coach Matthews for the first time when I arrived in training camp, and soon found that he aroused strong emotions, not always positive ones. That's one view. In mine, he was and is the best coach I've ever played for at any level. He brought leadership, knowledge of the game, and the ability to win; he motivated us and recognized talent. There have been plenty of other guys who could do one thing or the other better than he could, but in terms of being able to put everything together, he's number one, and beyond doubt the most important factor in my career success. He gave me the chance to do all the things I'd done in high school and at college, plus a little more. He made the decision not to go looking for someone to replace Fenerty. He thought I could get the job done, even though nothing suggested that I'd be tough enough to last. After all, I'd missed eight of eighteen games. He told me up front that he'd bring in other guys to compete with me at camp, and that it was my job to lose. By doing this, he got the most out of me that season and a couple more besides. He had confidence, and he put that confidence in me.

So training camp came and went. I played well and felt well, no problems. That is, until the first game of the season, when I (1) was named player of the game, and (2) got hurt. I sprained my knee. The club's response was to slide me over onto the practice roster, but at full pay, not the $500 a week. Then, when I mended, they said that I could sign back to my original contract, which was due to expire in this option year. I agreed to this, largely because I didn't know any better. Two weeks (and two missed games) later, my knee was healed.

Then the Argos proposed that I sign a new, longer-term contract that represented a very modest series of increases over my starting salary. I wasn't at all pleased with this. Yes, I'd had the injury bug, but I'd also been a starter with great promise. I wanted to be able to progress, to prove that I was of value, and be paid accordingly. I knew I was durable, even though nobody else had reason to believe it. A sprained knee is a freak occurrence. It happened only because I was working hard. I didn't want to be tied down for three more years, at a salary that I felt no longer reflected my worth. So my agent got involved again, to little effect, while I continued to work on my knee and ponder another offer from — of all places — Hamilton.

Very few people know this; as far as I'm aware, the Argos didn't know it at the time, although eventually they probably heard about it one way or another. It's one of history's mildly interesting "what ifs." The Tiger-Cats found out that I was on the practice roster — in effect a free agent. They called up and offered me more money, which is usually an inducement. What they didn't know was that money wasn't the only issue. The fact is, I'd fallen in love with Toronto, with Mom Crow, with the idea of staying with the team for as long as possible, since Coach Matthews had given me the opportunity to start as a running back. I kept this fact from the Argos, too. So I can't say that I considered Hamilton's offer too seriously. I wasn't calling anyone's bluff, or trying to use this as a negotiating ploy, since I didn't really want to pursue it. My agent's idea, by the way, was to sign a one-year deal only, after which he wanted to get me back to the NFL. So for a time everybody was talking at cross-purposes. In the end, we signed back a three-year deal covering 1990 through 1993. This involved only slightly more money, but it was heavily laden with personal performance incentive clauses.

The long and the short of all this was that I came back in the fourth week, and stayed healthy all season long; I wouldn't miss another game. The newspapers took to calling us the city's best-kept secret; Matthews went around proclaiming that we were going to shoot out the lights, win them all, and score 40 points a go. In fact, we'd scored 60 in the first home pre-season game against Hamilton, and managed to do so two more times during regular play. Once we rolled over Calgary, 70 to 18. We set a club record for the most points in a single season, and we did it with about six different quarterbacks, because Dunigan was ailing much of the time. We finished 10 and 8, including four losses to Winnipeg, who really had our number. The Blue Bombers were our nemesis all season long and would be our nemesis until the end.

Reggie Pleasant and I continued to be good friends, and our friendship would continue to blossom in later years. The guy who was the biggest influence on me now was Jeff Boyd, who'd moved into the Crows Nest. He'd been there the previous year, yet I'd barely met him because he'd been hurt and returned home. He was then in his early thirties, and I was twenty-five. He'd been in the league for quite some time, and had enjoyed success; he'd also had a chance down south, where his roots were. His family — his wife, Saundra, and three kids — lived in Los Angeles. During the off-season, he ran programs for wayward youth, some of whom had been in gangs. In many ways, he reminded me of Coach Cox, and reaffirmed all those positive lessons about the good husband and father, the loving and close black family.

Jeff taught me a great deal about life and football, and in return I was able to pour into him spiritually. At this point, I suppose I was a bit further along than he was. As a result, we both managed to grow, and I grew intellectually as well by virtue of his lessons. We began to team up on club promotions, which didn't pay us a penny but allowed us to eat well for free. This was much to be desired, as my eating habits were and are the worst. I'd grab anything in sight; I was famous for showing up with fast-food bags in hand even before a game.

Jeff was the person who first got me thinking about my place in the city, the first to suggest that I'd do well to live here year-round. I was, to a degree, his protégé; he steered me toward things he himself might have done, had his family situation been different. Roughly, this is what he said: "All this is going to pass sooner than you think. Take advantage of it while you can, and be a part of the city. People have accepted you; they like who you are. Not only can you play ball, you can speak well, which will take you far if you use it correctly. Don't worry about putting yourself forward. Don't think of this in terms of using people. It's not that, any more than they're using you. Make the most of this time, to everyone's benefit. Start now to build something here that will last after football."

This year, I began to follow his advice. The Athletes in Action Pro Week sessions had whetted my appetite; going out into the community held no terrors for me. The Argos have always had more requests for personal appearances than they could possibly handle. They're glad to see players involved with worthy causes. Many guys are reluctant to go; they're ill at ease appearing in public at such events. I was more than not reluctant — I verged on eager. When I went somewhere and enjoyed myself, and it looked as if the people there were enjoying having me there, too, this was seen as very good for the team. So Jeff and I wound up doing more and more. Soon, other guys began to get more excited also, and the whole thing snowballed, very spontaneously. There was no master plan on my part. People have said, "Oh, you've been so smart at marketing yourself." Well, thanks, but I was simply being myself. I was happy to get out and meet people and promote the team. It was easy. Everybody was cordial. I was small and non-threatening, still a bit of a novelty, and the Pinball monicker didn't hurt my recognition factor.

On the field, the biggest factor for me was Coach Matthews, who gave me the opportunity to shine. He could have relegated me to returns, pure and simple. Or he could have given me a shot at running back, while keeping me miles away from returns, on the theory that I couldn't do both. He could have said, "All right, we'll let him do both, but the minute he gets hurt I'll pull the plug." When I was hurt, that didn't deter him from letting me keep on doing everything at once.

Adam Rita, the offensive coordinator, had devised a very dynamic approach. In his scheme of things, the tailback — my official designation — was as much or more a receiver than a running back. Now I was in the optimal offence to display my strengths. That's why in 1990 I had close to 1,000 yards receiving as opposed to 500-odd rushing. We threw the ball all the time, and I caught it and ran. That's why we scored so many points: we were wide open, and very creative in our strategies. The more Rita found I could do, the more he thought up. It became something of a challenge to see if he could expand his game plan beyond my means, so I got new and different responsibilities every time he went to the chalkboard.

Another factor was the presence of so much success around me. Darrell K. Smith rebounded and had a phenomenal year. This meant I wasn't the only offensive threat, which challenged the opposition. Matt Dunigan, obviously one of the greatest quarterbacks in league history, and arguably the greatest leader at that position, was on the job; I'll have more to say about him in a minute. When he got hurt,

Rickey Foggie came in and tore the place up. Then we had all our stalwarts on the special teams — Carl Brazley, Reggie Pleasant, Doran Major, and others. Usually, veterans want no part of special teams; each has staked out his territory as a cornerback or defensive back. They say, "Wait a minute. My job is to knock down and intercept passes. I don't run around making blocks for some silly little runt who thinks he can return a ball." But these guys, whose livelihood is special teams, liked to see me run. They wanted to hustle down and block for me, so I could take off. They were excited about executing the basics that let me shine. A lot of those 3,300 yards belong to them.

So, after a triumphant season, away we went to the Eastern semifinals. I think I'd been averaging about 200 yards a game during the year. In the first playoff game, against Ottawa, that rose to 300, which helped us to win, 34 to 25. The next week, as we were getting ready to head to Winnipeg for the Eastern final, I caught one of the worst cases of flu on record. I was trembling, running a high fever, and aching all over. We lost that game late in the fourth quarter. Tom Porras threw a screen pass to Kevin Smellie, who had an open field to the Blue Bombers' end zone. He was all by himself, because Winnipeg's entire front seven were following me. But the ball got lost in the sun and went sailing over his head. That play should have put the game away. Instead, we were forced to punt. Then Winnipeg elected to run a quarterback draw, which would usually have got them nowhere fast, because Tom Burgess wasn't noted for being fleet of foot. This time, though, he sailed on down to our 35-yard line, where the Bombers kicked a field goal to make it 20 to 17 with no time left on the clock.

We had ended up mere inches and seconds away from a Grey Cup berth that year, and would have to wait until next time. And so ended 1990. I collected my awards, and the Argos' management decided to tear up my contract.

You'll recall that my agent, sitting down in Texas, had negotiated a three-year deal for me for 1990 through 1992. After this, to be frank, I can tell you he'd done squat. He was out of touch, had no idea of the way the CFL worked, and couldn't grasp what I'd been doing. He had no clue and no clout. He'd done some good for some of the people he represented, but I wasn't one of them. I was giving him five percent of not very much, most of which I'd hammered out all by myself. Mind you, I ought to be thankful for small mercies. I might have been in Calgary. Once again, I sought the advice of Jeff Boyd, who'd been represented by agent Gil Scott for many years. Jeff thought I might be able to renegotiate from a position of temporary strength, so he put me together with Gil. After a fair bit of to-ing and fro-ing, which included the issue of how much of any further increases, if anything, my former agent would be entitled to, Gil took over. I've been with him ever since.

7

Off-Season 1990—June 1992

Then began the busiest off-season in history. I'd been talking about coming back to Mom Crow's over the winter, because a lot of different charities had asked me to help them out. I'd signed up with the Canadian Cancer Society, the United Way, the Red Shield Appeal (the Salvation Army), the Juvenile Diabetes Foundation, Big Brothers, and the Special Olympics. We always tried to slate five or six events within a given week. Someone might agree to fly me in to deliver a speech; then I'd piggyback everybody else, so that it wouldn't cost them any money.

Before I went home in December, I'd done color commentary for the Grey Cup game on the old Canadian Football Network, along with the commentator Dave Hodge — something I might like to do more of later on. I'd also attended the Sports Celebrities Festival dinner for the Canadian Special Olympics, the best-run event of its kind. I felt as if I'd finally arrived — or, rather, as if the organizers had made a ghastly mistake and didn't know who I was! I met all the Special

Olympians, and there was an immediate bond between us. I know many of them by name now, and we exchange notes all the time.

The dinner features legendary performers from every era. There I sat, next to Althea Gibson, Nadia Comaneci, and Willie Stargell. This was an eye-opener, my first big-time event, and a humbling experience. Someone would say, "Hey, you're doing great," and I'd say, "Yes, ma'am, Miss Gibson." I just pretended I was supposed to be there, along with the likes of Roger Clemens and Donovan Bailey. All this was broadcast live on TSN, after which, of course, I received even more requests.

Then it was time for Christmas at home, followed by another Athletes in Action Pro Week, this time in Belleville. So the Special Olympics and the Pro Weeks become ongoing commitments, my first opportunities to go beyond the stage of shaking hands at various functions, and to really get to know people outside the world of football.

By now, though, the rumor mill was awash in murmurings about the ownership of the Argos changing. Harry Ornest had been in control since 1988. Suddenly we began to hear the name Bruce McNall, which then rang no bell with me, as I wasn't a hockey fan. When the names John Candy and Wayne Gretzky started popping up in the same sentence, even I started to pay attention. Excitement and anticipation mounted daily. This Dream Team would lavish money upon us; celebrities would flock to the stands, as they'd done when Gretzky headlined for the Los Angeles Kings; we'd be the hottest ticket in Hollywood North.

On NFL draft day, the biggest story was the CFL. The Dream Team went out and scooped up the showpiece from Notre Dame, the most celebrated player in college ball that year — even though he wasn't the Heisman Trophy winner — none other than Raghib (Rocket) Ismail. The deal made the cover of every major sports publication throughout North America. There he was (and, very soon, here he'd be), along with the owner of the L.A. Kings, Uncle Buck, and the Great One.

Quality costs, so this very quickly became the real story. The inevitable questions arose: Was Rocket — could he be — worth the money? He'd been guaranteed U.S. $4.5 million a year, more than the entire team put together. More, in case you hadn't figured it out already, than I was being paid. Given that I'd been named Player of the Year and knocked off 3,300 yards in the process, how could they possibly justify paying Rocket the sun and the moon, and what were they going to do for me? Was I beside myself, livid, ready to take my case to Mr. McNall? Ready to pack my bags and go elsewhere in the CFL or back to the States? Going to hold out for more money?

Some people said, "Well, you're too much of a team guy, you're not selfish enough. Anyone else would look to be traded, or at least be paid a portion of the new guy's salary, or at least what he'd proven he was worth." I always believed my position was clear. Toronto was the city I wanted to play in, and Rocket's contract, once the dust settled on the negotiating table as well as the field, could only improve my position. I consider the highest court to be the court of public opinion. Everyone was building a case for me, so there was no need for me to say a thing. If I did, I'd have been seen as yet another egotistical athlete who thought he was worth more than he really was. By keeping quiet, I could remain true to character and true to my teammates. By making an issue of it, I might have made a few more dollars; who's to say? I also might have ended up flat on my face somewhere I didn't want to be. If I let matters take their course, I could avoid creating dissension just when the team was building momentum. I felt (and events would bear me out) that I'd still be able to achieve what I hoped for: a slightly better salary, a slightly better pay scale that would slowly but steadily rise, eventually making me the CFL's highest paid non-quarterback, excepting only Rocket.

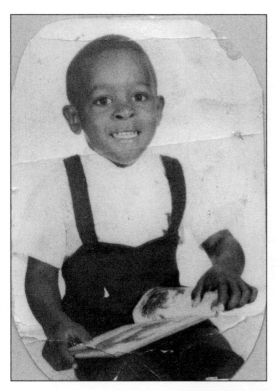

Reading at two years old—okay, just the pictures.

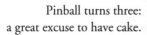

Pinball turns three: a great excuse to have cake.

Distinguished and dapper
in the courtyard of Shiloh
Missionary Baptist Church
at age four.

Proud portrait. Our fifth-grade class at San Jose Elementary School poses
in front of the American flag representing the thirteen colonies,
made by the student body from popcan tops.

She's my hero. A movie star—no. It's just my mom and me, at nine years old.

"I Love This Game." As an eleven-year-old with the Dunedin Golden Eagles.

A ten-year-old speedster playing Little League baseball. The bat was just a prop, because I couldn't hit!

A seventeen-year-old phenom, or so I thought,
runs for daylight as a senior at Dunedin High School.

Behind a shy, almost innocent smile,
hopes and dreams abound!
Senior picture at Dunedin High School.

Running the open field at the SkyDome, but expecting some unwanted company real soon.

Thanking the crowd for an undeserved ovation for breaking the Argo great Dick Shatto's record for career receptions. After all, my teammates were the ones who made it happen.

My offensive line makes me look good as I turn upfield.

Up and over—
one of 15 TDs in 1997.

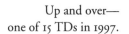

Back-2-Back. Toronto Argonaut
President and *mentor* Bob Nicholson and
me with the Grey Cup in 1997 after
back-to-back victories.

Please sit down.
The usual long-winded
Pinball giving an
acceptance dissertation
after receiving the Tom
Pate Memorial Man of
the Year Award at the
1996 CFL Awards,
aired live on TSN.

June 7, 1992:
"Wedding Day"

It couldn't get any
sweeter than this.
But it has!

Rachel at one-and-a-half years, sound asleep in
her favorite chair.

Rachel and Dad on the sidelines.
A post-game photo-op during
the 1996 season.

Visiting Reebok with Raven at three weeks old.

Rachel, the proud big sister,
holding baby Raven at three days old.

A Clemons family portrait.

What would have happened had Rocket not appeared? Reality suggests that I could have hoped to make, at most, $90,000, roughly what Fenerty had been paid. Did I really deserve more? Sure, I was Player of the Year — once. That might have been an aberration. If Rocket hadn't arrived, maybe my contract wouldn't have been conveniently shredded. Management might have strung me along for a year or two to see whether I'd continue to deliver. The fact is that Rocket did arrive, and he increased my market value overnight. Whether his salary was fair or not was beside the point. If for some strange reason the Argos had decided to give me $4.5 million, I wouldn't have made the cover of *USA Today*, or shown up as the lead item on every American TV sportscast. The publicity generated by Rocket's signing drew more television viewers, put more fans in the stands. The team was more popular, more identifiable, and I could go out and endorse more products for more money in my own pocket. With him, we stood a much better chance of winning the Cup, which would bring even more opportunities. As far as I was concerned, this was a win-win situation.

Some people said that Rocket was unproven. I beg to differ. This is a sore point among those who can't see young guys getting paid so much money, right out of college, without a single pro game under their belts. At the time, Rocket's salary did seem off the scale. No one could hope to receive it in the CFL today. For example, Doug Flutie was getting $1.1 million in Canadian dollars in 1997. As everybody knows, the league has a salary cap, and there are only so many ways of making an end run around that. As everybody also knows, CFL salaries lag far behind those in other professional sports. The Blue Jays are paid collectively $25 million; the Toronto Raptors, somewhere between $15 and $20 million. The Argos, when last I checked, come closer to $2.1 million. Nonetheless, some of the current figures that float around down south are difficult to relate to — until you start to think about them in context. What were the outraged protesters doing when the athlete was working at his game from seven in the morning until seven at night, elevating his skills to the point that he could command big money in the open market? He made countless sacrifices while others were busy enjoying other things. If someone else had worked as hard in his field, maybe he'd be equally well paid. We don't argue about a computer whiz who does this; he or she can demand huge rewards from any company in the land. We don't begrudge movie stars paid incredible sums for a four- or five-month film project, during which they very seldom face danger or pain and are waited on hand and foot.

The trouble was that, having been offered all that money, Rocket was supposed to appear as the savior of the team, and angelic, if you will, too. When he fell short, as we all do, he was dubbed a fad, and to some extent a mistake. In fact, he was just shy. The media misinterprets this as aloofness. He was four years younger than I was, and in some ways, younger than that. While he was no dummy, he wasn't yet ready to assume a leadership role emotionally, as much as some people seemed to expect it of him.

McNall had no illusions on this score. He'd brought Rocket here for a reason — to achieve the same effect he'd seen work before. He had paid Gretzky more than anyone else thought *he* was worth, even though the Great One was acknowledged as the greatest hockey player ever. McNall upped the ante, and in doing so revolutionized the game. That's why hockey is now so widely accepted in the States; that's why there are all the expansion teams. To McNall, Gretzky's salary was an investment. He lost money up front so he could gain it over time. This was his vision with Rocket, although it didn't pay off quite as well. For the moment, though, it paid off for me. McNall had invested in the business I worked in, increasing its value and mine.

That's why I didn't stomp out in a snit when Rocket came to town. He helped his own cause by his demeanor. He seemed very meek, harmless and playful, almost a big kid. He drove a truck and wore a plastic digital watch; he dressed in sweats or a baggy shirt and jeans. And he obviously played ball on a whole different plane in terms of skill. He had physical tools I hadn't seen anywhere, including the NFL. That doesn't always translate when it comes to playing the game, but it's a good start.

Let me explain what I mean. Rocket was a raw talent; in a lot of ways, he was green. I've seen guys who had quicker hands, who ran better routes, and had better moves. In terms of fluidity, the way he went from A to B was just unparalleled. He got there faster and with more style than anybody else. He cranked up to full speed before you knew it. Guys who can do that usually aren't all that fast over the long haul, just as guys with a high cruising speed can seem methodical, almost slow at first. Yet nothing about Rocket looked slow. His nickname described him exactly, although the mechanics of his running are hard to explain. He had tremendous pickup, he could just flat-out run, but not like a track guy, who just races along unimpeded. Rocket could run like that while he was playing football. This is a rare combination. He always made it look effortless, as if he wasn't expending much energy. During one game, the opposition targeted him and he was bounced around. That didn't get to him. He said, "If they make me mad, I'll just run faster." That was the thing — you felt he could if he wanted to, that he had even more in reserve.

So away we went to training camp, with the media in hot pursuit. They kept following Rocket around, not me; he drew their fire. There were a lot of reporters from the States, and some talk of our games being televised there, so McNall's plan seemed to be working. Don Matthews had been relieved of his duties by this time, owing to a dustup with Mike McCarthy, and Adam Rita had taken over as head coach. It became clear at once that Coach Rita was in control. He simply turned his mad-scientist act up a notch; now he had doubled the possibilities in Rocket and me.

But Rocket proved to be slow out of the gate. He got hurt, missed all the pre-season games, and didn't play the first game against the Rough Riders in Ottawa. They played hard and the game was close, when I took a punt on the first bounce, looked at an absolute wall of guys in front of me, and deked sideways, as I tend to do. I split the Rough Rider wall and took the ball 95 yards down inside the five-yard line. I was winded, and had to come out on the next play. We scored, and went on to win the game. As had to happen, a number of people started voicing variations on "I told you so."

But not for long. The next week, at our home opener against Hamilton, the Blues Brothers were belting it out to 40,000 fans, and Rocket was ready to go. His first big play was a reverse on a punt return. He was up on the line of scrimmage, as if he was about to block the kick. The plan was that I'd catch it, he'd trail back and loop all the way around, and I'd hand off the ball on a reverse. This works if the opposition obliges you with the perfect kick, which the Ti-Cats didn't. The ball angled toward the sideline, where I got it on a bounce. I thought, We're still going to do this. I froze for a moment, which froze the coverage team. I could see Rocket coming out of the corner of my eye, and I pitched the ball to him. He caught it in full stride and tore 75 yards downfield. This was what we'd signed him for. He went on to make another big diving catch and a couple more plays that got the crowd really excited. Throughout the first six or seven games we worked well together. It had become evident that I was the better punt returner; I took yet another one 95 yards in the fourth game against B.C. So Rocket saw to most of the kickoffs. All season long he hustled like mad, and it was plain that there was no animosity between us. This attitude fed through the entire team.

Meanwhile, Matt Dunigan was back in form, and making a huge difference. This is a good place to talk a little more about him. The key to his leadership lay in his voice; he had a commanding, drill-sergeant-like way about him. Any quarterback has got to make himself heard on the field. When Matt spoke, you knew he was taking charge.

He'd say, "Let's get out there at five-thirty in the morning," and you'd think, "Oh, no. He'll be there at four-thirty, waiting for us, champing at the bit." Whether or not this was true made no difference; that's the feeling you got. He was a sort of Neanderthal Man who'd stop at nothing to win. He prided himself on his physical condition; he always came to camp in tremendous shape. You felt as if you could never outrun him. Not only would he get the ball to you, he'd throw it right through you. You sensed that whatever it took to win, he'd do it. He was relentless on the field. He played the game with almost reckless abandon, which to some degree explains his problems with injuries. Amazingly, he could still function as leader when he was hurt and had to be replaced. He conveyed the impression that he'd give anything to be out there with you in the thick of battle.

Matt was all for blood, sweat, and tears. Otherwise, the mood in our locker room was very loose, very upbeat. Carl Brazley had us working out to an invention of his own, the Ghetto Stretch ("Okay, now extend your leg and get ready to grab that TV set!"). Donnie Wilson was the resident dance instructor, who favored us with a little Michael Jackson or John Travolta, a little of yesterday and today and what might be tomorrow. Watching him was like putting a quarter in the ride.

Another almost fictional character was Chris (The Joker) Gaines, a middle linebacker from Tennessee with a pronounced southern twang. He was maybe the toughest guy on the field, a reputation his bald head enhanced. He was white, but he had grown up in the 'hood and listened to rap music. Before every game, he did a routine called the New Jack Swing. He would stress that nobody else knew how to do this; various people did not understand it (Oprah, Dini Petty, and Arsenio Hall, plus every major rap musician), but *he* would show us how. Then he'd go into a dance of his own devising. Not only were we good, we were having fun. Toronto was the team you could not stand if you had the bad luck to be anywhere else.

Then, around the seventh game, I caught the injury bug again. I was running ahead of my all-purpose yardage pace from the previous season, and ahead of Rocket, for that matter. I'd just had a good game against Saskatchewan, and scored three touchdowns (actually four; one was called back) in our 62 to 10 victory. This meant that I could give a ball to my mom and Kelli, who were visiting, and to Diane. Then, the next time out, against Edmonton, I got hurt. I'd been tackled, and I was down with my leg in the air when somebody piled on. It was a borderline late hit, and totally unnecessary. I couldn't watch the play on tape; they tell me it looked really nasty. At least it wasn't a break. We waited it out for a couple of weeks, in hopes that it would mend, which left a hole in our offence. Rita brought up a couple of different people in an effort to fill the gap, among them Paul Palmer, with whom I'd played in Kansas City.

When it became apparent that the leg wasn't healing as we'd hoped, I had to face arthoscopic surgery. The worst part was the anesthetic. They wanted me to count backwards from 100, and I got halfway to 99. This was my first experience with a general, and I woke up feeling flat-out icky. There was a fair amount of post-operative inflammation and I couldn't straighten my leg, but in fact the procedure is relatively simple. It was major to me because I'd never had anything like it. As far as I know, it was a complete success; it just took a while to heal, and slowed me down more than it would have another guy who didn't depend so heavily on lateral movement.

I was back in the lineup for game 14, against Winnipeg. By game 16, we were in a position to clinch first place in the East, which would have enabled us to skip the semifinal, host the final, and sail on to the Cup. All we had to do was beat Calgary, an assignment I wasn't quite prepared for. I was more inspirational than functional, hobbling around the field and balancing on one leg. Thanks largely to Rocket, we won. He scored his first and only punt-return touchdown as an

Argonaut. It was a close game, and went down to the wire, and he broke it open — a fine run, perfectly timed, and the biggest play he'd made all year. Final score: 34 to 27. Mark McCormack, the author of *What They Don't Teach You at Harvard Business School*, talks about what separates the good from the great in any field, and he singles out the ability to deliver consistently peak performance. Rocket had that ability, and his effort helped us to finish the season on top of the standings at 13 and 5.

I sat out the next two games, and got ready to confront our arch rival, Winnipeg. They had a tough defence — an infamous crew including Tyrone Jones, James West, Greg Battle, and Paul Randolph. This was supposedly the matchup — our potent offence versus this incredible linebacking corps. We had a potent defence, with Ed Berry on one corner and Reggie Pleasant on the other, along with Carl Brazley, Rodney Harding, and The Joker, smack dab in the middle. This enabled us to take command at the outset.

I came back, feeling much better as far as my knee was concerned. But, on the opening kickoff, I got turf toe, which sounds even sillier than a pulled hamstring. It isn't. It comes from the toe's being hammered down repeatedly onto artificial turf, under which there's a base of unyielding concrete. The joint opens up and the ligament is exposed. I played the second half with my foot shot up, but it continued to swell throughout the game, and I could put no weight on it. It felt as if I was running on top of a tennis ball that was wedged into my shoe. This might be the most uncomfortable I've ever been during a game. Matt Dunigan, who threw for three touchdowns, went out as well, with a separated shoulder, and Rickey Foggie took over. The game wasn't even close. We won handily, 42 to 3, and we were off to the Cup.

The Cup that year was held back in Winnipeg, against Calgary, which had just upset Edmonton. We were the favorites among the betting fraternity. Among the fans, we were the team they loved to hate. We were booed more than ever before or since — worse, even, than the last couple of years in Hamilton.

Danny Barrett was the Calgary quarterback; this was the first year the team had come on strong. (In 1992, of course, they'd get Doug Flutie, and become an even greater force to be reckoned with.) We were wary of being overconfident, partly because we were. Self-doubt was not a problem this time around. The playing conditions were cold and ghastly, and we were going to be hard pressed to pull off a win.

I still had turf toe. I hadn't worn a shoe at all between the Eastern final and the Cup; I was on crutches most of the time. My usual shoe size is nine. For the Cup, I wore a size eleven, and went out to do what I could. It wasn't much. At halftime it hurt very badly, so the doctors shot it up again and away I went. Unfortunately, this time the numbing didn't take; later on, my foot blew up as big as a soft-ball. The swelling rose all the way up my ankle nearly to my calf.

My reputation preceded me despite this, and helped to take one of the Stampeders' top defensive players out of the picture. Darrell Hall was man-to-man on me for the entire game. So I obligingly played decoy, and he followed me everywhere. If he'd known how I felt, he wouldn't have bothered. In a sort of masochistic way, the pain helped since it took my mind off the unbearable cold.

Dunigan was still hurting; most people thought he was foolhardy to play. He let the world know he was getting shot up, which in itself helped to rally us behind him. True, it was almost overdramatized, but we all knew that it was for the sake of the team. That's how he played; he was willing to jeopardize his health, maybe even his career, to win. I suspect that he couldn't even feel his arm. Despite this, he threw a couple of balls up for grabs, which Darrell K. and Paul Masotti caught for touchdowns. He played a brave game, in which no one could function properly. Reggie Pleasant got frostbite in his toes, partly because he likes to wear a smaller-size shoe when he plays, to get a nice, tight fit. He thinks this helps him run, but he regretted it that day.

People say, "Well, everybody has to play in the same conditions, that's what Canadian football is all about." I say it's crazy. I love this game and I love Canada, but playing outdoors in that kind of weather is insane, it is not normal, it does not make sense. Having said that, I have to admit we've played some of our best games in near-arctic temperatures.

Given all these woes, it was a miracle end to a dream season when Rocket again peak-performed for us. We'd been ahead from the opening play, when Ed Berry intercepted a pass and took it for a touchdown. But the Calgary defence was tough, and as the game wore on, they pulled to within a single point, making it 22 to 21. On the very next kickoff, Rocket put on his cape and flew down the field, narrowly avoiding a beer can that sailed out of the stands to land just behind him. This was not a popular fan move, but we were off to the races. The final score was 36 to 21, and made a fitting climax to a video titled *The Glory Days*, a kind of "as it happened" movie focusing on the '91 season.

The on-field celebration is a special, great thing. Watch the footage and catch the expressions on our faces. There's a feeling of giddiness, almost of senselessness. We're grabbing anybody within reach, hugging them, jumping and shouting, jubilantly. Money can't buy that experience. Nothing can equal the sensation, and it's shared equally. It's all-encompassing, all-embracing. When you win the championship, everybody shares alike. The feeling is indescribable, and it's the one important thing, the memory that will stay with you forever.

The postgame celebration was difficult for me. All the numbing went out of my foot, so I went back to my hotel room with Mom and Diane. I was reflective rather than celebratory. I couldn't believe that after all these years, I'd helped to win the final game. We'd had great teams in high school, but we kept finishing one or two games shy of the state championships. At William and Mary, we never quite got there; in youth football, we went to the championship twice and never won. Even in 1990, my personal-best season, we couldn't crown it for the team. Now, after seventeen years of football, I'd finally played a part in the big one. I felt complete; there was no "but" at the end of the sentence: "It was a great season, but . . ." At long last, there was just an exclamation mark.

I didn't travel east with the rest of the team. Jeff Boyd and I stayed behind and saw my mom off on the plane for Florida. Then Diane and I went back to Mom Crow's, and got ready for the parade. If Toronto was out of practice, the fans made up for lost time. The welcome we got re-kindled the feelings we had on the field moments after winning the Cup.

Then the parade route was swept clean, real life resumed, and I went on a three-week blitz of personal appearances, wearing my Bozo the Clown shoes — size eleven Reeboks with a touch of lime green that made me stand out in any crowd. I was penciled in almost till the end of the year; I think the grand total was 21 appearances in 20 days. By the end of the first week, everybody else had wisely gone home, and I was alone in the spotlight. This is when the media really began to peg me as different. The Jays had yet to win a World Series, the Leafs hadn't brought home the Stanley Cup in a couple of decades, and we were the only game in town. So they took to following me around, which was good publicity for the charities involved. I was dog-tired, but this sort of thing gets you into the Christmas mood; it's nice to be able to give something back and be a part of a lot of worthy undertakings.

*   *   *

The next few months were spent in Clearwater, because I knew that if I came back to Toronto I'd jump onto the treadmill again. Then, in

March, Diane and I attended my first Pro Conference, held by Athletes in Action just outside Los Angeles. This particular get-together was in conjunction with NFL players, and we weren't sure at first how we'd fit in. It turned out to be a very comfortable situation, because I roomed with Darryl Ford, an Argo linebacker, and Diane stayed with his girlfriend. In fact, things went so well that we couldn't believe we hadn't gone before. There were so many like-minded and joyful people there, all eager to know more about God and have a good time in the process. When the conference ended, our plan was to spend a week with Jeff Boyd (who'd retired after the 1991 season) and his family before returning to Clearwater. As it turned out, we did this and therefore were able to surprise them with an unexpected development.

For the past few years, Diane and I had been talking about marriage. Lately, she'd been throwing me some pretty heavy hints. I knew very well that some day I'd get around to a proposal. I wasn't afraid; at the same time I wasn't ready. My dream was to be able to offer her a total package. I wanted to be more settled, more prepared, with a stable career, a nice house, and something resembling security. I knew these delaying tactics were a character flaw. She felt, with some justification, that I was running out of excuses.

On that final night of the conference, we were alone out on the balcony; Darryl had gone to visit his girlfriend in the other apartment. It was a beautiful night; the moon and stars were visible despite the smog. It suddenly seemed as good a time and place as any, so I got down on my knees and asked Diane to be my wife.

This was entirely spontaneous; I didn't have it in mind until it happened. I suppose I'd always thought that I'd plan something really way out and different. If I'd decided that night that the time was near, and then run off to design some elaborate scheme, I'd have missed the moment. I had no ring, no flowers, no limousine, no horse and carriage, yet none of these things seemed important. What was important was that I loved her very much, that we'd grown in our relationship and were mature and truly comfortable with each other spiritually and emotionally. To me, any other time would have been too late. Right then and there, it was right.

Of course, she thought I was fooling. I've been known to do so. She didn't say yes because she didn't want to be disappointed. I assured her I was absolutely serious, so we embraced and cried and hugged and all that kind of stuff. It was sort of dreamlike, and I kept marveling at how everything had come together over my whole life. None of the bits and pieces were perfect as I went along, but they seemed to match perfectly in the end.

I'd proposed with no earthly idea that we'd be married by the time I got back to training camp. My timetable was the following year, during the next off-season. That's not what Diane had in mind. She wanted to be a June bride, and not in 1993. Just as Mr. Sazio had given me three hours' notice to get on the plane to Toronto two years earlier, she now surprised me by specifying a three-month countdown to the altar, so the perpetual daters had their work cut out for them.

After we'd told our families, it was time to find the rings. In 1987, I'd bought Diane a promise ring at a shop in Kansas City, a petite ring with a beautiful stone that everyone commented on. I called the jeweler, Gary Penar, and asked him to provide the engagement ring. I knew exactly what Diane wanted, because she had been hauling me around to other stores for some time. I had nodded evasively and come up with reasons for not buying a ring on the spot, which had dismayed her to no end. I'm sure she thought I was having second thoughts. At last the ring arrived, gold with a one-carat marquis solitaire. That night, we went down to the beach. I had the engagement ring hidden in my hand. I asked her if she could see one particularly bright star, and pointed skyward. And pointed, and pointed. She looked and looked, to no avail, until, finally, she spied the diamond glittering between my fingers.

Compared with the rigors of planning and organizing the

wedding, that was the easy part. To complicate matters, we bought a house, after weeks of searching both new and existing construction sites. We settled on a place that was "build to suit" in a new subdivision just north of Dunedin in Palm Harbor. Suffice it to say, we could have put both the homes we grew up in inside it with room to spare. The house was my main concern; I delved into the final modifications and spent many happy hours with the builders and contractors. This kept me out of the way of the wedding juggernaut, except for those crises with the schedule, when we'd sit down together and work it out.

My Honeywell training paid off: I was the behind-the-scenes orchestrator. The day itself was Diane's, and the order of the day was perfection. Occasionally I'd try to oversimplify the issues, with soothing pronouncements along the lines of "Well, there are a lot of wedding dresses in the world, and you will be wearing one of them on June 7, 1992, and there are a lot of other dresses in the world, and at the very least your bridesmaids will be wearing the requisite number of them, and if things come up, we will deal with them one at a time." After receiving a brief lecture on male insensitivity, I'd go back and play subcontractor some more, and matters would proceed. We also attended marriage counseling sessions with both our pastors but, in truth, we felt we were pretty much prepared. We realized that our commitment was first of all to God — that we'd spend the rest of our lives together according to His will. Everything else would flow from that.

Then came the thorny question of the guest lists. I felt positively outnumbered on this score. My family tree is sort of overgrown — there are a lot of branches but not much of a grand trunk. Not so with Diane's. She is one of eight brothers and sisters, as were both her parents. When the Lees and the Bullards get together, they need a parade permit. To make matters even more interesting, three Lee brothers had married Bullard sisters, so there were cousins who looked like twins. Any list was going to be miles long. At first, Diane thought we could hold it down to about 200 people. I said, "Not a chance." This rose to 250. I kept repeating myself. In the end, there were 400 at the reception and 500 at the wedding. Neither of our churches was large enough to handle the crowd, so we managed to find an accommodating Lutheran pastor who'd take us in.

I'm sure you can sympathize with Diane's frame of mind on the day itself. Her biggest worry was that her 6 p.m. wedding would start at 9:30, because her punctuality-challenged bridegroom would be running late, as usual. In fact, everything went off without a hitch. With rain forecast, the day was sunny. Diane and her mother rode once around the block in a horse and carriage, which pulled up to the entrance of the church just as the bells rang out. Their arrival was a traffic-stopper; people clapped as the procession went by. Then the music began, and Jessica Pleasant started into the first song. I was actually at the church two hours early, a never-to-be-repeated occurrence, in deference to my bride. I nearly disappeared in the midst of the wedding party, which was thirty people strong — twelve groomsmen and an equal number of bridesmaids; two best men; a maid and a matron of honor; and four ushers. All of my childhood buddies and fellow teammates who could get plane tickets attended. As presents, I'd ordered nice, subdued Reeboks for the whole cast, which went well with the tuxedos. We contemplated changing into them for the reception, and the groomsmen did, but I decided not to — one of my more intelligent decisions.

My pastor conducted the actual ceremony, and Diane's pastor added a few words — a very funny ten commandments for husband and wife. The whole setting was beautiful, filled with fantastic floral arrangements. Then, as icing on the cake, a saxophonist played, and everybody started to dance. We got to the reception late, but nobody cared. It was at a hotel on Clearwater Beach, and half the county showed up, with or without invitations. We propped open the doors and let the people come; the chef had assured me he'd cope with however many arrived, and he did. Then, after a limo ride over to our suite, we began our honeymoon — all seventy-two hours of it. A June bride has her day, and then it's her football-player husband's turn to spread his belongings all over the floor, pack them, and catch a flight for another training camp.

8

SUMMER 1992–FALL 1993

Leaving my bride was admittedly a bit of a jolt, no question about it. Instead of carrying Diane over the threshold of our brand-new (and as yet uncompleted) dream house, when Diane joined me, we took up residence in the Crows Nest in west-end Toronto. This was a bittersweet reunion. Pop Crow had died during the off-season, and Mom Crow had prepared their own room for us to live in. We were so grateful for everything she'd done that we never even thought about taking an apartment elsewhere.

And what did the team face, as defending Grey Cup champions? Adam Rita had returned as head coach, assisted by Dennis Meyer. Nobody seemed upset that Matt Dunigan had chosen to go to Winnipeg on short notice. Rickey Foggie was still in place, and had seen heavy duty the previous year as starting quarterback. Chris Gaines had been forced to retire with an ankle injury. While Doran Major and Carl Brazley were no longer with us, we still had Rocket Ismail, Darrell K. Smith, Paul Masotti, and the great defence, the nucleus of a winning team. We were a confident bunch — big guys in the big city, ready to kick it into high gear, to go out and make it two in a row.

The little guy wearing number 31 had a couple of minor problems, but he kept quiet about them. My turf toe had lingered throughout the off-season as the scar tissue worked loose. For three months, I'd been in real pain and unable to run at all. By this time, I was okay when it came to plunging straight ahead, but lateral mobility, the mainstay of my game, still gave me grief. Plus, I was slightly chubby. I came in heavier than ever before, and my back was tight and out of balance, the result of a slightly rotated hip joint. Overall, though, these were minor aggravations, and I could lick them in a week or so.

This is the year that kind of put me in the closet. I remember wanting the ball a lot more, and not getting the opportunity to be in situations where I could be effective. In the first game — which drew a smaller crowd than the previous year's opener, a portent of things to come — I had slightly over 100 yards, much more receiving than rushing, and then the door started to close.

We started to struggle, and the more we struggled the more we depended on Rocket. While he could still come up with the big play, in terms of carrying a team, game in and game out, he lacked consistency. But he was our big gun. We lived with him or died with him, and we became very predictable on the field. We all thought in the back of our minds that we were too good not to get it together, but it never really gelled.

At home, I was happy, coming out of my Alice-in-Wonderland wedding, experiencing marital bliss, and wondering why I'd waited so long to tie the knot. Diane and I were in our cozy room at the Crows Nest, and I wanted more than anything to share with her the things I'd been talking about in previous years: How fabulous the city was, how well the team was doing, how rewarding it felt to be on the winning side. Now all of a sudden, we'd hit the wall for no apparent reason. We begin to slip away from what made us successful. We were reeling, trying all sorts of stuff, losing games in the craziest ways.

At this point, less than halfway into the season, Adam Rita was abruptly fired. This provoked an unprecedented backlash. That afternoon, guys refused to practise. Dennis Meyer stepped into the breach, a very tough position, and suggested that we carry on business as usual. The team rebelled against him. I'd never seen this before, and haven't since; when the head coach speaks, you listen. Considering the way things had been going, we certainly needed to practise. The players interpreted this as insensitivity on Meyer's part, an example of his taking advantage of Rita's misfortune. He lost credibility as a leader instantly. We hadn't gotten to know him very well, despite the length of time he'd been with the club. We realized he had a good, sound, defensive mindset, but the team as a whole hadn't connected with him as a person. He was cast in the mold of traitor. A lot of guys decided that Meyer had long wanted to be head coach, would have done anything to get there, and was now seizing his chance with unseemly haste. For them, that fatal first impression never changed.

In fact, Rita was fired out of desperation. He was an easy target. It's far simpler to replace one coach than thirty-seven players. Whenever things aren't going right, people will say — literally, in our case — "Well, you gotta mix up the boat." They'll holler for new blood and a different direction, criticize the coach's failure to reach the team. Something isn't clicking, the mix isn't quite right. The most obvious scapegoat is the coach, just as, on the field, it's the quarterback who's singled out, although so many other factors determine wins and losses.

The trouble is that a mid-season coaching change almost never works to the advantage of the team. This makes you question its validity. Should you just hang in and play out the year, which is probably shot in any case? That way, everybody maintains integrity. What will a major upheaval really accomplish? Are you trying to show the fans that you care, that you're committed to winning? You know it won't make any difference in the standings, unless the interim guy can actually make an impact. Maybe you've found yourself a new coach without having to go shopping in the marketplace. If he can't do it, at least you've confirmed that you have to do just that — which is about the best that can be said for the experiment.

The time to switch coaches is during the off-season. Everybody knows it. Matthews turned us completely around between 1989 and 1990, when there was time to prepare, time to put his system into place from the beginning. That's why you come to training camp — to build a relationship, to learn and become comfortable with a regimen, to understand a coach and his philosophy. A coach's system is working perfectly when he doesn't have to teach you a whole lot, because you're thinking the way he is. You can finish his sentences.

More accurately, although it sounds demeaning, the coach doesn't make you think — it's all reaction. There's an old saying: "Analysis is paralysis." When you're thinking too much, it impedes your play. In order to make plays, to be quick and creative, you've got to reach the point where adjustments are second nature. It's hard to concentrate deeply and exert a lot of force at the same time. During a game, you receive a lot of input — so many signals and diverse visual clues. If you're lost in thought, it slows you down immeasurably. Coaching gives you a bank of information to fall back on, resources that will help you on the field. In the back of my mind, I know what the opposition is going to do; I've been educated about their tendencies, the intricacies of what's likely to happen. I register these things unconsciously; I don't have to actively think about them. It's a bit like driving the same route to work each day. You know when a bend is coming up; you know at exactly which point you can speed up again.

The coach puts this sort of information at your disposal; he makes the game easier for you rather than tougher. Coach Rita had a knack of doing that. That's what we thrived on, knowing the other guys so well that we could create, and then take advantage of, mismatches. Instead of worrying about the perfect 30-yard pass, we'd just hand Rocket the ball, which put a defender who had to confront him one-on-one at an instant disadvantage. This is the sort of thing we went away from. Under Rita, we'd showed a lot of different looks, but the basic elements remained straightforward and clear-cut. It was simple for us, complex for our opponents. Now, we'd abandoned these proven strengths. We became too smart, and the game became too complicated for our own good.

We never got any sort of fluidity going in 1993. Many people tried to pin the blame on ownership. The theory was that McNall had lost interest and enthusiasm. Gretzky, the polished pro who always said the right thing, declared, "I bought the Argos so that the overflow from the game would go down to my restaurant. Now the overflow from the restaurant is going to the game." This dismissiveness was very unlike Wayne. It was, however, indicative of our woes. We weren't dealing with the same excited, committed management, with the exception of John Candy, who loved, lived, and breathed Canadian football. He didn't change; he was always the same to everybody. Overused as that phrase is, in his case, it's apt. He really cared about the people he came in contact with; he gave you that good, warm, fuzzy feeling. That's not to say that Bruce McNall didn't. He had charisma of his own. The difference was that when he wasn't there, there was some question of his commitment. When John wasn't there, there was never that doubt. The bad tone was coming from the top and filtering down.

The year wasn't a total loss. We had several chances to get back on track, and we even came close. Ottawa was bogged down as well, and we almost made it to the playoffs by default. To be fair to Coach

Meyer, he did his best. I've argued against a mid-season coaching change, and I stand by those arguments. Oddly enough, though, the statistics actually favor a team winning their first game after the new coach takes over. It's a combination of back-to-Eden, survival of the fittest, and gotta-play-for-my-job. Meyer's position was probably untenable; on the other hand, someone who comes in from the outside carries no baggage and writes on a clean slate. At best, he projects an air of fresh possibilities.

So much of this game depends on confidence — just believing that you're going to win. A team is composed of thirty-seven guys, all of whom can run and jump and tackle with more or less equal skill. If you put all the teams in a row, they'd look pretty much alike; you couldn't spot the sure winners at a glance. The vital factor is the team element, the way everybody comes together and functions as a unit. This hinges on attitude, which a new coach can feed. He almost represents a freedom from bondage, a release from the shackles of all the bad stuff that's gone down up to the time of his arrival. Everybody's said, If only I could do that over again. Well, now you can, so you go out and win the first game. Then comes the tough part — you have to sustain that energy and momentum. That's tough, and in most cases an insurmountable task. You may win a game. Then you think, Well, we're still 2 and 8, we're still not very good, and there's a long way to go. Maybe the coach has half a dozen good stories in him, six tricks to get you up and moving. After he pulls them all out of his hat, the novelty wears off, and it's harder to motivate the team over the long haul.

So we just kept running into new and different obstacles. During our game against Calgary, Rocket was upset by two instances of pass interference that went unpenalized. If they'd been called, we'd have been first and goal. Later on, one of our guys was hit — in Rocket's view, illegally. He sped to the rescue, and there was a skirmish on the sidelines. In the confusion, he appeared to jump on somebody's head. This made both the Canadian and the American national news. His resulting fine was unprecedented in CFL history, and the incident marked the beginning of the end of his career with the Argos.

Why did this year fall apart? It was the usual combination of circumstances, which are easy to analyze after the fact. First, we lost Matt Dunigan — a much greater leader on and off the field than anybody gave him credit for. People began to appreciate that fact when we got into this dreadful lull or spiral and couldn't find our way out. Second, we didn't achieve success early on. We could have won the first two or three games easily, and then we'd have been off on the right foot. Instead, we were deflated from the outset, which made us change our game plan. We got all tangled up in what we seemed to be doing wrong, rather than bearing down on doing it right.

Personally, I didn't have that bad a season. My rushing yardage actually increased: I led the team with 572 yards. I could reel off the other stats, but they didn't matter overall, because we ended the year at 6 and 12. I still think that, given more opportunities, I could have done more. We'll never know. I do know that, whether I wanted to admit it or not, I wasn't playing at peak — turf toe takes its toll on a twenty-seven-year-old.

My biggest confidence shaker is more difficult to explain. In 1991, when Rocket arrived, we were seen as the dynamic duo. I was on par with him for most of the season, despite my injuries. Even if I wasn't 100 percent fit, I seemed to be the pulse, the fight of the club. Then we won the Cup on his heroics. Because of that, he became the man, and I slid back to number two. I didn't feel like number two, but my way of dealing with that perception, unlike other guys who'd have fought back or argued with Coach Rita, was to retreat into a shell. I didn't say anything that might have detracted from team chemistry. If I had, maybe I'd have played better, with better results for everyone. But I accepted a diminished role and let Rocket have the spotlight. The previous year, I'd been as much or more a part of the game plan than he was. In 1992, he handled the bulk of both kickoff and punt returns. I wasn't playing with nearly the same regularity or confidence. I think the whole team lacked confidence, for different reasons. Rickey Foggie had his big opportunity, yet he didn't win games. Most of our losses weren't his fault, but the measure of a quarterback is whether you win or lose, and we just kept on losing.

Two other factors entered in as well. In 1991, our big year, we hadn't been that much better than our competition. We won eight games in the final three minutes, squeaking through by the narrowest of margins. By 1992, this fact had slipped our minds; we started off thinking that we were light years ahead of anybody else. The maxim is that five plays make the difference in any given game — you just don't know which five they're going to be. We didn't care. We thought we were better than we actually were, with the result that the other guys pulled off the majority of those five vital plays. Sometimes you have a swagger about you that means business: You just go out and get the job done. That's what we'd done in 1990 and 1991. Other times, it's a selective swagger. You're saying, We can afford to lay off a bit; we can turn it on whenever we need to. Not necessarily, as we learned to our cost in 1992.

In retrospect, the abrupt manner of Adam Rita's dismissal doomed us then and there. He'd stood behind us all the way; he commanded admiration and respect from everyone. Coaches very often blame players so as to save their own hides, or make an example of someone, cutting him to get the others' attention. Rita never did this, which helped to explain the rebellion against Meyer. We knew that Mike McCarthy, the general manager, made the calls when it came to talent. He felt that certain guys weren't performing, and urged Coach Rita to replace them, but Rita was determined to stick with the lineup he had. He'd searched all off-season long, added new talent to the carryovers from 1991, and formed a group that he considered the best available.

He knew we were in a slump, and he also felt that it was a cycle, something we'd pull out of together or not at all. He told McCarthy that, if there was a problem, it should be placed directly on his shoulders. Then he quite rightly put the pressure on us. He'd gone to bat for us, and expected us to reciprocate. We didn't have time to do so. Basically, he'd said to McCarthy, "If you want to get rid of someone, you'll have to fire me." Eventually Coach Rita would get his own back, after his move to Edmonton the following year.

In December, Diane and I headed for Florida to see how our dream house was coming along. The contractors had been at work completing all the modifications we'd specified. We saw it for the first time at night, after a marathon drive. It was everything we'd expected, and this helped to put things in perspective. Despite the grim season, things weren't so bad on balance. The nice thing was that, unlike any other business, football losses don't carry over. When the clock starts running the following season, a ten-game deficit doesn't count; you come back and take a fresh run at it. My plan now was to settle into the house, spend time with my beautiful wife, and get back in tune with our families; I didn't want to hustle back to Toronto as much as I had in previous off-seasons.

I also had some thinking to do. This centered on the question of how much was enough on the field. I'd never expected to play at this level for so long. I'd always understood the brevity of a football career, the necessity of having something else in my pocket. By this time, back in Toronto, I'd met Paul Phillips, and created with him a business that would become Cableguard Marketeers Inc. Today, it's doing very well; we employ hundreds of people at a location in Barrie, Ontario. At the time, though, it was a two-man operation that barely paid the phone bill, and I was looking at all sorts of other options. I went so far as to get a license to sell life insurance, and thought about taking the securities exam. Little as I wanted to be an insurance salesman, it was better than sitting idle, and infinitely better than working out. I was swinging back to Mr. Pragmatic again, the side of me that had never been lost or disappeared, looking for safety nets to serve me after my playing days.

This was the longest period that Diane and I stayed in our house, from mid-December of that year until late May of 1993. It was wonderful for us to spend time together, to learn more about each other, and to do this thing called marriage. People had warned us that the first year would be terrible, that we'd get on each other's nerves. There'd be minor irritations, little things that would drive us crazy, fights over which way we wound the toilet paper. We waited patiently, and discovered only that we really loved each other. We also found that another timetable went out the window. Our plan had been to wait three to five years before we had our first child; we wanted to travel and see whether Diane would resume her studies. Then we began to babysit our niece Zoe, her youngest sister's child. She'd take naps in the bed with us; we played with her all day long, up and down the house. Diane decided that someone small would be a useful acquisition. I thought that sounded great, and six weeks later, we were expecting a new arrival.

*   *   *

Meanwhile, in Toronto, there were more departures. The big news during this off-season was an eight-for-eight trade with Edmonton — the largest swap in CFL history. The guy at the other end was Adam Rita, who'd resurfaced with the Eskimos as head coach. He knew us all. He still had confidence in us, so he went after us. In fact, he went after me, as a courtesy; I suppose he didn't want me to feel left out of the action.

The Argonauts' thinking, if you could call it that, ran roughly along these lines: 1992 was horrible, so let's look for someone to blame. We didn't win because Matt Dunigan wasn't there. Rickey

Foggie was, so he's the problem; he didn't measure up. Let's be rid of him, and bring in Tracy Ham from the Wild West, to help execute a brand-new strategy. Seven other guys will keep him company. This will solve all our problems, and we'll live happily ever after.

Who did we give up in the process? We lost linebacker Donnie Wilson, our showtime guy, who played to every whistle and every down. We lost Darrell K. Smith and Ed Berry, mainstays of the team for so many years. We lost Bruce Dickson, a young Canadian player who went all-out on special teams. He didn't show up in the stats, but his block could turn 10 yards into 35. No one notices, yet that can make the difference in a 3-point game. Football is a game of inches.

These truisms are repeated over and over. Some have no merit, while others are so simple and so accurate that they're profound. We gave away not only talent but heart and desire, the qualities that determine who's the winner and who's the also-ran, that allow you to pull off those five game-winning plays. Impossible plays happen because somebody keeps on going. It's part of human nature to want to quit when we've done enough, when we've reached the status quo. When things get sticky, we think, "That's good enough, nobody will fault us if we take a little rest." They say that quitters never win and winners never quit — another cliché that's true. That's why we go on playing even when we're 10 points down with two minutes to go. The one thought in your mind is, How do I get the ball? Nothing is impossible. Pinball can take it back 95 yards. Masotti can catch anything that's airborne. We can score. Then we can kick a field goal. Never say die; never think you're out of it; never admit defeat before you step out on the field.

How one-sided was the eight-for-eight trade? Other than Ham, the former Edmonton players arrived with varying degrees of ability and commitment. Some were on the verge of retirement. Only three of the guys made it through camp. A couple didn't show up at all.

Not to Adam Rita's surprise, all eight of the guys we sent west made it onto Edmonton's roster. A year later, with the departure of Ham to Baltimore, we'd have nobody left. Only Ham was still playing two years later, whereas six or seven of the guys we traded were still on the field.

Now the club, not content with keeping Dennis Meyer at the helm, brought in a new offensive coordinator who was going to turn it all around. This was Darrel (better known as Mouse) Davis, the guru of the run-n-shoot offence. Great things were expected of this strategy. Tracy Ham was in fact the best runner in the league, and we had him. As backup, we also had Mike Kerrigan, who was no slouch himself. Unfortunately, the run-n-shoot offence doesn't mean that the quarterback runs the ball. Quite the opposite. He's very limited in what he can do as a runner. Run-n-shoot is a quick-release technique that involves reading patterns on the fly; it speeds up the game, and severely limits your options at the same time. Now we had a first-string quarterback who was capable of doing many different things, locked into a system that accented none of his strengths. It was like designing a high-powered motor, putting it in a car with a cramped engine compartment, and driving around in stop-and-go city traffic. It served no purpose, and was poor coaching at its worst.

Mouse Davis was not to be denied. He was a larger-than-life character who'd been around for a while — a student of the game, yet very one-dimensional. He had no desire to assimilate at all; all he knew was run-n-shoot. The great coaches design their offence and defence around their players; they adapt as circumstances warrant. When they have great runners, they run the ball. When they have great passers, they pass. When they have a combination of the two, they mix it up. They get more out of their players than other people can, more than the players knew they had in them. Not so Davis — and we were lost from the start.

It's interesting to compare Davis with O'Billovich, who was about to return to the scene. He had a system also, but within it, he was a little more reasonable and a lot more fair. He tried to pick the best talent to execute his plans. Davis almost tried not to pick the best, so that he could credit his system, and not the players, when things went well. Run-n-shoot would work despite, not because of, anybody else.

His and Obie's broader schemes or ideologies were outwardly similar, but the two men differed totally in the way they treated people and responded to situations. Obie's presentation was much more selfless. Davis was more concerned with himself and the system and how it ran, with who got the praise and how he'd look at the end of the day. Run-n-shoot meant Mouse Davis, not Tracy Ham or Mike Kerrigan or even the Toronto Argonauts. Obie understood that he and whatever system he might devise were only as good as the guys who did the job. He didn't mind changing people — as I've said, he was often overly eager to make the attempt — always in aid of improving the club's performance.

I'm not sure what Davis's agenda was. Obie had nothing to prove; Davis did, from the very first day. With Obie, nothing seemed seemed personal; with Davis, everything did. Obie was a team guy, and Mouse Davis was a Mouse Davis guy, with seemingly no one to answer to. Mike McCarthy had personally chosen Mouse as his man. In doing so, he also undermined Dennis Meyer. Davis was more recognized than Meyer was; he had at least equal authority. So now we had a body that was bleeding before we'd played a single game.

The Argos were ill advised to embark on this adventure. I'm not arguing for doing nothing, or for loyalty at any price. If something is bleeding, you move decisively to stop the hemorrhage. But everything in life is cyclical. In the case of Adam Rita, we'd had a great coach who was experiencing problems. He'd been at a peak, and seemed to be heading for a valley. Inevitably, though, the good companies, the good teams, and the good people straighten themselves out and climb back up again. Even a good stock takes little dips, but you hang in with it over the long haul. Eventually, Meyer might have found his feet, exercised good leadership, established credibility, and shaken off the perception that he was Rita's nemesis. Time and distance heal many wounds; you want to let the bad stuff pass. Davis's arrival threw a wrench into this process. There was no sense of hierarchy and continuity. Several other long-term players had retired. Carl Brazley was gone. Ian Beckstead, the center, was gone. Dan Ferrone, the guard, was gone. Even our great hope, Rocket, was gone, back to the States, on the grounds that he wasn't living up to his end of the bargain in terms of making personal appearances. In fact, his $4.5 million U.S. wasn't being recovered at the gate. So there we were, in serious disarray, with nothing to fall back on.

Looking back on 1993, it seems as if I didn't play much at all. This was the case for the first half of the season. I did my thing, and I did it in the return game, 77 punts for 716 yards and 30 kickoffs for 604. Once again, the stats don't look all that bad. I finished first in the East in all-purpose yards, third in the league behind Henry (Gizmo) Williams and Derrick Crawford. I caught 32 passes and racked up 481 yards on 89 carries. So much for me. The team finished in the basement at 3 and 15, our worst showing since 1981.

It's a wonder I got those yards, because I spent the first ten games at odds with Mouse Davis. First, he claimed I didn't catch the ball well, which, if he'd been paying attention, he wouldn't have said. He knew my work; he'd been up here before. He'd been a lot of different places, and there may be a reason for that — if all you have is one string to your bow, and it's called run-n-shoot, the other guys eventually catch up with you, and you have to seek greener pastures to do it all over again.

Davis seemed to have something personal against me. He started calling me the Mayor of Toronto, and not in a pleasant way. He tried not to be openly spiteful about it, yet then he cut back my playing time, on the grounds that I might get hurt. None of this made sense. When he played me, infrequently as that might have been, I was averaging 10 yards per carry, partly because there were gaping holes. Thanks to our reliance on run-n-shoot, the opposition expected us to throw all the time. Davis kept looking for excuses not to put me in the lineup. He tried everybody and his brother back there at my position, with varying results. The only reason we scored any points at all was that run-n-shoot suited Paul Masotti's skills, and Mike Kerrigan's also — which was just as well, because Ham was injured (as eventually was Paul), and Kerrigan had to soldier on in his place.

Halfway through the season, the light dawned in the front office. It was time for yet another coaching change. The call went out to O'Billovich, who'd been biding his time in British Columbia until the right opportunity presented itself. This time around, the opportunity was double-barreled: He came back as both head coach and general manager, ousting Mike McCarthy. Meyer remained as defensive coordinator, and Mouse was free to pursue other options.

Obie had his work cut out for him. At this point, we'd managed to salvage exactly seven wins in a season and a half. As might have been predicted, we won the very first game of his regime, 35 to 26 against Winnipeg, who had been playing very well. We began to show some signs of life, Obie brought me back into the mainstream, and I saw more action as the season drew to a close. At least our attitude was better. By that time, unfortunately, it was too late to pull things together as a team.

The first half-season had been trying for me. I tried not to let it show, which is probably a failing. I had to exercise self-control, or I would have shown my disrespect for Mouse Davis overtly. I didn't confront him, I just came to work and did my job. That's what leads people to think that nothing affects me, that I'm happy and smiling all the time. In fact, I was still enjoying the game, although not as much as before. I just counted my blessings. It's easy to say, So-and-so is out to get me — and I try to avoid doing that at all costs. In this case, I don't have a whole lot of reservations about believing this, given the things that Davis said and did. His reasons for not playing me were very strange. So many people played for us that year that I lost track; it was unbelievable. I almost feel as if Davis tried to make the system tough on purpose, that he tried to confuse us, to make it hard for Tracy and for me, because he was in love with his precious system. All he had to do was plug in the interchangeable parts, and it would run like clockwork. Given the situation, I think my stats were halfway decent and a step up from 1992. I came back and played hard, with emotion and respect, even though I don't feel that my respect was reciprocated.

When you play this game as hard as you can and still wind up 3 and 15, you wonder whether your identity hinges on what people say you are, what the media say about you, how the fans react to your fortunes on the field. That year, I had to decide whether I was a sort of potluck package known as Pinball, or whether, deep down inside, I was Michael Clemons. The answer was, I was me, because I had to be. All along, I'd been thinking: I'm solid, I'm grounded. I'm a Christian guy. That's hard to hang on to; at a certain level, any athlete is tied to his success or lack of it. Negative comments hurt, no matter what their source, so I wasn't immune to media speculation, fan disinterest, or anything else that conspires to bring a team down.

In 1993, some important elements of my success were taken away. The year before, I hadn't been the man, the go-to guy. Rocket was. At least he was paid more than the rest of us put together, and the team was of a higher caliber. This year, until O'Billovich returned, I wasn't the go-to guy, either, and the team was by any measure much worse than before. Matter of fact, I was the furthest thing from being the man, the first time since my rookie season that I wasn't on the field with any regularity. Davis patronized me, almost suggesting that my success wasn't because of my play but because people liked me.

He prevented me doing what I do best, and had done many times before. But through all that, I was able to content myself. I felt it as much as anybody when we lost. However, I was able to go beyond the misfortune and move on. This season might have taught me how to lose. I don't know whether that's a good thing or not.

Can you care deeply about the game and still smile when you're 1 and 9? I could. To me, the guy who's faking it is the guy who walks around in a bad mood all week and then dogs it on game day. The guy who's letting the team down is the guy who doesn't believe that, in spite of everything, we can win. I just can't stand this. When a guy is scared and doesn't want to be there, you can see it in his face, down there on the field. It's highlighted and magnified. When you put your all into something and your success is inextricably linked to somebody else who couldn't care less, you get a little testy.

Of course I get disappointed sometimes — mostly with my own performance. If I do my best, and we lose, of course it will affect me. My feeling is, work as hard as you can. Then, when you come to the sidelines, you can be mad, happy, sad, whatever you want to be. Just give what you've got when you're on the field. This is why we're out there. Too many people want to judge things that are around the game, not the game itself.

Besides, I had other responsibilities now, and another job title: husband and father-to-be. During the season, Diane was very ill, pregnant with our first child. She didn't have morning sickness; she felt ghastly morning, noon, and night. We stayed with Mom Crow for the first six games. When Diane needed space and privacy, we moved to the SkyDome Hotel in mid-August — not the homiest of surroundings, but by far the most practical solution.

So there we were, calling up room service at odd hours, losing every game (some of them literally in sight), with Diane in awful shape, and thinking about a strategic withdrawal to our dream home in Clearwater. We missed family and friends who could lend much-needed hands. Yet, in the midst of all this, amazingly enough, we began to talk about what was on both our minds — the prospect of staying in Toronto full time, probably for the rest of our lives.

This is hard to explain now. When I first came here, I had absolutely no intention of staying. I'd come to play ball; I'd put in my time and go back "home." Two years later, I was totally convinced that Toronto was a marvelous city, but home was still in Florida. I wanted very much to remain with the club, while I wasn't convinced that I should be here year-round, let alone after my playing career ended. I saw the virtue of maintaining a semi-permanent base here, and that was about it.

Why was this? Because all the examples I had to go by were pointing me south. Carl Brazley, Jeff Boyd, and Reggie Pleasant were great friends, wonderful husbands and fathers, strong family men, and exemplary Christians. When they finished a season, they went back home. Home was simply somewhere else. This was a real hurdle for me to overcome. Most important, I wanted to be close to my mom and my sister, Kelli, to be able to affect their lives positively, now that my mom's relationship with my stepdad showed signs of breaking down once and for all.

Now, in 1993, when things were at the lowest point on record — Diane deathly ill, the team on another planet, and our families thousands of miles away — we talked it over and decided to put down roots in Canada.

I think the most obvious reason was our love of the city, a love affair we embarked on immediately, and which endures today. I think we were responding to the affection we felt here, the reception we'd been given. We felt a part of things. It's the reason why our children are Canadian citizens, and why Diane and I — given my genius for procrastination — are landed immigrants. (Perhaps by the time you read this, I'll have wrapped up the necessary paperwork.) We've burned our bridges now; the Florida house has long since been sold.

But over Christmas 1993, we went back to it, and spent a good portion of time there, pacing the floors and wondering whether we'd made a mistake in deciding to set up shop so far away. The more we paced, the more something kept calling us back.

So back we came, in February 1994. Diane was due to deliver the first week of April. As the countdown continued, we moved out of the SkyDome Hotel. It had served its purpose. It seemed an inappropriate spot for a nursery, so we found a furnished apartment on Jarvis Street, a place where other players had stayed and that catered to visiting executives.

Diane still felt miserable. The doctors had put her on medication to control her nausea, because she'd actually lost weight over the first three months, and she's a small person. This helped. She tried to take as little of it as possible, as she was worried about its side effects on the baby.

I felt I was underfoot, so I began to do tons of stuff, which was misinterpreted at the time. If the team is in a trough, it's supposed to be less desirable for players to show their face in public. They should be concentrating on football day and night. The perception in football circles is that, when you're losing, you're no good, so you can't do good — which is, of course, nonsense. At any rate, I was running all over the place, helping Big Brothers, and Diane was scared to smithereens that I'd be off and grinning at a charity event when the big day came. I promised not to schedule anything for the three crucial weeks, and it was just as well, because the day came two weeks early. Besides, we had a lot more plans to discuss as the deadline approached. This period marked the real transition from contentment in football with the Argonauts to contentment with life in Toronto, our wish to be Canadians and to become part of the community.

We discussed names. I told Diane that the child would be hers to name, that I had no rights in that department. I'd had very little to do with the baby's coming to fruition; she'd carried the burden for nine long months, so whatever she picked was more than fine with me. So Justin Michael was slated for a boy, and Rachel Chantelle for a girl.

After all the tumult of those months, the last few weeks were probably Diane's most comfortable. While we were in Florida, on top of everything else she kept having asthma problems. One time we were in the countryside, half an hour from the nearest hospital, and she started having terrible trouble breathing. I was Mr. Calm, telling her to relax and wait for the ambulance, while things kept getting worse. This was the most frightening moment of my life. We couldn't afford to wait, so my cousin drove us at hair-raising speed into town. Thank God we made it safely. This resulted in yet another round of medication, and more worries as Diane's time to deliver grew short.

March 25, 1994, proved to be just the calmest day. Diane's water broke at seven in the morning, and then we lay back down for a bit. Around nine we got up, with the bags already packed. We had two little outfits, for a girl or a boy, along with slippers and an overnight bag. The only thing missing was a videocamera. It all seemed to unfold so methodically. Off we went to Queensway General Hospital in Mississauga. I looked after the room; we had a tape recorder with calming music. Then Danny Webb, the Argonauts' equipment manager, brought us a camera to record the occasion for posterity. Truth to tell, Diane thought that if I left to get it, I'd find a charity event along the way and come back sometime the next week.

She went into labor about one o'clock in the afternoon. By three o'clock there was no doubt that we were into the countdown. We walked the floor and did a little taping, knowing full well that seeing ourselves on tape wouldn't be the same. The most important thing for me was to be part of the moment. I held her hand and fed her ice chips as things moved gradually along. We were prepared for twelve hours' labor with the first child, but soon the pains became more intense. She was almost apologizing for hurting, so we told her she was doing a great job. She didn't want to take any painkillers; it was amazing, the way she was handling the pain, with no relief at all. I'd try to tell her to get ready, but the contractions were coming right on top of each other and she had no time to relax. Finally they had to give her an epidural injection, which conked her right out. When something says on the label "may make you drowsy," it puts her to sleep immediately. Now she could hardly push at all, much as she kept trying for two solid hours more. The medicine sapped her last remaining strength. The scariest part was when they started talking about a Caesarian and other procedures. They were concerned about the baby's heart rate, and I was wondering about how this would affect Diane, and whether the baby would be okay.

At last Rachel appeared, safe and sound. The nurses put her on the table, and I danced around hugging them, kissing Diane, and loving everybody in sight. Pathetic! Then we got to hold her, and I could not believe that this child had anything to do with me, because she was much too beautiful.

9

1994–1996

It's a pity that Robert Drummond wasn't yet with the team in 1994, because he'd have had the perfect weather report for July 16. Rob's way of suggesting that it's ultra-balmy outside is to say he saw the Devil at a lemonade stand. That's the kind of hot it was in Shreveport, Louisiana. It was a scorching, searing, burning heat that seemed to rise up and get you. If it didn't, something else would. We went to a little soul food restaurant in the middle of the 'hood, where they served us heart-attack toast, saturated in butter. This might have been a plot to slow us down. After we'd eaten, we were standing outside, and a carload of guys cruised by and threw us some gang signs. Titus Dixon said, "If they're going to shoot us, let's make them look for us," so we huddled in the parking lot until the van arrived to take us back to our hotel. But football players have their priorities straight. The food was so good that we returned the following night.

This was the Shreveport Pirates' home opener, and the stadium was still in the process of being refurbished. There'd been an awful amount of rain, and the red clay was showing through the turf. The groundskeepers were relining the field to CFL dimensions, with mixed results. We didn't care. It was too hot to think.

It was so hot, our trainers had broken out an intraveneous drip. I'm not exactly certain what it was, and I gave it a pass. I don't like a lot of tape or pads, and I don't take a whole lot of stuff. Some of the guys got it before the game when dehydration was predicted. Some got it at halftime because dehydration was imminent. Some got it post-game because they'd lost fifteen pounds. I probably lost about eight, and I was getting a lot of exercise; I covered 221 yards. We got clobbered in the first quarter, 20 to 7. But we went on to win the game, 35 to 34. People in the stands were curious about me. By the end of the game, the tune had changed from: Why can't you tackle the midget? to Why isn't the midget in the NFL? We gained a lot of fans that day, and signed a lot of autographs—so many that my fingers cramped up because I'd disdained the drip.

Then we went to Baltimore, Maryland, and ate seafood down by the waterfront redevelopment. Later on, we went to Memphis, Tennessee, and ate ribs at Corky's Barbecue. In Sacramento, California, we wound up at a Denny's restaurant. If you haven't been to Sacramento, don't worry. The next year, when the Gold Miners pulled up stakes and resurfaced as the San Antonio Texans, we ate Tex-Mex along the Riverwalk. We never did go to Las Vegas and eat at a hotel buffet. Instead, the Posse came to us at the Dome, and separated my shoulder.

How quickly memories fade. Someday, I'll tell Rachel and Raven's children about the strange years that their grandfather played on both sides of the border, not the ball, and the Grey Cup was snatched away by upstart Yankees. I'll explain that the CFL split first east–west, then north–south. They'll ask, "Isn't that the way you used to run?" I'll say, "Yes, but," and start all over again.

The season of 1994 marked the league's first concerted stab at its ill-fated expansion, which had begun the previous year, when Sacramento came on-stream. We'd played there the night the Blue Jays' Joe Carter hit his World Series–winning home run; they showed it on the giant screen, to make us feel at home. Baltimore, Shreveport, and Vegas signed up next, and Memphis and Birmingham followed in 1995.

The expansion concept stemmed from Bruce McNall. It was his vision that U.S. markets that weren't large enough to support an NFL team would become CFL franchises, on the plausible theory that Americans would flock to football of any variety. It's easy to be wise after the event, but I believe that this could have worked, had it been introduced the right way. A two-year countdown seemed in order, but there was no process in place to educate the market, no period of acclimatization. We got expansion monies in March, and took to the field in July. Despite all the rosy projections, no one grasped what we were getting into. Fans never understood the history, the unique qualities of the Canadian form of the game. Given time, they might have, and the idea might very well have flown; in my opinion, the Canadian game is more exciting. There's more happening, more to enjoy, mainly because there's less emphasis on defence. Very few people are defence-minded, and can watch with interest a 0-0 tie. At the risk of sounding biased, I believe most fans like to see teams score lots and lots of points. The Canadian game lends itself to this. Its strategies may be less complex; the American game may be played at a somewhat higher level. By any objective standard, though, the CFL offers more pure entertainment.

What would have happened, had the expansion teams succeeded? This wouldn't have accelerated or made inevitable the absorption of the CFL into the NFL. From a business point of view, it doesn't make sense for the NFL to invest in a lot of far-flung and sparsely populated markets that won't significantly affect its television revenues. More likely, franchises will continue to move around within the States. Right now, the NFL would probably welcome expansion—nine CFL teams north and nine south of the border. The NFL would continue as the premier league; expansion wouldn't substantially detract from, and might even augment, the NFL's fan base. Good football is good football. The Canadian game would find its audience.

By the way, we'll see a Toronto NFL franchise within a decade, but not by the turn of the century. It seems a bit of a reach to say so when the Argos have been drawing only 20,000-odd fans per game, yet the two leagues could coexist and complement each other, as long as there isn't an ownership conflict of interest. We could work out the scheduling problems inherent in both clubs occupying the Dome. Toronto has the ability to support even more sports, if Chicago, which isn't all that much larger or wealthier, is anything to go by. I think that a fondness for the CFL might reassert itself if the two games could be compared side by side. This would mean more fans for the CFL who would also be more knowledgeable about the game.

Meanwhile, back in 1994, these things were far from our minds. To recap: Diane and I moved from Jarvis Street to a rental condominium in Mississauga, just west of Toronto, soon after Rachel's birth. The following year, we'd sell our Florida dream home and settle down for good. Up in the Argos' front office, the Dream Team was about to decamp. The actual sale of the team was delayed by John Candy's untimely death. As I understand it, he'd have been part of the new ownership, had he lived. I never got to know him well, because everyone wanted to be close to him, and there was a lot of traffic at times. I know he was always extremely supportive. In 1991, when I'd won the Player of the Year award, we had had a banquet in Saskatchewan, sponsored by the players' association. Candy arrived there in his private jet and flew Darrell K. and me back to Toronto. This was typical—he was overly accommodating, very generous. I found it intriguing that he didn't try to be funny all the time. He had a very serious side, bordering on pensive; he wasn't "on," like so many comic performers.

At any rate, the sale was concluded in May, and training camp began in June—not much time to implement new plans and ideas of any kind. The problem was exacerbated by this being the middle of baseball season, with the Blue Jays defending their World Series championship, and both clubs were owned lock, stock, and barrel by the same beer company.

Which was fine with us. The previous ownership had proven to be as disenchanted as it was economically starved. Unsure where the club was heading, we more than welcomed the change, which promised immediate credibility and stability. The immediate principal was TSN Enterprises, the largest sports network in the land. TSN was owned, in turn, by Labatt's, which had scads of money, and was led by Paul Beeston, arguably the most influential and dynamic sports administrator in Canadian history. Equally important, his right-hand man, Bob Nicholson, now the Argos' president, had a passion for the CFL and would work to make things happen behind the scenes.

Elsewhere, the Labatt's riches were viewed almost as a threat. There'd been a salary cap of sorts in place since 1992; I believe it was $3 million per club. Now, even tighter restrictions were established. The league's reasoning was that the ownership with the most resources would win; community-owned teams out west couldn't hope to compete dollar for dollar. Nor could the U.S. franchises, because they'd be overly dependent on gate receipts. The league's TV contracts were mainly with Canadian networks—and Shreveport, for example, didn't receive a TSN feed. So a new, scaled-down cap was instituted. It was the same for every team, and allowed for a single marquee player (usually a quarterback) on each. He could be paid whatever he could command. The problem was obvious: Everybody didn't have the same ability to buy a superstar. This, however, was the most palatable compromise that could be reached on short notice.

To put it briefly, the 1994 Argos were all over the map. Marvin Graves ended up being quarterback most of the year, after Mike Kerrigan got hurt. O'Billovich was still with us, as both head coach and general manager. It was sort of a turnaround year for me, after the Mouse Davis debacle. I made the Eastern all-star team and wound up with 2,400 yards, including 787 yards rushing, more than anyone else on the squad. We ended the season 7 and 11, went to the Eastern semifinal against Baltimore (coached by none other than Don Matthews), and came back defeated, 34 to 15. What I can replay most vividly in my mind, though, is yet another game, which took place in Baltimore's Memorial Stadium in mid-August.

Baltimore had played against us in our season opener. I had two consecutive punt-return touchdowns, but one was called back, and we lost, 28 to 20. The return engagement in Baltimore saw more than 40,000 fans in the stands—not surprising, since the club managed to average 30,000 a game over the two expansion years. People had arrived a couple of hours early, whereas in Toronto, they'd amble in with five minutes to spare. The stadium smelled like football; there was a freshness in the air and the grass was soft. It was warm, but not oppressive, and I function better in the warmth. I'm more aware of what's around me; my reactions are quicker and more precise.

The enthusiasm and energy there in Baltimore were something I hadn't experienced in a while. The game was being played in the evening, too, the same time we used to play high school ball. So that game—the first time I ever rushed for more than 100 yards—remains without question my favorite. Not only did we unexpectedly win, but everything was right—the atmosphere, the whole approach. You didn't mind the partisan fans; it felt more like college-to-college-team loyalty than a big city-to-pro-team connection. It was an event, a destination, a chance to belong to something bigger for an hour or so. In the States, there's always a small-town feel to a game, no matter how large the city. A stadium becomes a community in and of itself.

Racial, cultural, and socio-economic factors don't really matter. People come together, wearing the same T-shirts and rooting for the same team; they are excited and passionate. You only tap into this every so often, and I did that night.

Otherwise, this was not the greatest of seasons. I was lucky, in that I had a secret weapon at home, one Rachel Chantelle Clemons. It's hard to let the game's disappointments spill over into the next day when there's a baby who needs changing, who doesn't know or care what the score is, or how many times you fumble. So this year marked the beginning of life together as a family. The previous two years had been more of a continuation of Diane's and my formal courtship; all we had to worry about was ourselves. Now, I found that I was married to Supermom; she welcomed my help but didn't expect it. I didn't mind diaper duty, but Diane kept beating me to the punch. She was so devoted, absolutely in control. I still struggle to do my part, but find I'm usually more trouble than I'm worth, strewing debris in my wake. By this time, of course, we'd received a fresh set of dire warnings about parenthood—yet as far as we could see, the only downside was wakefulness. Rachel suffered from colic, and thinking back it was the best sleep I ever lost. I'd sit there rocking her at three o'clock in the morning. I could cradle her head in my hand like a football, and her little legs would straddle my forearm just about as far as my elbow, and nothing bad ever lasted long while we were together like that.

By the way, the other big news on the home front this year was Rachel's "disappearance" from a SkyDome washroom. I was on the field, and Diane was in the stands, with Rachel more or less on her lap. But Rachel was up in arms that day, so Diane took her for a stroll to give the people around them a break. A woman approached her and said, "Give me that child, and go and watch your husband play." You may wonder why the ultimate mom would surrender our firstborn to a total stranger. That's because you haven't met Shirley Forde. I hadn't, even though her son Duane was busy blocking for me; he'd joined the club the previous year. When Mrs. Forde tells you to do something, you do it, no questions asked. This marked the beginning of our most important relationship since Diane joined me in Toronto. Here, we found family. Shirley and her husband, Arnold, are our personal angels — God-sends. They're extremely special—loving, open, and so generous that we worry about imposing on them or over-stepping the bounds. Rachel still belongs to Mrs. Forde, and her husband, not to be outdone, has since kidnapped Raven, our second daughter. If we arrive for a visit in the afternoon and leave in the late evening, we'll seldom catch a glimpse of her. What we do see is really quite amazing. If she's fretful, he calms her instantly; he entertains and challenges her, sits rocking with her for hours at a time. The kindness that he and Shirley have shown overwhelm us, and our gratitude really can't be put into words. These few will have to do.

* * *

Pretty soon, 1995 was upon us. Along with it came new hope that the new ownership would work its magic. We'd really bought into the idea that great things awaited us. Paul Beeston had built championship teams: witness the Blue Jays. He knew it took time. Now, during the off-season, Bob Nicholson acquired Kent Austin, one of the best quarterbacks in the CFL, and one of the few who'd ever thrown for over 6,000 yards. We'd done some things well the previous year, doubling our number of wins. Marvin Graves had brought us back when we were 21 points down in the final quarter against Hamilton. He had a promising future, as did we. Austin could guide him, and with both of them in form, we'd be contenders again, having turned the corner and begun to move in the right direction.

Meanwhile, O'Billovich had relinquished his coaching duties, and headed upstairs as general manager. The choice of his replacement was somewhat strange, but everybody bought into it. Mike Faragalli (who, you'll recall, coached me at William and Mary in 1983–84) was well respected.

However, in training camp, Faragalli's inexperience began to show almost immediately. He chose a committee composed of a number of players—in his judgment, team leaders—who were supposed to work with him in some ill-defined way. The choices were suspect at best. He conducted his camp as if it were a throwback to college ball. A professional schedule isn't ten or eleven games, and professional athletes aren't in their late teens, with a resilience verging on fool-hardiness. You don't beat yourself up with full contact from the word go, and you don't expect a thirty-one-year-old offensive line-man intimately acquainted with knee surgery to go through knock-around drills for twice as long as a university student would. We faced two pre-season games, then an eighteen-game schedule, and then the playoffs, if we played our cards right. That made a grand total of twenty-three games, if you counted semifinal, final, and Cup.

Quite a few guys got the idea that this was a case of too much, too fast. Among them was Austin, who wasn't at all shy about stating his opinion. This caused a problem that persisted throughout the year. Austin felt that he knew and understood the game better than Faragalli. In general, quarterbacks are given a little greater latitude, a little more freedom to implement their own designs and to augment what's already in place. That sometimes works, but the tug-of-war between Austin and Faragalli was off the scale. It became a battle within itself. Austin would try to rally guys to his point of view, and convince them that this or that should be in the offence. Soon, however, he got hurt, in a way that revealed how counter-productive Faragalli's scheme was. We were dead tired, having taken a red-eye flight back from out of town. Then we'd had a full day of meetings, followed by a strenuous practice. There was some question as to whether we should have been on the field at all. Austin was caught in a run-down and pulled a calf muscle, which sent us into another quarterbacking tailspin. In fact, Austin had a whole string of injuries this year, which he attempted to remedy with the famous oxygen tank. This was a very expensive gadget — big enough to get into and small enough to make you claustrophobic at the same time. It was supposed to speed up the healing process. You'd shoehorn yourself in, put on a mask, and breathe pure, colorless, odorless, and tasteless gas for as long as you felt inclined. Austin swore by the thing and spent an inordinate amount of time inside it.

This season illustrated yet again how a team's leadership starts from the top, and how, in many instances, the team dynamic is much more important than is the talent level, as such. We never became a cohesive unit, never had a strategy we were comfortable with. Faragalli wanted offensive balance; Austin wanted to throw the ball all the time. We passed to set up the run instead of running to set up the pass. We had no signature, no confidence or continuity. This was apparent in our inability to perform in the clutch. We were hanging tough in games, but could not win them. We dissolved into factions and let minor squabbles escalate into conflicts.

One day, a rookie named Jermaine Younger got into an altercation with Jason Colero, our assistant equipment manager. Younger had asked him for a rain jacket, and somehow Jason (who'd been with the club forever, starting as a ball boy, and was everybody's little brother) took exception to his tone of voice. Words were exchanged, and Younger slapped him. Everybody sprang to Jason's defense, and the episode got wildly out of hand. A meeting was called, which involved two black and two white players, and it degenerated into an airing of every long-suppressed point of contention, real or imagined, that could be dredged up between newcomers and veterans, and, worse yet, between blacks and whites. Masotti, who doesn't have a prejudiced bone in his body, went nutso. Gerry Townend, the trainer, and Danny Webb, the equipment manager, were incensed.

I was none too pleased myself, because I was trying to explain Younger's point of view without condoning his actions. This was symptomatic of our woes that year. We were looking for someone to lash out at, to serve as scapegoat for the fact that we were once again on a downhill slope.

After nine games with Faragalli at the helm, O'Billovich came back downstairs and onto the sidelines, as coach. We finished the season at 4 and 14, well out of playoff contention, and returned home to await brighter days.

This spelled the end for Obie within the organization. He would soon be fired — a dismissal, the reasoning went, that was doubly justified. As general manager, it was his decision to hire Faragalli. As coach, he then attempted, and failed, to work with the talent that he himself had selected. That makes it sound as if the club was looking for an excuse to fire him. I am not suggesting that; they wanted him to succeed. They did feel that they'd given him two chances, and things had gotten worse instead of better. They didn't believe they had the time or the patience to wait it out.

Obie's downfall helps illustrate why coaching is an inexact science at best. He'd been putting marvelous talent in place for years, dating back to the acquisition of Condredge Holloway, Gilbert Renfroe, and Joe Barnes. He'd chosen Carl Brazley, Donnie Moen, and Terry Greer. All these and more helped establish his reputation; a coach's success hinges on how others perform. Were we not talented enough to deliver for him in 1995? Possibly. We felt we were, but maybe that wasn't the case.

Still, consider the talent he had to work with. Obie and Beeston and Nicholson had already laid the groundwork for the team as it would evolve. Marcello Simmons, Pierre Vercheval, and George Nimako were on board during 1995. So were Duane Dmytryshyn, Norm Casola, Chris Gioskos, Jeff Fairholm, Noah Cantor, and Mike Morreale—the list goes on. So was Donnie Wilson, back where he belonged after his sojourn in Edmonton. Given so much skill, how could we possibly lose? I don't have the answer now, and I certainly didn't at the time.

At no time do I look at revolving-door coaches and think, I can do better than this. I'd coached youth football and youth soccer, and helped out at William and Mary. It's a tough job, and excites me. I try to be honest in my appraisal of performance, but not critical. I think I may have a talent as a coach because I have an ability to simplify things, which may come from my facility for mathematics. In high school, I couldn't understand why the teachers made it so hard. The concepts weren't all that tough. If teachers who, I assumed, understood these principles at least as well as I did, took the time, they could make sure you grasped them, as long as you broke them down into manageable pieces. The same could be said for football. Take it back to the basics: If the other guys don't score on you, you can't lose.

But how do you win? You believe in yourself, even though you may not be as talented as players on the other team. There's a difference between being skillful and knowing how to win. Skill and will are only part of the equation. The other component is knowledge and understanding of the game and its context. If I've got incredible skills in basketball, I can take shots from way out. I may be more proficient in doing this than anybody on the other team, but if I do so all the time, and they take shots from way in, chances are they'll come out on top. You have to know what works successfully, how to take advantage of an opponent's weaknesses and camouflage yours as well as you can. And you can't be scared of losing. Many people are, which is in itself a big deterrent to winning. You have to be aggressive and assertive in order to prevail.

At that point, I had no desire at all to coach. First, I hate giving up. Even while we were losing to the tune of 4 and 14, I carried the ball more than in any other year—181 times, for 856 yards. I got my second of three Ironman Awards, presented by the ALS (Lou Gehrig's disease) Society. Baseball's remarkable Gehrig played 2,131 straight games for the New York Yankees before succumbing to his illness. The award is given for perseverance, leadership, and being— that suspect term—a team player. It also implies a degree of durability and skill, a love and passion for the game. Unlike other awards, it's voted on by fellow players, and it is all the more appreciated for this reason. It's a heavy thing, too, actually made of iron. It really weighs down a fellow of my stature who hates exercising. I put it up on the shelf alongside the 1995 John Candy Memorial Award, naming me the team's most valuable player, and the 1993 Tom Pate Memorial Award for community service. I seemed to be building quite a nice collection, and this seemed like a bad time to throw in the towel, especially since I'd been telling everyone we were going to turn things around.

The clincher was that if I were to coach, I wouldn't want to do so at a professional level. It makes for a hectic family life; it requires too much of you too much of the time, and you have no chance to let off steam or think about anything else. Don Matthews has tremendous focus; I don't necessarily enjoy that kind of single-minded concentration. The player-coach relationship is much more intense and diverse than most employer-employee interchanges. In other arenas, you simply relay the necessary instruction or policy direction. You give the guidelines; you don't sweat the details. As a coach, you share your own philosophy, techniques, style, personality, and belief system. You spend time in ways you wouldn't as a business superior. You're in control as well as on display, whether you're winning or losing, in informal settings or the heat of serious battle. How you behave in all those circumstances is critical. On the one hand, it's vastly rewarding. On the other, it's terribly draining. If I were ever to contemplate it, I think I'd look at coaching at the high school or college levels, where players are looking actively for direction.

Maybe that's why, in 1995, my role within the team began to change. Earlier, it had been pretty much limited to the field. Now, I'd been assigned some younger players to help along the way, as befitted an old guy who'd just logged his hundredth game. I started to become a mentor.

The process began with Jimmy (the Jet) Cunningham, who joined us in the waning hours of the season. I remember talking with him about football, finances, family, and God. Surely it was only yesterday when Jeff Boyd and I were sitting at the Crows Nest, covering much the same ground. But with Jimmy, the burden of the conversation shifted to me, especially when we were counting down to a game. He was like Reggie Pleasant, only worse. The day before we played, he didn't mind being out and about. On the day itself, he turned into a hermit; he didn't stir from his bed or say a word. I'm silence-challenged, so I kept on chattering just to fill the void. When he recovered his powers of speech, I found that Jimmy had an infectious enthusiasm for the game. He got a charge out of everything, and made me appreciate the smaller things all over again, things I'd forgotten about in the course of too many losing seasons. He jump-started me, so I was happy to be thrown together with him.

I wasn't supposed to do all that much—just be there over the long haul, and give them someone to talk to and lean on if necessary. I suppose I was pointed out as a sort of example for other guys as well. To some extent, you're cast in various roles because of your age; years of service have a lot to do with this. With the vast majority, it's just a matter of the way you carry yourself. You take the time to sign autographs; you behave in a civil manner; if you have a family, you don't go on the road and forget you do. That's the role I'm most comfortable with—just being myself. I don't like giving rah-rah speeches; that's out of character for me. I like to clown a little or be the best supporting actor, but not the guy leading the parade.

*　　*　　*

In early 1996, Bob Nicholson brought the players he considered leaders on the team together—Paul Masotti, Donnie Wilson, Chris
Gioskos, Pierre Vercheval, and me—to talk about a successor to the
head coaching position. There wasn't much of a debate; Don
Matthews was everybody's first choice.

He had coached the Baltimore Stallions to a Grey Cup victory over
Calgary in 1995, and the year before had lost by a field goal to the
B.C. Lions in the Cup game. The only other solid possibility was John
Hufnagel, Doug Flutie's offensive coordinator in Calgary. The theory
here was that, if we got him, we'd have a better shot at attracting
Flutie. I thought it was time for Hufnagel to become head coach
somewhere, as he deserved it. But coming off our last three or four
seasons, the brightest of which had been 7 and 11, this was no time
for experimentation. We were under the impression that Obie would
remain as general manager. We had no idea that a vote for Matthews
was in effect a vote against Obie. Perhaps our conviction wouldn't
have been as strong, had this been put to us directly; we don't take
anyone's livelihood lightly. So it came to pass that when Matthews
came, he'd wear two hats, and Obie would go his way.

With Matthews on board, there was real, justified optimism in the
air, the kind you could see and taste—particularly since we then did
add Flutie to the mix. That in itself went quite a distance toward
making us pre-season Cup favorites.

One of the things that allowed Matthews to excel so quickly was
fortuitous timing. He came to us just as the American teams were
dissolving, and their players were about to go into a dispersal draft
that took place in March. Shrewd choices there would enable us to
improve faster. Matthews went shopping with a view to defensive
players, and came back with the pick of the crop—notably Ed Berry,
Alex Gordon, and Donald Smith. Next, as free agents or as trades,

would come Demetrious Maxie, Rob Waldrop, Tim Cofield, Kenny Benson, Mike O'Shea, and the rest of the Smith "brothers," Adrion and Lester. Soon, only Donnie Wilson remained as a carryover on defence from the previous year. Our every move seemed to be charmed—player after player would prove to be all-star after all-star. Mike Vanderjagt, who'd been cut twice before, was about to blossom into the most accurate kicker in Grey Cup history.

These were wholesale changes, a fresh start on both sides of the ball. Our offensive lineup also bore little resemblance to 1995's, with the addition of Robert Drummond, Mike Kiselak, Chris Perez, and Tyrone Williams. So many people seemed to be on top of their game. I don't think anybody knew how good Drummond was, with the possible exceptions of Matthews and Drummond himself. Young or old, in camp everybody seemed to thrive on the competition, which was even more heated than usual. This year's roster was 36, with room for only 18 imports, one fewer than before. Matthews made a number of tough decisions right away. He'd already spotted his favorites, and felt that the newcomers were better than what he'd inherited, so not everything was sweetness and light.

So there was number 31, the senior statesman, surrounded by all these speedy young guys, with no clear indication of what lay ahead for him. I knew it was going to be an interesting year, because Adam Rita was back as offensive coordinator. This meant a return to his signature touches—weird formations and unaccustomed, almost impenetrable wrinkles. He had so much in his mind that never reached the table, so much that made the table but not the game, and so much that reached the game but was unlike anybody else's scheme. Rita had a sort of *Mission Impossible* approach. His scheme was ever-changing, and everyone was interchangeable within it, apt to show up anywhere on the field. This forced us to grasp the total offensive picture, which we'd execute more effectively because we understood what was going on around us, or so the theory went.

A week earlier, I'd asked Rita for a playbook. He'd put me off. "Don't worry," he told me. "You'll have no trouble picking the plays up." On day one, I learned that I was going to be a receiver. This presented a totally different learning curve—I'd have to run routes for a living! And so I did, all throughout camp and both pre-season games, interspersed with dusting off my old duties as a running back, because I was supposed to know both positions, when and if somebody bothered to give me the ball.

The Mouse Davis episode of 1993 was far less stressful than the first four weeks of 1996. I had no idea how, if at all, I was supposed to fit into the strategy. I was out there hustling to and fro, wide open half the time and looking for the ball, which failed to come my way. The only times I got it were in short-yardage situations, where I didn't want to be, given my size. Meanwhile, Drummond was tearing up the field, and Cunningham was handling most of the return game, in between catching lots of passes. Partly as a result of this, we won our early season games — a good-luck sign. Whenever we win these, we have great years. Whenever we don't, we stink. As a player, I was happy with winning. As an individual, I was lost at sea. I couldn't make head or tails of what was happening.

Maybe the worst part of all this was that great things were expected of me. The combination of Flutie and Pinball was supposed to be deadly, yet we weren't connecting. Others were, and I was doing squat. I tried to keep my feelings to myself, but it was apparent that I was unhappy and confused. This was commented on in the media, and at least one article, by Steve Simmons, hinted that I was past my time. Meanwhile, neither Matthews nor Rita said a word until a meeting that took place after our first regular-season loss, a 38 to 36 squeaker against the Tiger-Cats. I'm told that Matthews jumped on everybody from a great height. He really read the riot act. After a loss, the one thing he demands is undivided attention. If you value your job and don't want to add fuel to the fire, you arrive there early, looking suitably contrite. That day, I was booked at a charity event that I'd agreed to attend ages before. It was off in the suburbs, and coming back, I hit a brutal traffic jam on the highway. I got to the meeting ten minutes late, and Matthews went berserk. Before stalking off, he told me that I had a choice: Put football first or retire.

I went home, and pondered the ultimatum. For about thirty seconds, I actually did contemplate retirement. I could have walked away that week, and still have fed my family. I realized I didn't need football to live. With that came the greater realization, however, that I didn't want to walk. I resolved to work within the system, although exactly what it was remained obscure.

All of which may sound rather odd to those who don't know the game. Surely a quick fix would have been for me to collar Matthews and ask him outright what he had in mind. I'd been working my butt off to no avail. I had no desire—and no right—to question him about my role. That, to me, is a very bad attitude. To carp and whine about not getting the ball is selfish. My job was to keep on doing whatever he wanted me to do—in this case, so I thought, to run routes all day long. If I was discontented, I had to deal with that. His job wasn't to make me or anybody else happy. He had made me well and truly unhappy by questioning my commitment, though, and I thought he was wrong to have done that.

And what if I'd demanded to be given the ball more often? There's another nice, quick fix: Matthews collars Flutie and tells him to do this. Unfortunately, that doesn't work either. You have to allow a quarterback, particularly one as good as Flutie, to do his reads honestly. You can't force his passing game; it has to unfold according to a natural flow. You can decide to run the ball a certain number of times a game; that's different. It's when you make up your mind beforehand to throw to a certain place, come what may, that bad things happen. Nor was it Matthews's job, given the chain of command, to go directly to Flutie. That's why Rita was there, as offensive coordinator. And let's face it — we were winning.

No matter what had been happening on the field. I'd put myself in the wrong by showing up late for the meeting. With Matthews, football always comes first. If a tornado strikes, football comes first. All his players have to share and act out this attitude. He also understood me personally; he'd coached me and played against me. He and Rita had a plan for me when they moved me to this position. They knew it would add longevity to my career. Maybe they also knew I wouldn't clue in quite as quickly as they'd hoped. For the moment, Matthews was trying to light a fire under me. If you have somebody who doesn't care, you have to deal with it right away, because the further away you get from the incident the less they care and the less they'll respond. If you have somebody who cares, let them stew a bit, let them think about it—which is what I proceeded to do.

Game five of the '96 season, against Saskatchewan, was my coming-out party—9 catches for 106 yards. The next two games were more of the same—another 9 for 89, then 7 for 97. Doug was calling plays with the intention of looking for me first; I was a primary receiver instead of an afterthought. I began to feel guilty about getting the ball so much, and depriving the other guys. I also felt more and more stupid about how I'd behaved in the beginning, how nearsighted and petty I'd been. Matthews's system had been working even then. I had thought I was being totally ignored, when in fact (with one exception) I'd been catching five balls a game. Multiply that out over the course of the season, and you get 90. The all-time league record is 126. Despite all my talk about knowing the game up, down, and sideways, I'd failed to adapt to changing circumstances. As a rusher, I'd been accustomed to handling the ball twenty times a game. So actually the work was being spread around. Drummond, Masotti, Cunningham, Fairholm, Williams, and I were all pretty much in the same ballpark—the sign of a good team.

So now the big picture was becoming clear, and football was fun again. It's always so much better when you win, and we were winning every game in sight. Even practice became a joy, because Matthews was exercising his usual philosophy. When we practised, we practised hard, focusing on every detail. Then we could do whatever we wanted—relax, lie down on the field, chew straws, or put our feet up—anything as long as we didn't get in the way of the drill. Nor did Rita believe in beating up his players all week long. He wanted our very best when it counted, on game day.

So this was the tempo of things—a very relaxed, convivial atmosphere, lightened up by rituals such as Hat Day, which is when you have to wear a hat, or donate twenty dollars to the Chicken Fund if you don't. Hat Day took place the day before a game. It included entertainment, songs, jokes, and skits. But it was eclipsed by the advent this year of the infamous Who's Daddy—one of those male-only-because-women-wouldn't-be-stupid-enough-to-come-anywhere-near-it rituals you've always suspected infest the sports world. I not only participated, but led it. It's a sort of chant that goes back and forth, getting progressively more up-tempo and tangled as we run through Daddy's many and varied activities. By season's end, it's more like a cross between a song and an epic poem. It hinges on the notion of being in charge. A good father doesn't spare the rod; he has to lay down the law, which is what we have to do on the field. We don't want to chastise our opponents, but they'll thank us in the end.

In other words, we were loose again, in high spirits, and spreading fear and despondency among our foes. Momentum built, as Matthews's scheme continued to work to perfection. Somewhere in mid-season, it was decided that Jimmy Cunningham needed a hand with returns, so I began to handle kickoffs while he concentrated on punts, just to keep everybody fresh. We won nine games in a row, before hitting the wall in the form of the British Columbia Lions, who really took it to us. While I personally didn't have a bad game, we were beaten pretty handily, 35 to 11. This was doubly galling as they hadn't been playing very well, but upsets are funny that way.

The reality is that at the pro level, any team can beat any other team on any given day. There isn't a staggering or overwhelming difference in talent level from team to team. That's why *upset* is really the wrong word to use. It would be an upset, for example, if a CFL team was soundly whipped by a high school team.

At the pro level, there are individual players who stand apart. A defence or offence or special team can be, on balance, and by accepted standards, better than somebody else's, but at the same time, no one particular player is absolutely unstoppable, off in a league of his own. All the teams know basically what their opponents are going to do. They decide where they can attack you; they see at least the possibility that they'll do so successfully. Maybe you become complacent, make half-hearted plays, or commit sloppy errors. That's when your opponents smell the chance for victory. If they think they can beat you, they might. If they believe it, they very well might. Hypothetically, any game could go either way. These same factors account for the ridiculously lopsided scores that crop up every season. Sometimes you spring something new and totally unexpected; the other guys can't figure out how to counter it, and start to reel. More often, though, turnovers are the key to a landslide victory. Injuries are crucial, too. If your quarterback goes out, the defence wears down, and the points start to pile up.

Speaking of injuries, to my knowledge no one's ever tried to do me deliberate harm. There have been plenty of late hits and cheap shots, and the thinking behind them could very well have been "If we can shake him up, we won't have to worry about him for fifteen minutes." That's within the rules, fair game. We play a contact sport, and hard knocks come with the territory. Most cheap shots are spur-of-the-moment and are committed out of frustration. The other guys are having a tough season, a tough game, a bad quarter. Maybe your guys have been draped all over them. Maybe you got past them once too often and made the play look easy. We have a saying: "Keep your head on a swivel." You don't amble around; you hustle all the time and stay on the alert. You look for trouble coming at you.

Certainly I've taken some ugly shots after the whistle. Once, not very long after I'd joined the Argos, a guy named Tank Landry, a beast of a linebacker, hit me so hard that (to put it delicately) mucus emanated from my nasal cavity. I was miles away from the ball at the time. Darrell K. Smith jumped all over Landry. Then he turned around and jumped all over me, for being dumb enough to let it happen. But we don't have goons or fighters or enforcers. Compare the amount of brawling that goes on in football with hockey. We have so much contact as a matter of course that matters get worked out without people coming to blows. If a guy *is* notorious for cheap shots, his number goes into the memory bank, and what goes around, comes around, one way or the other.

But I digress, as I have a habit of doing. We'd just been knocked around by B.C., but we came back in game 13 and won a squeaker against Calgary. Jimmy the Jet made a 93-yard touchdown return, a huge play. Masotti had another fantastic outing, with 6 catches for 174 yards. I caught 6 also, for about a third that distance. This was the long-awaited East–West showdown between the clubs with the two best records. We won by a single point, 23 to 22, setting ourselves up as the premier team, and looked forward to seeing the Stampeders again in October.

The following week we beat the Blue Bombers pretty soundly, went back to Calgary, and proceeded to lose, 30 to 23, thanks to a couple of questionable plays. That was okay; we'd clinched first place in the East. Then we hung around in Red Deer, Alberta, for a week, took care of Edmonton the next week by a score of 24 to 17, and returned to host B.C. at the Dome. We had something to prove, and we managed to prove it, if only by 4 points. Some teams match up against one another really well; their strengths are more or less on par, and you know you're going to get your money's worth as a spectator when they meet. This year, although they hadn't capitalized on the fact, B.C. was a club quite similar to ours. (In this game, they got a lot of help from suspect calls—not your normal bad calls, but real howlers that almost spelled another loss.)

Next came Hamilton, and a game that wouldn't affect our standing one way or the other. We went down to "Never Win" Stadium and hammered the Ti-Cats 47 to 14. This was the day that Drummond rushed for four touchdowns and I set the Argos' all-time record for season receptions—116 catches, which surpassed Terry Greer. The season ended 15 and 3, the best results in club history. I'd covered 2,626 all-purpose yards, 12 yards short of Jimmy's mark, which put us first and second in the entire league—final proof, if any were needed, of Matthews's scheme.

So here we were, closing in on another Cup after a long, hard drought, and witnessing Matthews's Jekyll-and-Hyde transformation. At playoff time, the easy-going players' coach turned into a Marine (which he in fact was, in his youth) before our startled eyes. Mandatory curfew came into effect, and he highly recommended that we put in more than the normal maximum of four or five hours of practice time. He did this the same way my mom used to recommend that I go to church. Everything that had come before was insignificant. In 1991, we'd been almost fearless, to the point of being ripe for the picking. This time, we were workmen with a job to do. To accomplish it, we knew we'd have to buckle down. With this in view, we waited for the Montreal Alouettes to arrive at the Dome for the Eastern final.

We jumped on them from the start and never let go. I took the opening kickoff back 91 yards for a touchdown, which helped when it came to selecting the top player of the game. Our special teams were in fine form, and we took advantage of several turnovers. The key factor remained that Montreal couldn't move the ball. Bill Bradley, our defensive coordinator, had done a fantastic job all year long, and this game marked the culmination of his efforts. We absolutely nullified Montreal's attack, rolled up 43 points to their 7, and were on our way to The Show.

Meanwhile, just to keep us on our toes, the best from the West had been unseated, when Edmonton beat Calgary. I'd predicted that this might happen, because of the Eskimos' superior defensive strength. This set the stage for an evenly matched encounter in Hamilton on November 24.

What is it about Hamilton, anyway? Masotti is practically a native son; he lives on the outskirts, in Stoney Creek. Toronto is forty-five minutes up the road. Yes, we'd given them a bad time throughout the season, but now we were the Eastern representatives. Are there no regional loyalties these days? Could we not have expected some infinitesimal hint of support and good cheer? Couldn't they let bygones be bygones for a couple of hours? No, to all of the above. Hamilton hated us with a vengeance. Those few Torontonians brave enough to creep down the highway were forced to adopt protective coloration, telling reporters they were from Edmonton, to avoid being jeered at in public places.

The weather forecast for November 24 wasn't bad: cool and not much in the way of snow. Nothing could go wrong. Drummond had had an incredible year, as had Cunningham. Masotti's stats were pretty much as usual—1,000 yards receiving for the third straight season. Flutie, as expected, had been more than outstanding, and our defence was ranked number two, second only to that of our opponents. All we had to do was go out and work for sixty minutes. If we did this, we could win.

For most of us, the Cup was a new experience. A lot of the veterans had come close, getting knocked out of contention in the finals. Then there were all the recent arrivals, who'd never known the joys of pitched battle against both hostile elements and an even more hostile opposition. I think Masotti and I were the only ones who'd gone all the way with the Argos. Of course, Flutie had won the Cup in 1992 with the Stampeders, as had Robert Drummond, Ken Benson, and Lester Smith with Baltimore in 1995.

During the week leading up to the game, Matthews tightened the screws. No one slept in his own bed. From Tuesday night on, curfew was a way of life. This was no honor system; we waited for the knock on the door—which we could seldom hear, because our hotel was within earshot of the celebrants down at street level, all of whom, as noted, were firmly against us.

When we got up on game day, we smelled snow in the air. No problem. If you clean an artificial-turf field, the footing is great; it doesn't get slick, the way frozen grass does. Next came chapel, which always draws a crowd when the Cup is at stake; it's like going to church at Christmas and Easter. We were greatly in need of spiritual guidance; the day before, we'd let off steam by recapping the highlights of what had gone on all year, climaxed by an extended and even more raucous version of Who's Daddy.

The big dilemma, as always when the footing is unsure, is the issue of footwear. We keep a special stock of shoes that went out of production twenty years ago. While they aren't esthetically pleasing, they work. (Danny Webb, the equipment manager, keeps them under lock and key, and doles them out as if they're worth their weight in gold.) Should we wear them, or wait for an updated report on the snow? It was coming down more heavily with each passing minute.

How much ought we to wear? Just a shirt underneath? Long- or short-sleeved? If you wear two shirts, which goes underneath? Do you wear something that repels water to some extent? What about gloves? What kind? Do you wear a warming pack? If so, do you put the heat flint inside it? Will the heaters on the sideline keep you warm enough? Can you get away with wearing fewer clothes? What if the heater goes off? Will you be under-dressed? Will that affect your performance? These things affect you to some extent at any time, and now they're magnified out of all proportion.

You want to have a great game, so you try to get your thoughts in order. How to prepare? How to properly focus? How much water will you need to drink? Should you eat fruits and vegetables to maintain your energy level?

Questions gnaw at you during the week like gnats. They fill your mind. You're tired of waiting, you want to get out there and get things over with at last. You burn more energy before than during the game. There's so much tension leading up to it; there's tension in trying to relax. When can you take a nap? How far before the game do you eat? Will the nap make you sluggish, or give you extra zest? All this preys on your mind, toys with you, in a contest between you and endless trivialities.

Then, when you get to the stadium, which seems to take about five days from the time you wake up in the morning, your mind begins to ease a bit; you start to get in the flow. You try to think about the event itself, its history and importance. What should you be noticing? What should you remember about this moment? All these things may vanish if you don't hang on to them, things that you're trying to pay attention to now and relish so that you can go back and tap into them and recreate all this same energy and enthusiasm and euphoria at your leisure.

Suddenly, you're dressed, and all the trivial matters have been resolved. You've chosen your attire. Some you've worn all year long; some is experimental. You test your shoes during the pre-game warmup. You test your gloves. It's cold and wet, and the snow is falling and falling. You decide to wear a T-shirt under a long shirt, made of water-repellent material. You can roll up the sleeves up if you want to. There'll be a jacket on the sidelines. No gloves. You'll use a warming pack, as you have all season long.

The snow is thick and the crews are out clearing the field. They start at one end, and when they get to midfield, the area they've worked on is covered again. They're only ten yards ahead of the falling snow. You begin to realize that the surface will be a nightmare. You may not be able to see. It's snowing harder all the time. Now you have this sick feeling that maybe you won't be able to perform well—well enough to stand up, to not be ashamed, well enough to win, maybe not well enough to do that great move you've always wanted to make in the Cup game with the whole country watching and everything at stake, so that you can replay the tape for your kids and say, "Look, this is what it was like and over there, that's me."

Now it's close to game time. I start to think about all the little things, the automatic things I'm not supposed to think about. Stop thinking so much; go on automatic pilot. When I don't have the ball, block for the other guys. Be smart, play to every whistle. Look alive. If I see the ball coming to Masotti, who makes every catch, I've got to run after it, because he might just bobble this one and I want to be there to salvage the play. Four or five plays will determine the outcome. I've got to hustle all the time.

I begin to rehearse this in my mind. This is the one. More than in any other game, I don't want to wind up saying, Coulda, shoulda, woulda. Everything is more acute, more aroused, more important, and I want this to translate into my effort on the field. I want to play the greatest game of my life.

That was the dream. The reality was that the snow was crazy and the wind was up. All bets were off. We thought that our defence would neutralize their offence, but it didn't happen. We also thought that the reverse would be true to a degree; it didn't happen, either. We thought the score, if it was close, would be 7 to 6. But both offences started going nuts, and didn't stop.

I didn't feel as if I was much a part of what was going on. I wanted to be able to make some plays, but no. Just as in the the 1991 Cup game, I was spinning my wheels. History was repeating itself. All this week, I'd been running around like a teenager. I felt primed and tuned, and now here I was, not accomplishing a whole lot. I made a couple of catches, a couple of important plays, while the game mostly see-sawed back and forth without me, a very nerve-racking game, one of the strangest ones I've ever played in, because everybody moved the ball.

Edmonton made big plays, even freak plays. Eddie Brown almost missed a pass. It brushed his fingertips and was falling to the ground, but he kicked it up with his shoe and caught it and kept running for a long touchdown. Jim Sandusky caught the ball and went 75 yards when two of our defenders collided with each other. Gizmo Williams made an epic return and neutralized Jimmy Cunningham's punt-return touchdown. You felt that anything could happen and probably would. It was so wet, so messy. Ordinary plays required an element of luck to pull off; we never had the feeling that this game was ever in hand.

The biggest play came in the fourth quarter, after we'd finally taken the lead. I think the score was 36 to 30. Edmonton was about to score, when Adrion Smith intercepted a pass and returned it for a 49-yard touchdown, putting us up 43 to 30 with less than three minutes to go. Then Edmonton marched all the way down the field and scored, with still a minute left.

In the CFL a minute can be an eternity. Edmonton would try an onside kick and gain excellent field position if they recovered the ball. I was designated as the player to receive the ball on our special team to defend an onside kick. Our strategy was to create a wall of guys in front of me, to block Edmonton's rush. All I had to do was hang on to the ball. With less than a minute on the clock, Edmonton tried the onside kick. The ball seemed to float above us. As it came down, I focused in, until I could almost read the lettering. Then all I saw was a shadow, and an Edmonton fullback named Tony Burse ran right through my chin—the hardest hit I'd received all year, and totally illegal. A penalty flag was thrown, and we took possession of the ball. The scary part was that if Burse had been looking at the ball instead of me, he could have caught it on the run and possibly scored. Edmonton was that close to being able to tie the game with a touchdown and win it with the convert.

I was dazed from the hit. As with the hit laid on me by Micah Moon so long ago, I had to get up. Burse weighed about 230 pounds, and he was as strong as an ox. I was knocked silly, and everybody was upset by the hit, but the last thing we wanted was to take a stupid penalty. Now we could run down the clock. So I got up, not entirely certain where I was, and went and finished off the last two plays. For the first ten minutes of the victory celebration, I wandered around aimlessly. My postgame party didn't start until eleven minutes after the final whistle. That didn't matter. We were Grey Cup champions again.

Everything was very different from the Grey Cup we'd last won. The first Cup happened before I could turn around. One week I was at William and Mary; the next I was riding up Yonge Street as thousands cheered. It was an ascension, an uninterrupted success, like going to the moon. We had blasted off and I'd hung on for the ride. The first time, everything came so easy. Back then, we thought we were unbeatable. This marked the beginning of a dynasty—same time next year, and nowhere to go but up. Now, I understood that 1991's win was a feat that's seldom accomplished—the exception, not the rule.

There's a feeling of indomitability when you take it all, even though one foot can make the difference. You score 800 points throughout the year, and the Cup can be decided by the narrowest of margins. If your kicker changes the ball's trajectory by a fraction of an inch, the chip shot becomes a missed field goal. You win all, or lose all. If you win, everybody loves you. You ride in the parade and go on radio and TV, people want to pay you money to speak, you get sponsorships, ticket sales hit the ceiling, and you feel unstoppable.

So, after all those losing seasons, this was a whole different level of appreciation. Those four years had taught us how to savor the victory. Suddenly they made sense and seemed worthwhile. Even the bitterest disappointments made sense; a burden was lifted from our shoulders. This was why I'd stuck it out, this was why we kept on playing through 3-and-15 seasons. This is a feeling you experience very few times in life.

10

Have I told you enough about Paul Masotti? The temptation is to say, "It's third down, and Masotti saves the day," as he very often does. He'll be there when I arrive at a new training camp, and we'll probably start off talking about money and stock markets. In real life, he works with an investment firm, managing people's investments. He's my financial adviser, and I trust him implicitly.

What can be said about a guy who's always been there? We've seen literally hundreds of players come and go—young guys on their way up the ladder, old guys looking for their last grab at the brass ring. Our sticking around with the same team as long as we have is an exception to the rule. In future, it will be unheard of. I miss the bonds that I developed early on, and I'm more apt to maintain those bonds than to develop new ones, because I know the new ones will be severed by choice or chance. Those early days won't come again. It took time for me to get to know Reggie and Jeff and Carl, and we had the time then. Now they're long gone, and time's running out.

The only constant is a hot-tempered Italian who throws his helmet around on the sidelines and then laughs about it a minute later, who's a pillar of reliability on and off the field, who'll hang his cleats up when I do, who shares my values and my sense of loyalty, in whom I can confide and I respect more and more as time slips away. There aren't Masotti stories; there's just Masotti.

Paul used to catch balls thrown by Doug Flutie, and there are a couple of Flutie stories to tell. He too will remain a good friend when football is a thing of the past. After the rough beginning to that first year together, he found that I shared his understanding and love of the game. The breakthrough happened one day as I was running a pattern and turned to look for the ball. The instant I moved, Doug threw to the open spot. Pretty soon, we were on the same wavelength, feeling the ebb and flow of the action, responding with the perfect counterstrike

He's gone to Buffalo as I write this. Whether he'll get the chance to play or not hinges on many factors—the coach, the general manager, the system as a whole. He'll enhance the NFL, and he wants above all else to prove absolutely that he can make it there, as he did before. In Chicago, Coach Mike Ditka tried to retain him, but management made a different call. Because the other quarterback wore bubble shades and head-butted his offensive linesmen, he went into the lineup instead of Doug. That was Chicago's mistake. Doug's the best player I've ever seen, and I never begrudged him a single penny of his $1.1 million salary, which he earned time and again. In fact, he deserved more.

While he was here, I got to see a side of him that few would suspect existed—his insecurity. You'd think that a guy who'd achieved so much wouldn't care what others thought and said, but he constantly worried about his performance, about how his teammates and the media reacted. This was exceptional. In another way, too, he was unique in my experience.

Doug has a pure and boyish enthusiasm for football that you just don't see in a thirty-five-year-old. At that age, the game has got the better of you. Its flaws and compromises have worn you down. You liked it in the beginning, and there had to be a degree of passion involved for it to carry over into adulthood. In your mid-thirties, you have no more illusions. You know too much. Doug is almost oblivious to all that stuff. His enthusiasm supersedes all the garbage that goes along with a decade-plus of playing pro ball, all the injustices, all the politically motivated decisions, all the right decisions that still carried a taint of unfairness.

What about the guys you wanted to see given another kick at the can because they were good players and decent people? At the same time you knew in your heart they weren't as good as or better than the younger guy hot on their trail at training camp. Away they went, cut to fit a limited roster, and thanks for the memories.

Any business is cutthroat in its own way, but even so, these hard-and-fast decisions are particular to the sporting arena. Anywhere else, you can move people sideways, slide them upstairs or out of the line of fire. Not here. Every strength, every weakness is exposed. We're playing a primitive game in which only the strongest survive. Everything is based on production and outcome—who finishes first, who runs the fastest and jumps the highest, or at least shows the most promise of doing so. Friends and kindred spirits fall by the wayside, more with each new season. And what remains of your enthusiasm diminishes because you know the reality.

When you're twenty-two, football is just a game, perfect and unblemished. Sooner or later, you realize that it's life, and life is hard. Doug has somehow managed to escape that process. He's maintained a sort of oblivious pride. To him, the game remains untainted and unsullied. It's still just a game—running out to the lamppost and turning out and catching the ball by the tree. I envy him this. It's as much a part of his success as his skill.

Which, by the way, is formidable. People talk about his age, and wonder whether he'll be able to cut it in Buffalo. I suggest that he'll be the fastest quarterback in camp. He runs, he throws off-balance, he jumps, he scrambles, he does things guys did when they were coming out of college, and now those skills are all based on years of hard-won experience and in-depth knowledge. Doug is a manic watcher of films, even though he already knows the moves of every opposing defensive back. He watched every CFL television broadcast. When the rest of us trooped in to study the next day's screening of our performance, he'd probably seen it two or three times already, plus a rerun of the commercial feed late the previous night. It's no fluke that he's as good as he is—yet it's his enthusiasm that rules his personality.

Most people would say I've retained my share, although not as much as Doug. I have a keener awareness of the game's shortcomings, or at least tend to dwell on them more. I like to think this only makes me work harder to put them aside, and makes success the more special when it comes.

Doug was closely followed in enthusiasm by Jimmy Cunningham, with whom I had the traditional year-end conversation about what he should do. He loved Toronto and he loved the league; he was kind enough to say that he'd like to be in my position. Exactly where he ought to achieve this end was on his mind. He was looking for stability, and the Argos offered him a measure of that—a good, sound future and a slow-but-sure climb to decent money. More important, he knew that, financially, he could prepare himself for life far better and faster if he went south of the border. In 1992, a report stated that three out of four NFL players were flat broke two years after their careers ended. Jimmy didn't want to be among them. He asked me point blank if I thought he should come back. Being selfish, I thought he should; he'd help us win. Being a friend, I told him he had to make his own decision. I did give him some information to help him decide. I didn't talk about his becoming me—I talked about his being better than I was. He had the potential to do greater things on the field. He has a slightly different makeup than I do; he's very shy, not as outgoing or comfortable speaking. These are skills that can be learned. His upstanding character would be apparent, even without much polish. Shyness is rare these days, and could work in his favor. If people perceived him as humble, quiet, and reserved, that would be all the better. There were advantages and disadvantages to both staying and going. Once he decided to leave, I stepped aside.

In December, Diane and I were planning to take a second honeymoon, our very first cruise, to the Caribbean and Mexico. But our expectation took second place to an illness in the family. All year long, Diane's sister Vernette had been having trouble shaking some sort of flu. This condition worsened, and finally proved to be far more severe than anyone had realized.

We flew to Florida at once. Surgery was scheduled for Vernette for the following week, and we were supposed to leave on our cruise that weekend. We boarded the vessel with great misgivings, although her other siblings were with her and there was nothing we could do. The surgery revealed full-blown stomach cancer. In the middle of this, Diane's mom was rushed to the hospital as well. She's diabetic and asthmatic, with a history of heart trouble. After exploratory surgery of her own, the doctors determined that she had to have an immediate triple bypass. She pulled through, and we returned the following Sunday morning. That same night, Vernette passed away, leaving a husband and three young children.

A few months earlier, Diane had decided that she wanted a second child. The day before Vernette's funeral, we learned that she was pregnant. We decided to keep the news to ourselves until everything was settled. The only person we told was Rachel. My mom was holding her during the funeral, and she let slip the fact that she was going to have a baby sister, so the word very quickly spread. Diane then decided that, if the child was a girl, we ought not to name her Vernette. She wouldn't want to subject the child to the pressure, the constant reminder of having been named after someone so kind and loving who had died so young. I agreed. Similarly, if Diane and I should ever have a boy, he won't be named Michael Junior. In the meantime, simultaneously grieving Vernette's passing and looking forward to the blessing of a new life, the family came together and we made it through.

Soon we were into yet another difficult pregnancy. At first, Diane felt better than she had with Rachel. After a few weeks, I had to return to Toronto and honor various commitments, so she stayed in Clearwater to help her mom, who needed special care and attention. By the time another three weeks had passed, she was violently ill again, so sick that she didn't know if she could fly home. I came down, we flew back together, and everybody got on the treadmill again, with Rachel in daycare, Diane pondering the merits of adoption next time around, and me running hard to get everything done before another football season began.

*   *   *

At 1997 training camp, I couldn't understand why I felt so good—a typical reaction. I hadn't done much work off-season. Matthews was muttering darkly that my load was about to increase; I think his phrase was, "You'll be doing it all." With Jimmy gone, that seemed likely; I'd been doing most of it already. You'll remember that I was a dozen all-purpose yards behind him the previous year. The whole idea of shifting me to receiver was that I wouldn't, at my ever-advancing age, get bounced around quite so much. Now, it looked as though I'd have to run the return game single-handedly, if *plantar fasciaitis* didn't lay me low. Nobody could spell this, so the story went out that I had trouble with my heel. In fact, it's an inflammation of the tissue on the soles of the feet. It lasted about a week, and I missed a couple of days. After that, I stayed on course.

Meanwhile, Matthews was casting about for the next Jimmy Cunningham. After a couple of false starts, his thoughts turned to Derrell (Mookie) Mitchell. Fifteen hundred yards and the Rookie of the Year award later, everyone would realize that this was a good choice. Mookie's one of the most likable guys you'll ever meet, and turned out to be our most naturally gifted receiver, including Masotti, because of his breakaway speed. Andre Kirwan looked steady as well, Adrion Smith had proven himself, Felman Malveaux looked as if he could fly, Robert Drummond was back in action, and the rest of the team was relatively intact. If a thirty-two-year-old could keep his eye on returns of all descriptions, we were ready to roll.

Strangely, because it's obviously the most recent, this past season is something of a blur to me. I guess that's because it was so insanely active. Here are a couple of daily conversations. "How are you, Di? How you feeling? How's the baby doing? Is she moving all right? That's great! Bye." "Hi, Paul, how's it going? Is the business okay? How's the cash flow? How's the funding? We're okay? Hmmm. Bye." In fact, the cable business hovered close to the brink for a week or so, and we didn't know whether we'd be able to meet the payroll. I'm happy to say it's much healthier now and growing.

Then the games were underway, and I became aware of the fact that, if I was going to do everything at once, I'd probably top 3,000 yards once again. If so, I'd be the only person ever to do it twice. Meanwhile, Mike Pringle in Montreal had topped it also. As I'd been there, done that, my thoughts turned to the next plateau: Was 4,000 yards possible? Of course, I wanted to do whatever was necessary to make the team better.

That's the politically correct answer, and not so far from what I really believe. I didn't need the accolades, didn't feel I had to validate myself as an athlete or make my mark. I'm not exactly driven by personal goals and targets, but neither am I oblivious to them, if only because people remind you of them day and night. I certainly realized that I was nearing records of significance and import. I think that's a good thing; it shows you care about what you're doing, as long as it's not your focus when you're going in. Still, if I was saddled with returning both punts and kicks, catching 100-odd passes, and playing running back when Drummond needed a rest, I wanted to do something that hadn't been done before.

I'd worked this out; I'm an economics major, so I can count pretty well. In 1991, I missed two games, and still managed to log 3,300 yards. That's 200 a game, even with a lingering knee problem. This year, if I stayed healthy, played all the games, and kept up the same pace, we'd arrive at 3,600. Add a few more for luck and good judgment, and 4,000 sounded not only possible but within my grasp.

Matthews knew this. He was there when I covered the 3,300. He likes his to see his players in the record books, without dwelling on statistics; he's forward-looking to a fault. He had a Grey Cup ring for every finger, and never wore one, because he believed that would mean he was thinking about yesterday. You never become complacent about success; you build on it and keep moving on. Every season is a stepping-stone, not a tombstone. Tomorrow is another, better day.

And it wasn't long before better days were upon us. We were back in stride again, hearing the word *dynasty* more and more. Once again, there was talk of winning every game, and once again, we proved to be human, because an oblong ball takes funny bounces.

I just kept at it, and the yards kept piling up. I was trying not to think too much about the record books, and thinking a lot about Diane, who constantly suffered false contractions. On two occasions she went into premature labor. I drove from Barrie at breathtaking speeds, and joined her at the hospital. We were afraid that she might be losing the child. The hospital even notified our gynecologist that this had happened, which mercifully wasn't true. I slept in her room, tiptoed off to practice, and came back to the room again. After a couple more days, she was free to go—to face another month of false alarms before the real thing came along.

Which, just to jump ahead a bit, it did, on August 28. Having weathered all the ups and downs, Diane was having full contractions, with no sign of actual labor. It seemed as if she might go beyond the due date, so our doctor suggested we speed things along with an intravenous drip to induce the proceedings. We had a plan of attack, and just as with Rachel everything was quite predictable, only much faster. Rachel took twelve hours to join us; this baby took only four from start to finish. I'd have thought that this would have taken less out of Diane, but it was even more taxing. The pains were intensified because she couldn't walk up and down as we'd done before, thanks to her IV connection. First, she squeezed my hand. Then she held my arm. Then she hooked her arm around mine and grabbed my shoulder, then my head, then all of me. She asked for medication at the end, and the doctor told her, "By the time you get it, the baby will be here."

I felt the worst at the very last. She'd gone through nine months of stuff that only women know, and it was almost over, and she'd been so brave and strong. But she was so tired, one step away from the top of Mount Everest and unable to take it, at the point of sheer and utter exhaustion. And there's nothing a husband can do. But finally, Raven Cymone Clemons came fluttering into the world— really fluttering—her tiny body in motion from the first breath. You think you can never recapture the first time, and you're wrong. The next time is no different. You have the same flood of emotions, the same overwhelming love for this new little person and the woman who carried her, the same awe before such beauty and courage, the same awareness of the presence of an all-powerful God.

*   *   *

Whereupon Raven's old man bought a box of cigars for his team-mates, headed down the road to Hamilton, and handed it to the Tiger-Cats, 46 to 3. You see the problem here. It's hard to remember exactly what went on in a year so filled with wonderful and miraculous events. The yardages just kept creeping up, week by week—257 against Hamilton, 280 against Saskatchewan. Somewhere along the line, I passed Dick Shatto's all-time club reception record of 466, and they stopped the clock to show a "Best of Pinball" video on the giant screen. Somewhere else, I broke my own record of 3,300 all-purpose yards, and wound up with 3,840, more than anybody's ever logged in any league. If I hadn't had any return yards called back, I'd have been close to 4,500. Somewhere else, I became the first player in history to cover 1,000 yards in three different categories—receiving, and punt and kickoff returns. Somewhere else, I passed Gizmo Williams and became the all-time CFL leader in career all-purpose yards, with 21,266. That one definitely crept up on me. Gizmo was 800 yards ahead when the season began. Around the fifteenth game, somebody said, "Hey—you and Gizmo are tied!" We had the exact same number, after all these years, all the different situations we'd played in. I'm not sure where we are now, other than one and two.

What else can I say? I broke my own record for team receptions, with 122 for 1,085 yards. Toward season's end, I became a running back again, when Rob Drummond was hurt. Maybe that's what I'm proudest of—being able to step into his shoes on zero notice, and gain upwards of 15 yards a carry—700 or 800 all-purpose yards over three games, in two of which I was named offensive player of the week. That sort of thing can turn around and bite you if you're slowing down.

During the last two regular-season games, I made no returns at all, and very few while I was replacing Rob. This raises another interesting "what if?" At least, I was rested for the playoffs and other guys got a shot at gaining some experience. Matthews knew exactly what he was doing. If I'd been injured, who'd have filled my shoes? If I'd been hammering away at my usual hectic pace in games 17 and 18, maybe somebody would have hauled me down in Montreal on November 9th. We'll never know. What we do know is that 4,000 yards will have to wait a bit.

So the year wound down, and a Montreal-versus-Toronto Eastern final grew from a probability to a certainty. We were supposed to have their number, but our meetings had grown progressively tougher as we went along. They beat us at the season ender on October 26. We said, "That doesn't matter. We're number one in the East, at 15 and 3." They said, "In the playoffs, we'll do it again." If we'd won that game, it would have made us complacent. Because they did, it made them *confident*. They seemed to be adjusting successfully to our scheme. Last year, we'd buried them—only because of our defence. This time, it was assumed that because we had Flutie and Drummond and the rest, we'd mow them down again. Not necessarily. Offence sells tickets; defence wins championships. That's not sports jargon; there's a lot of truth to it. Montreal had the second-best record in the league. They'd handled everyone but us, and on close inspection, they were a pretty good squad, if you count Tracy Ham, Mike Pringle, a defence laden with all-star-caliber players, and a couple of receivers who knew what they were doing. Suddenly, it wasn't a matter of marching unimpeded toward the Cup. In fact, the final was shaping up as the real Cup, the real showdown and the one to watch.

We felt we measured up well against them, and we hit the field at the SkyDome feeling pretty good about ourselves. Then things started to unwind. Uncharacteristically, Drummond had a couple of fumbles. We didn't control the Alouettes defensively as we'd done in the past; they were moving the ball far more capably than we'd thought possible. The year before, the game was over at the opening whistle. It kept on rolling from the first touchdown. This time, we were stopping ourselves. Little miscues and misfires were thwarting our drives. There was a sense that we should have been leading by more than we were.

If I remember correctly, we led 20 to 9 at halftime. That was the good news. The bad news was, this was the same margin we'd enjoyed when we played them two weeks earlier and lost. There was an ugly feeling of déjà vu. We'd kept them in the game; we hadn't put them away.

They rallied in the second half, and scored a touchdown. We answered with a field goal, which made it 23 to 16. Two touchdowns later, they were up 30 to 23. They'd scored 21 points in the quarter to our 3. Then we tied it, and they came right back, marched down the field, attempted a field goal, and missed. We got the ball and returned it, but couldn't score. Back they came, and missed a field goal again. We were see-sawing back and forth with no results. By this time, there were only a few minutes left, and we were tied at 30-all.

At this point Doug showed his leadership and took over the game. He said, "Pin, it's just me and you, down the field, you and me all the way. I'm either going to run or throw it to you." We'd been backed up in our own end. He made two great runs, one for a first down, the second for 9 yards and a bit. Drummond got another first down and then, on the fourth play of the drive, Doug called a play we ran quite often.

I ran a deep crossing route and realized Montreal was playing a man-to-man defence. I was shouting in my head, Doug, you gotta see me! In this matchup, the receiver should have the advantage, and I was *willing* Doug to look at me. I made my cut and turned cross-field. Doug picked me up, and winged the ball toward me. It seemed to hang in the air forever, refusing to come down. I was miles downfield, and I went up for it just a little bit, to secure the catch.

When you're reaching for the ball, as soon as the ball touches your fingers, a defender can hit you and knock the ball away. Catch the ball against your body, and you can hang onto it. As soon as I caught it, I was thinking, All I have to do is hang on. We were in field goal range, and we had the best field-goal kicker in the league. So then I thought, Just don't fumble. I knew that my defender should have been trailing me; I'd beaten him on the break but he should have been right behind me, so I wanted to wheel around. You can sense someone coming although you can't see him, and in this case the free safety was on my tail, too. I made my move, wheeling around and back into the field, leaving both Alouettes tangled together.

I remember wondering, Where is everybody? There should have been someone else. Later on I'd find out that Montreal had blitzed, and their coverage was chasing after Doug, so I was pretty much alone. Mookie was downfield trying to block, screaming "Run, Pin! Run!" I picked up a little speed and hit the end zone, only half aware of where I was. I'd made a 58-yard play altogether, the most nerve-racking open-field run I'd ever made, because nobody was there. I thought surely somebody would appear, and if he was smart, he'd try to jar the ball loose, so I was waiting for the hit that never came. Instead Mookie jumped on top of me, and then everybody else piled on, and I began to cry like a baby, just lying there. We had been in tough with the Alouettes, yet we'd squeaked through. This had been the game-winning touchdown, the knockout blow, and the single biggest play of my career, with forty seconds left on the clock, making it 37 to 30 and putting us into the Grey Cup game again.

*   *   *

After which, in all honesty, the Cup itself turned out to be something of an anticlimax. We'd seen Saskatchewan unexpectedly beat both Calgary and Edmonton (who'd finished first in the West, and was hosting the game), and prepared ourselves for the worst, or at least the unexpected. Anything can happen in the Cup, particularly outdoors, particularly after we'd just gone through what had been billed as the real Cup, and had emerged physically and emotionally drained. The Roughriders had played us hard all year, beating us on their own field. They seemed to be on something of a roll. The Cinderella Syndrome was at work; but we were still favored to win. Still, we never took them lightly, or viewed the game as a foregone conclusion—although, to be honest, no one would ever talk that way about a truly formidable opponent.

We arrived in Edmonton on a Tuesday, and stared at an icy field. I went out on it wearing brand-new shoes that Reebok had just developed. They kept your feet nice and warm, but they were an uneasy cross between overshoes and spats. They slipped on top of other shoes, and zipped up above your ankle. I felt as if my feet were shrink-wrapped, and I very nearly killed myself by falling down and landing on my elbow. I tried a different pair, and wiped out again. At least it wasn't all that cold—though who knew what might blow up between now and Sunday? This wasn't East versus West; it was everybody against the elements. Again.

I'll say this about the Wild West: the fans know how to stick together. The Edmonton fans had mourned the previous weekend's defeat at the hands of Saskatchewan for about seventy-two hours. Then they threw themselves behind the Roughriders long and loud. By Thursday the hotel lobby was filled with green and white, and the festivities began in earnest. These people like to party. As a change of pace, and to get us out of the line of the media fire, Matthews whisked us away on Saturday afternoon to the children's ward of a hospital. We walked out with practically no clothes on our backs, and minus fistfuls of tickets. I think we managed to cheer up some kids, who were kind enough not to boo us. We knew that the next day there'd be 59,900 rabid Roughriders fans in the stands and maybe 100 lonely easterners.

On game day, it seemed to turn bitterly cold; foul weather follows the Cup around. After the traditional space-at-a-premium chapel service, we headed to Commonwealth Stadium, found out that the sideline heaters didn't work, and started thrashing out the issues at hand.

There's so much to comprehend about your own game plan, your own scheme. You wonder about what the opposition's going to do. What will that be? What have they done before? Do they have new tricks up their sleeves? Will they poach the tactics that other teams have used successfully against us recently? Are they emboldened by their successes in recent weeks? How, given their personnel, will they attack you? How do we counterattack? How will they deploy their defence and special teams?

All these things are in your mind—and then, suddenly, everyone's talking about shoes. Not again! The game is so much bigger than footwear. The West Edmonton Mall is full of shoes. Surely we can each find one pair that will enable us to stand up throughout the most important game of the year. We take refuge in shoes now. Everything else is internalized. We've gone over all the variables till we're blue in the face. Now we're blue with cold, and in doubt about our shoes. People are sent to scout the field, and come back with conflicting reports. Shoes are different for everybody, everybody has different needs, different tasks to perform. You need to dig in or glide, plant your weight or keep your footing. Besides, the field is pristine. Its condition now proves nothing; the game's the thing.

My final choice, as in 1996, was the good old rubber-soled shoes with gobs of knobs on their bottoms. They're unattractive, but still the best thing for snow or frozen surfaces. Finance ministers wear new shoes when they deliver their budget speeches; we wear *these* shoes when we go out to win Grey Cups. Sometimes they work, sometimes they don't.

On the opening kickoff, Saskatchewan fumbled and fidgeted around with the ball, and it looked as if we'd take over from the first play. Unfortunately, their returner recovered, and away he went. The Roughriders scored first on a field goal. Late in the first quarter,

Mookie Mitchell scored on a 14-yard pass from Doug Flutie. Before long, we gained control of the game, and maintained it throughout. We executed and performed well. Everything was very businesslike. In the Cup, there's always an uneasiness, a refusal to feel settled until it's done. You can't relax too soon; you've got to play until the last whistle. Even so, the game was never in doubt, and ended 47 to 23. So that was that— the end of a particular road. Low drama? That's the way it was.

The high drama was provided by Diane, who I suspect was tired of my hogging the spotlight and wanted to upstage me. After the game ended, the people in charge of distributing championship hats started tossing them into the stands where our supporters were sitting. The man next to her jumped up to grab one and hit her on the forehead with his elbow. By this time, I was trying to fight my way through the mob to meet her. I saw Ken Benson's wife, Erin, walking with a security guard, who was carrying an apparently unconscious spectator in his arms. Then I saw who the spectator was. Diane was starting to come around, and still slightly glassy—so to be safe we loaded her into an ambulance and rode off to the hospital for a quick checkup. She kept on apologizing, and I kept thanking her for giving me an excuse to skip the media frenzy. The ambulance drivers were very kind, and took us back to our hotel, where we made a grand entrance—the post-trauma wife and her addled husband, still in uniform. And it's true; I had to keep waking her up throughout the night, to ask her if she knew who and where she was.

* * *

So now I had three Grey Cup rings to wear on special occasions, and a rather special year to look back on. Because I did so many things that nobody's ever done before, people ask me how I did them. To explain, I have to draw a couple of parallels between this past year and 1990, my other record-breaking season.

The first and most important common factor is Coach Don Matthews. In 1990, I was just a little jitterbug who could turn it on in the return game, the perfect designated import. That's why the designated import rule was created, for the Pinballs and Gizmos of the world, guys who are great on special teams and can get a crowd to its feet. Matthews took a look, and became the author of my initial success. He gave me the opportunity to play running back full time as well as return kicks and punts—first of all in 1990, when I was too small, and again in 1997, when I was too old. He recognized what I could do, and put me in a position to accomplish it.

Then, if you're going to do fancy tricks with a ball, you'd better have somebody who can get it to you. I did, in both 1990 and 1997. The two greatest quarterbacks in recent CFL history are Doug Flutie and Matt Dunigan. Surprise! Let's not forget Rickey Foggie, either, who was around in 1990. Another point: During both these years, we had a lot of super-talented guys around. In 1990, there was Darrell K. Smith; in 1997, Robert Drummond; in both years, the hot-tempered Italian guy from Hamilton. The club had a variety of weapons, a complex arsenal. The opposition didn't know who was going to come at them. Yet another crucial factor was health. In 1997, I didn't miss a single game. You've got a better shot at racking up solid stats if you aren't flat on your back in the rehab room, or slowed down by lingering ailments.

I hesitate to mention the final point. There's no athlete I enjoy watching more, no athlete who's done more in his sport than Michael Jordan. I'm not drawing a direct comparison; I'm not in his league or at his level. But in 1997, I think I managed to capture some small part of what I admire so much about him. Even though he's the greatest player in the history of basketball, he came out every night— no matter who he was up against—and maintained the same edge. Every night, he played with the same passion and intensity and love for the game. His aim was always to put on a show—he was never there just to get by. If the Chicago Bulls were up 20 points with a minute left and there was a loose ball, he'd go after it as if the game had just started. A loose ball means nothing, but he risked injury nevertheless. He knew no other way to play. His game evolved; he became smarter and took it to a new level, playing within himself.

To some extent I think I've been successful in making that transition for myself. I've moved from being the young guy who's quick as a cat and has all the flashy moves, to the older guy who's still really quick, with good moves, but has learned to rely on other things, to be smarter when he plays, to pick his spots. There was a time when I'd never step out of bounds. I'd take a shot to gain another inch. Now I know that sometimes it's smart to step out. I'll get that inch back on the next play. I've learned the game so much more as I've aged. Before, as a running back, all I read was man-or-zone. I had a capacity for the game, I understood thoroughly what I had to do but now I understand what everybody does. I could go in as and emergency quarterback if I had to and understand what should happen— if not execute the play. I don't rely on the flashy play anymore. I've learned to take an 8-yard gain. Once, I'd see 8 and want 20, so I'd make a dash for 20 and end up getting 4. Now I know that you go for 20 when the time is right. I can *feel* that, sense it better than before. I've even become more north–south in my running. Coach Laycock would be proud, I think; I'm finally maturing as a player. I still travel sideways a bit too much, but I get to where I'm going. It's what I know best.

11

1998 Season

Doug Flutie. Robert Drummond. Rob Waldrop. Ken Benson. Mike Vanderjagt. Mike Kiselak. Pierre Vercheval. Reggie Givens. Johnnie Harris. All of them all-stars, and all of them part of yesterday. An ominous shadow was cast over the beginning of this past season. Thirteen starters were conspicuous by their absence, including ten who'd made the CFL all-star team — an incredible loss, and one that's probably unprecedented in league history.

These players left for a variety of reasons. Doug was the spearhead of it all. He had an opportunity to go on to the NFL, and everyone knew that he wanted it badly. Not because he believed that the NFL was a better league — far from it. He really appreciated his time here, and I don't think would have exchanged it for longer-term success in the States. The fact of the matter is that he's ultra-competitive and hated the whispering that had always dogged his career. Yes, people said, he was a great college quarterback. Yes, he won the Heisman Trophy. Yes, he did well in the USFL and was maybe the CFL's best player ever — but he couldn't cut it in the NFL. That suggestion ate at him absolutely past irritation. For years, he'd yearned to get back south of the border and prove himself once and for all, which as we know he proceeded to do in Buffalo.

His departure seemed to open the floodgates. Of course, you expect a certain amount of turnover each year. You lose guys, you get guys; that's the nature of the business. The previous season, Jimmy Cunningham had gone to B.C. — a major blow, but compensated for by the arrival of Derrell Mitchell. No team — especially a team as good as the Argonauts had been during the past couple of seasons — is built around a single player. Our difficulty this time around was both the sheer number of guys who went elsewhere and, even more important, their quality. I can't remember when we've seen two team members picked up by the NFL after the end of the season. After closing our 1997 season, there were four — five counting Adrion Smith, who joined Flutie in Buffalo, but later returned. Mike Kiselak, the CFL's best lineman, became a starter in Dallas. Mike Vanderjagt, who handled kicking duties, had an outstanding year with Indianapolis, and Reggie Givens made his mark as a special teams player in San Francisco.

Others were scattered around the CFL, in large part because they got better offers elsewhere. Robert Drummond headed for B.C. as well, although going into training camp we thought we might have succeeded in keeping him. Then Kenny Benson went to Saskatchewan, and Pierre Vercheval to Montreal.

Other guys were lost in curious ways. Johnnie Harris also wanted his chance to make it in the NFL, so he went to the States and played in the arena league, hoping to make the transition from there, and has since signed with the Oakland Raiders. Then there was Rob Waldrop, our best defensive lineman and arguably the CFL's best defensive player. Coach Matthews saw him as the man who drove our front seven. Even when he wasn't making plays himself, he required a lot of attention and that allowed others to make them. But after helping to win two Grey Cups (and having already spent a couple of years in the NFL), he decided to become a police officer, and joined the force in Los Angeles. This surprised people who saw him only as a very one-dimensional physical player. In fact, he was a psychology major who always traveled with a laptop computer. So there he went, still at the top of his game, because he chose to seek a new direction and be fulfilled in different ways in life.

These were huge losses by anyone's standards, and hard for us to contemplate or come to grips with. For the Argonauts, this was like being shipwrecked before we'd left port. The only saving grace on troubled waters was that we still had the best captain alive, in the person of Don Matthews. It's true that he hadn't brought a lot of guys back in 1998, and seemed to have let a number of our guys slip away. If he'd been acting only as general manager, we might have questioned whether he was doing his job. But as head coach we knew full well what his abilitites were, especially when it came to defence and special teams.

So we were extremely optimistic, because we thought we'd solved our quarterbacking problem with the acquisition of Kerwin Bell, who'd gone 13 and 5 with Edmonton three years earlier. He wasn't as mobile as Flutie, but there was no doubt that he could throw the ball. We still had (or so we believed) Drummond, who could run the ball, along with old guys like Paul Masotti and myself to provide a little support to Andre Kirwan, Duane Dmytryshyn and particularly Mookie Mitchell, who'd been outstanding the year before, and was only going to get better as time went on. Offensively, then, we felt that we were good enough to do what we needed to do. Defensively, we thought that Coach Matthews would bring in enough fresh faces to plug the gaps. And in fact, when camp began, it looked as if in some ways we had even better personnel in place. So, although it may sound odd, our attitude wasn't that we'd lost ten all-stars and would be lucky to survive. The idea was that, despite everything, we were still the most talented team in the league, and that we were going to go all the way again.

This was theoretically possible, because other teams had suffered losses, too. The current buzz-phrase was "greater parity" across the board. The popular wisdom was that every game would count, that nothing could be taken for granted, that the Cup was far more up for grabs than before. We felt that this was true to some degree in the East, where it looked as if Montreal was the primary threat, given that they'd played us so tough the past two years. On a personal, one-to-one scale, though, we thought we had their number.

Then there was Hamilton. Their tough defence was a Tiger-Cat tradition. But another tradition came to Hamilton — Ron Lancaster. A great competitor as quarterback with Ottawa and Saskatchewan, his coaching talents were sure to bring excitement and a desire to win to Steeltown. Hamilton also added quarterback Danny McManus, who was experienced and always had great composure, along with Darren Flutie, who signed as a free agent. In all, we felt that they might prove to be as good as or better than the Alouettes. So, in our minds, parity applied to everybody else. We honestly thought, at least at first, that if we weren't the best, we were certainly far better than the opposition thought we were.

I still believe that's true. This could have been the year that Coach Matthews confirmed his place as undoubtedly the foremost coach in CFL history. A lot of people won't believe me, but we could have won the Cup. We weren't that far away from winning it. You'll get arguments from those who say, "Well, you guys weren't that great; the whole thing was sort of up and down." That's a fair comment — and therein lay our failure. We simply had quite a few guys who didn't respond or rise to the challenge, which wasn't the case in the past.

What we didn't realize when we so drastically changed the makeup of the team is that you can get another guy in who may be as talented as the one he replaces, but the result will be a profound difference in chemistry. He's going to have a different work ethic, a different desire to win. There'll be a difference in the level of his knowledge and understanding — not only of the game, but of his position within it, of his role as a teammate. All these things are imponderables until you get together in a working atmosphere. Only then does a group dynamic emerge. Our immediate stumbling block was that we were young as a group, and unable to make the necessary adjustments in time. Nor, with the exception of the defence, did we improve as time went on. You've got to get better as the season unfolds; that's the essence of professionalism, of experience and veteran leadership. Instead, we got worse. When that happens, it suggests a lack of character. In this way, youth hurt us. I don't mean that we were young in age, but young in terms of the mental game. There were other issues that related to execution, to the way we played the game, that didn't necessarily fit the talent that was there — and some of them can be laid at Coach Matthews' doorstep. We did a number of things that were old, that were more suited to the team as it was constituted a year ago. They weren't our biggest problems, though. The biggest problems were our own.

It didn't take long for our weaknesses to become apparent, especially since we were plagued from the outset by appalling luck. As I've said, Robert Drummond left the team while we were at training camp, which did much to add to the idea of parity. Then the fun began. Kerwin broke his arm in the very first pre-season game, and wound up on the sidelines for six long weeks. Jay Barker stepped manfully into the quarterbacking breach, but everyone was all too aware of the fact that he was starting for the first time anywhere as a pro. Jay had been a four-year starter at the University of Alabama where he went 37 and 2 and led the Crimson Tide to a national championship. Although a rookie to the CFL, he did a remarkable job — even though, in the first regular-season game against Saskatchewan, he got knocked cold on a play, and Nealon Greene had to replace him. If Nealon had been hurt, I might have been out there taking snaps myself (as I actually did in the pre-season opener, with the Maple Leafs' Tie Domi as honorary coach).

As it was, with Jay at the helm we beat Calgary — who'd eventually win the Cup — in their own park. Later, with Kerwin healthy again, we took care of Hamilton 42 - 6. In that game, Kerwin threw for an amazing 445 yards. These performances were not flukes. Despite losing ten all-stars, and despite other departures and injuries, more of which were still to come, we were able to remain competitive. That alone attested to Coach Matthews' ability to keep us in contention.

Which brings me to my role this past season. At training camp, it wasn't etched in stone that I'd be for the most part relieved of my duties as a returner. Coach Matthews had decided that, in order to "prolong my career," we'd try to have somebody else take over the return duties.

And try we did. This is what I mean about young guys who may have had sufficient talent, but weren't strong enough mentally to pull it off. James Dye, the first of many potential replacements, had led the U.S. colleges in kickoff returns while he was at Brigham Young University. He ran the 40 in 4.33 seconds and had an NCAA-leading punt return average of 21.9 yards. He was amazingly fast and seemed to have a positive attitude. Unfortunately, he was also extremely insecure. I wish he could have stuck it out, but he had a lot of things going on in his life. He was married, a father of two with a third child on the way. He had all sorts of responsibilities and obligations, and they weighed heavily upon him. He felt that he needed security so as to care for his family, and also felt — wrongly — that he was going to be dropped from the team. So he left abruptly under what appeared to be mysterious circumstances, and was replaced in turn by Don (Kato) Hitson, Anthony Bookman, Steve Smith, Sherman Smith, Tony Smith and Lester Smith — and once or twice by me. It was definitely a position by committee.

Tony Smith was a former first-round draft choice of the Atlanta Falcons, and we looked to him as Drummond's replacement at running back; there was never any suggestion that I was supposed to carry that load. He was ideally suited to the task, because he and Rob were practically twins — big, strong and fast. But Tony managed to break his collarbone in our first dreadful pre-season game, and the call went out to number 31. Tony missed a total of fourteen regular season games.

Nor did our bad luck stop there. Kato Hitson turned out to be a diamond in the rough, and returned two punts for touchdowns in his first two games. We hoped and believed that he might be able to function as running back until Tony's injury healed; but then, his third time out, he broke his leg — a nasty, ugly break. This left Coach Matthews with few options, and meant that I was handed the ball more and more often. Besides, he wanted to have me there, close to a young quarterback— Jay —because I understood the offence and could add a degree of stability and continuity.

Then what happened? I believe that the majority of people would say I was playing out of position. They have a mental image of my grinding or slogging away, usually for short gains. There was a great deal of commentary along these lines; one newspaper article wondered whether I'd been sent on a "suicide mission." Maybe that's because I wasn't seen engaging in marathon returns; there weren't those bursts of activity to serve as a counterpoint. If you asked most people how many passes I caught, they'd answer, "precious few," and go on to roundly criticize Coach Matthews for misusing what talents I may possess.

The situation was more complex than that. First, let's not forget that I was no stranger to the running back position. That's how I started off with the Argos in 1989. In 1997, I'd averaged 6.3 yards a carry, more than in any other year except 1991. In 1998, I averaged 4, which was a very average performance. But, although it didn't seem to register in the public's mind, I accounted for 995 yards receiving as opposed to 600-odd on the ground. Not that this did us much good. The trouble was that, as the season wore on, we grew complacent about the finer points of our offence. We relied on the pass, while resorting to the run only to keep the opposition honest. When we elected to run, we didn't adapt to the loss of three vital components: Flutie, Kiselak and Vercheval. Without them, the dynamics of our running game had to change, but didn't.

Our problem wasn't my playing out of position, or Coach Matthews placing me in an untenable situation. It was our inability as a team to execute. We were reduced to a lot of juking and jiving in the backfield, which allowed everybody to catch up to us while we were going nowhere. The reason was twofold. First, having lost Flutie, we continued to use a five-receiver set. As a result, we could not control the backside defensive end. Kerwin was probably a better pure drop-back passer than Doug, but did not use the bootleg or roll-out pass to the same extent. This would have frozen the defensive end and kept him out of our backfield.

In years past, a defensive end used to be up on the line of scrimmage, concerned (with good cause) that Flutie was about to take off in some weird and unforeseen direction. With five receivers, it was virtually impossible for us to block the end — the guy who might have done so was out running a pattern. This was our wide-open style of offence — it hinged on the pass. And if we chose not to pass, what happened? Even though we didn't block the defensive end, he was taken care of by Doug himself, who might well run or roll out with the ball.

Without Doug's ability to run the ball, Kerwin was at the mercy of the defensive end, who single-handedly eliminated the possibility of a cutback run. The rest of the defence could stack themselves up to cover the front side, which they did with ease. Mathematically, the offence was outnumbered. It looked like a parade out there, and it was terribly difficult to move the ball. This is what happened to us, time and time again.

To compound this situation, we lost Kiselak, whose forté was punching through to the second level — getting past the defensive linemen to make life difficult for the linebackers. Chad Folk, a very promising young Canadian, did a great job at center. Then, to make matters worse, we also lost Vercheval, who was as skillful at run blocking as any lineman you care to name. This triple whammy was too much for us to overcome.

Watching tapes, a football veteran would say, "Oh! Now I see why you couldn't run the ball." The fans, watching the games live or on TV, would say: "There goes poor little Pinball again, slamming into a solid wall of very large defenders." That was quite often the case, because of what I've just said. But it wasn't always so. In 1997, three of my best and highest producing games were when I filled in for Drummond as a running back. The difference was that all three vital pieces — Flutie, Kiselak and Vercheval — were in place, which helped me immeasurably.

That's not to fault or attempt to pin the blame on Kerwin, who was more than competent. If anything, he threw the ball vertically better than Flutie did; he really stretched the defence. But overall, his talents were different, so we had to scheme differently, and we didn't. Nor, by the way, did the B.C. Lions, who had Drummond in their stable. The Lions ran a similar offence utilizing five receivers. As a result, Drummond struggled during the first five or six games. I believe that his best output was 37 yards rushing. Then B.C. belatedly switched to two backs, controlled the defensive end, and allowed Rob to run for 160-some yards his next time out.

So I don't think it was a bad decision on Coach Matthews's part to play me as a running back. It's what he felt the team had to do at the time — a decision that was forced upon him by events. Our inability to run the ball didn't relate entirely to a guy who's five feet five and 170 pounds, getting a trifle late in years and long in the tooth. We could still have run effectively, had we executed properly, but we never adapted our system because (thanks to Kerwin and Jay) we threw the ball so well. Using me as a runner was no misuse at all. Rather, it was the best use under the circumstances — in fact, the only use, given the situation we were in, having lost Drummond, Smith and Hitson. Besides, I looked upon it as a challenge and an opportunity. In all my years with the team, I'd never rushed for 1,000 yards, and I was looking forward to the prospect. It was the only landmark I hadn't reached as an offensive player. Actually, at one point in the 1998 season, I was hoping that I might reach 1,000 yards in both receiving and running, which no one has ever done before, but it wasn't to be.

If we did make a mistake, it perhaps lay in not taking advantage of the mismatches that arose because I was playing a bigger man's position. The guys who were paired off against me used to guard Drummond. They were much bigger and heavier than me — therefore, supposedly less agile and quick. They were also less agile than the guys who were busy guarding Mookie Mitchell, because he was almost exclusively a receiver, and I was a receiver/running back. Given that situation, we should have been able to take advantage of some mismatches, but we didn't. Changing quarterbacks is part of the reason why. Kerwin tended to throw to Mookie Mitchell, who had a spectacular season and carried the team in many instances. He was our focal point offensively, to some extent at the expense of Andre, Paul, Andrew and Duane. We didn't spread the ball around enough. It was also the case that I was kept in the backfield much of the time to keep the opposition on edge.

I come with a degree of baggage; there's an accumulation of past history that stands in my corner. Maybe our opponents thought, "Well, he hasn't broken loose yet, but he might." No one really feared us running the ball, but they feared me doing something back there. This perceived or potential threat didn't materialize for the most part, but in its own way it helped out the other things we were doing.

And so the year wore on. Tony Smith's broken collarbone took forever to mend. We hoped he'd be back in action by the sixth game. Actually, he didn't return until game thirteen against Saskatchewan on October 3. In his mind, the injury wasn't healing correctly. Then, when it finally seemed to be all right, he didn't produce. We tried to make a returner out of him as well as a running back, but to no avail. Other minor injuries plagued him also. Even though the trainer had given him the okay to play, he felt he wasn't ready. Finally, after I got hurt during our second-last game against Montreal, he would not dress. Here again we see the inexperience and lack of professionalism — as distinct from a lack of ability — among the younger members of the team.

The end of the season had been very frustrating for me, because I was hurt for the first time in four years — not counting the glitch during training camp, and the traditional Labour Day showdown in Hamilton, when I got poked in the eye and saw double for most of the game. As it was, I lost two full games, and was present but barely accounted for in a third. This was doubly galling, because I thought that at that point we were on a roll, finally coming together as a team. We still had a chance to finish in second and possibly first place when we went to Montreal in late October. During that game I took a hit from a defensive back when I was in a full sprint. I managed to twist away and make it into the end zone, but when I tried to get up, my calf cramped — or so I thought. It felt like a cramp, but it wouldn't go away, and it turned out to be a pulled or torn muscle. Worse yet, the game wasn't sewn up We needed to win in order to host the Eastern semifinal at the Dome, rather than go back to Montreal and face the Alouettes on their home turf. I went to the sidelines and the trainers tried to massage the cramp, but without success. At least we won the game, by a score of 40 - 13, and thought that we were on our way, because at this point Montreal was playing as well as anyone in the league, and Hamilton — who we were scheduled to play in two weeks, followed by Winnipeg — had fallen off a bit.

As it turned out, that's when the wheels fell off, for me and for the team as a whole. I had to sit out the following week in a re-match with the Alouettes, who beat us by 10 points — 38 - 28. I tried to come back the next week against Hamilton, because we could still mathematically host the semifinal, but the supposed cramp had become a knot, and I couldn't put any weight on my leg. I dressed for the game, but I was totally ineffective, and we got blown out — 45 - 8. That was worse than being stuck on the bench the previous week. I was unable to do anything to help, even though I was on the field. I felt as if I was hurting the team. Then I sat down again for the last regular-season game against Winnipeg, and again we were defeated, closing out the year with three losses in a row.

To add insult to injury I was five yards short of 1,000 yards receiving with 90-odd catches, but that was a non-issue, a sidebar, because now it was playoff time. I'd rested up, and had stayed off my leg, because I realized that I'd played at least a week too soon against Hamilton. Now I'd take a fresh run at it; nothing could go wrong. My leg ached slightly, but seemed to be getting a whole lot better. By mid-week I was flying around, feeling good — until I strained it again. During the semifinal, it bothered me quite a bit; I certainly wasn't 100 percent. I told everybody I was fine, even though I knew in my bones I might not be able to play at all.

In the Eastern semifinal against Montreal, I was able to get out there and contribute to some degree, but basically this was another exercise in frustration. In the playoffs you want to show all your wares, your ten best moves. This time, we played adequately; we had 435 net yards to Montreal's 420. I think I got 40 rushing yards on six carries and 50 in the air plus one touchdown — certainly not a stellar performance, but we had a chance to win. We were only a turnover away from advancing to play Hamilton, but did not come through in the clutch. I myself dropped a pass in the third quarter, one I should have had. This probably was symbolic, because we really fumbled an opportunity to make it three trips to the Grey Cup in a row. Even at 9 and 9 closing out the season, we still could have made it happen. Even having lost ten all-stars, Coach Matthews — despite having made a couple of questionable decisions regarding talent — gave us the opportunity. The potential was so great for us to rise above the losses and the mistakes; that's the real disappointment.

I did the analysis for the Eastern and Western finals and then went to Winnipeg to do game-day analysis for the Grey Cup. Of course, people asked me how I felt about sitting in the broadcast booth instead of being on the field. I said I had no grudge, because I felt that the best teams were on the field. Both teams excelled through-out the year and had the best records, and their playoff victories bore this out. But I didn't truly believe that. I thought that the Argos were our own worst enemy, but I also thought that there was no reason why we shouldn't have been playing that day.

Complacency breeds mediocrity. To say, "Well, all things considered, I suppose we did pretty good," is a poor excuse. The fact is that we had the talent to go all the way, but because of inexperience, perhaps because we lacked depth of character, we struck out.

*　　*　　*

In looking ahead to the 1999 season, one or two statistics may interest (or depress) you. In 1998, despite having won two Cups in a row, we averaged 19,000 fans at our home games, up slightly from 1997. In 1989, the year I came to town, we were averaging 35,000. The last two home games this past season, against Montreal and Hamilton, were much better attended — but for the first seven, we were averaging 16,200, in a metropolitan area of about 4 million people.

What can be done to rectify this? In my view, the problem is two-fold. The first can be summed up in four words: Kids don't play football. Instead, they play hockey and basketball and soccer and baseball and lacrosse. Many university football programs are in danger of being dropped because of expense. The same situation holds true for high schools across the country, where the level of participation has dropped off significantly. In minor leagues, parents can't afford to let their kids take part, because of the high cost of equipment and travel. Rightly or (as I believe) wrongly, football continues to be perceived as a dangerous game.

That's the first reason why you can usually fire a cannon through the Dome on game days. Kids aren't playing on their own, and they aren't urging their parents to take them out to see the Argos in action. Nor, I would imagine, are kids in Winnipeg clamoring to be taken to see the Blue Bombers. This lack of interest and involvement is more or less league-wide.

How do we fix that? First of all, you've got to have volunteers — people in all parts of Canada with the same passion that I have for the game, who are willing to commit the time to build youth football, to enthuse kids and to educate parents, guys who have sufficient charisma and ingenuity to raise funds, to outfit teams, to organize and manage the sport at a local level. If these efforts succeed, the natural desire on the part of young people to participate will drive new programs and revitalize old ones. The key is to get kids taking part early on, and the sooner the better.

The other difficulty is particular to the greater Toronto area, although it may also affect Vancouver to some degree. We've tried but failed to position an Argos game as its own individual entertainment package in a crowded marketplace. Let's say that you're trying to decide whether to go to *Phantom of the Opera* or *Les Misérables*. Both are excellent productions, and well worth seeing. You may prefer one or the other; you may choose instead to go to the opera or the ballet. But you don't make your choice because the rest of your options are second rate, somehow less deserving of your patronage. They differ in composition, not quality. They're comparable, and are seen as equals when it comes to an evening out.

Not so the Argos. We're seen as Tier 1-A. It could be argued that any CFL team is Tier 1-A — that is, not as good as the NFL. But — witness the many players who are successfully heading south — that's not true. In Toronto, though, you have the Raptors, the Leafs and the Blue Jays. That's the first string. Despite their wealth of history, despite their winning records, despite the fact that they play in the same venue as the Jays, the Argos are still perceived as one step down. But the Argos are clearly comparable in terms of professionalism, quality and so on. Plus they're a genuine bargain when it comes to ticket prices. But we haven't been able to stake a claim to that topmost rung of the ladder in the public's mind.

Many theories have been floated to explain why this is so. True, we play an 18-game regular-season schedule, and it may be difficult for people to lock onto or feel loyalty toward a team in that short a span. Half the games are out of town, and television coverage — or lack of coverage, given the local blackout of home games — is a whole other issue. But we can't play a longer season. It's a physical impossibility (as the NFL knows; they play only 16 games). Even if we doubled the number of games, we'd still pale by comparison with baseball, hockey and basketball, which involve 162, 82 and 84 games respectively. I'm not sure how to go about it, but we have to differentiate ourselves as the most exciting summer and fall participation sport or entertainment option available. The entire family can attend; it's not as expensive as other sports; there's a lot of energy in the Dome; there's a story line to each game; and each play is really important and key, related directly to the end result. All this is true, but we haven't been able to convince people of that fact.

Nor are we, or any other club, getting enough help in our efforts to promote ourselves. The CFL hasn't adopted the NBA model, which the NBA stumbled upon out of dumb luck, because they weren't marketing geniuses. They still aren't, which helps to explain why the league has fallen on hard times during the past two years. In part, this is because some of the players have proven to have feet of clay and are deemed to be obscenely overpaid. A couple of years ago, however, when Jordan and O'Neal were at their peak, the glamor of the game was at its height as well. Why? Because corporate North America had made stars out of basketball players and other athletes. The NBA didn't make its own stars, because it had no money. All it had was a bunch of teams that were in varying degrees of trouble. Nike and other advertisers made the stars. The NBA just tagged along for the ride and got priceless marketing for free.

What have the CFL and corporate Canada done? Very little. The prime example is Doug Flutie. He played to his usual greatness, but Buffalo got bounced in the playoffs. Doug was a novel figure and had a good season; he surprised people and became an instant media darling. Corporate North America latched onto him and marketed him by using the very assets we failed to appreciate while he was here. His skills, as I never tire of pointing out, are superb, which everyone admires. He is a little guy in a big man's game, and everyone likes an underdog. He is a quarterback, and any quarterback tends to stand out. He is nice looking, and so appeals to women who follow the game and who make important purchase decisions. Corporate Canada and the CFL missed a golden opportunity to promote Doug and raise the game's visibility a notch.

If there were any justice in the world, the Dome (and stadiums everywhere) should have been filled every time he played. He should have had the sort of impact in Toronto that Roger Clemens had when he was with the Jays. It didn't happen — in part because corporate Canada didn't see the virtue of getting behind the CFL, and the CFL didn't press its case.

As another example, let's consider Gizmo Williams. He's made some of the most electrifying plays ever in the game of football, taking the ball 100 yards, from endzone to endzone. He's done this more times than anyone. In fact, he's had more end-to-end runs called back on penalties than any other kick returner has successfully made. Not only is he an outstanding athlete, he's one of the funniest and most engaging guys you'd ever meet. I'm sure that he could have been a very effective spokesperson for the game. With promotion, people throughout the league would have been more eager to come and see him in action. But, like so many other players, he was (and remains) well respected and a great fan favorite in his home city of Edmonton, but virtually unknown elsewhere. No one thought to make use of him in this way — and this sort of non-thinking will have to change if the league is to break through to a wider audience.

Times have changed, and stars today are created by a media presence, by being seen on commercials that feature them, not as nice guys, but as stars. In fact, stars can be not-so-nice guys — we should all aspire to be a Wayne Gretzky or a Michael Jordan, but those are rarefied heights to climb. Fortunately, we've got enough highly talented nice guys to go around — but the CFL has got to get corporate Canada involved. In all my years with the Argonauts, there hasn't been a national television commercial (or radio commercial or print ad, for that matter) that featured a CFL player. There've been several local or regional campaigns and plenty of individual endorsements, but that's all. Nor are CFL players profiled in national magazines, except when they flee the country. I honestly don't know why, considering that we've had many Olympic athletes, who — not to belittle their achievements — take second or third place at the Games, but still secure national commercial contracts. This makes it tough for a fan in Montreal or Toronto or Hamilton to say, "I think

I'll go down to see a game because Edmonton is coming to town." Who, exactly, is Edmonton? The players aren't personalities. Basketball, baseball and hockey have personalities. All we have is teams — and that's the case in every CFL city.

*　　*　　*

So, where does that leave us, and what lies ahead? Don Matthews, as everyone knows, has decided to try his luck in Edmonton, where I wish him well. If that weren't enough, we've also waved goodbye to Mookie Mitchell, who last year turned in arguably the best single-season performance as a receiver in Argo history, Terry Greer notwithstanding. Mookie had 160 receptions for 2,000 yards and 10 touchdowns. His departure leaves a huge gap to fill. Also, Mookie is a great friend. He is the one I spent most of my time with on away trips, playing dominoes (at which I beat him constantly. That's my story, and I'm sticking with it.) But he's gone now, to the Chicago Bears of the NFL, part of another yesterday — as is Kerwin Bell, who'll next be seen wearing a Blue Bombers uniform.

Still, all is not lost. Kato Hitson has a very promising future, having worked hard to rehab a serious injury, and will be back in 1999. He reminds me a lot of Jimmy the Jet — a young guy who's dying to prove himself over the long haul. Another bright spot is Jay Barker, who'll be our first-string quarterback. He's a guy I'm extremely impressed with from two standpoints. He's both the most consistent individual in terms of his Christian stance and personal morality I've had the good fortune to play with since Reggie Pleasant, and a tremendous asset on the field because of his youth and mobility.

Several outstanding defensive players will also rejoin the club. Besides Adrion Smith, we have (for the first time since I've been here) three all-star-caliber Canadian linebackers — Mike O'Shea, Kelly Wilshire, and Glen Young. This is how you win football games. This is what Winnipeg did for many years, what Edmonton was so good at in their best seasons and what Hamilton was so successful at last year. Then we have the rest of the Smith "brothers" returning in the defensive backfield, which is as strong as it's ever been. Roger Dunbrack, another young Canadian defensive lineman who surprised everyone last year, will also be among us. So that, along with the presence of Demetrious Maxie, who I think may be the best defensive lineman in the league, bodes really well for the future.

Offensively, for those who are yearning for help and thought that I was in fact playing out of position, we got Eric Blount, formerly with Winnipeg, a guy who can not only run the ball out of the backfield, like Drummond, but who, unlike Rob, is also more than competent at returns, and last year turned in 3,816 all-purpose yards. Here's how diverse his talents are: 599 rushing yards on 133 carries; 78 punt returns for 1,051 yards; 64 kickoff returns for 1,695 yards, a CFL record; six touchdowns and one 2-point conversion. In my estimation, Eric, Mike Pringle and Mookie were the three best offensive players of 1998. Eric was certainly the best returner, Gizmo Williams and Jimmy the Jet included, so I expect that he'll play an important role in our success.

Meanwhile, back in the front office, we have a new general manager, Eric Tillman. This represents a gain. Eric was the Argos general manager in 1997 and prior to that he was the B.C. Lions general manager from 1993–1995. He won Grey Cups with both the Lions (1994) and the Argos (1997). His football experience began back in 1983 in player personnel with the Montreal Concordes. Eric engineered the trade with Winnipeg; he sent Kerwin Bell and wide receiver Reggie Swinton to Winnipeg for Eric Blount and slotback Mitch Running.

With Eric Tillman as general manager, our player personnel situation has definitely changed. If he'd been in charge in 1998, maybe he'd have been more aggressive about trying to keep the guys who went to the NFL or to other teams by signing them before they made their move. If you put enough on the table to attract a player, and he's generally happy with the club, he'll be more likely to stay put. In fairness, Coach Matthews wanted to give players the latitude to take their shot at the NFL if they wanted to, but I believe that Tillman will be more proactive, and more apt to secure the services of proven veterans. Matthews didn't need to do this. He thought he'd find new, young, moldable talent. Tillman is interested in young talent also, but in addition he'll look for experienced personnel such as Eric Blount. So we're in good hands when it comes to signing talent back and making the hard decisions that will make us better in other areas.

We also have a new head coach — Jim Barker — and to be honest, I don't know if I'd have thought to go this route. If I'd been present at the interview process, where I understand he stood out above the rest, I'd probably have come to the same conclusion, but I was looking outside the club — when all the while, probably the smartest guy was right in house.

Everyone knew that Jim Barker understood the game; as the Argos' offensive coordinator, he was both widely liked and well respected. Coach Barker joined the Argos for the 1997 season, having been with the Alouettes in 1996. He coached in Saskatchewan in 1994, interrupting a U.S. college career as a coach from 1978 to 1995. But I was naive; he wasn't first in my mind. I thought of him as my buddy, the guy I'd go and talk to as a friend. Actually, he was the obvious guy for the job. Apart from his knowledge and leadership abilities, he brings continuity, which is in short supply these days. He knows all our deficiencies as well as our strengths. He knows our personalities, having been there a couple of years as offensive line coach, so there's not as much of a learning curve; he's an instant, natural fit. He's paid his dues, even though he's still young by league standards, and might have been overlooked because of his age. Of course, there's an element of the unknown, but that may add to the excitement and rekindle the passion. Too much of a good thing is no good. With Don Matthews, our attitude often slid into overconfidence. Now we'll have to go out there and do it. Exactly what will happen remains to be seen, because Barker hasn't won a single game as head coach. The flip side — eternal optimism! — is that he hasn't lost any either.

12

TACKLE VIOLENCE AND GET MAD

When I was twenty-one years old, I thought I could change the world. I was silly enough, confident enough, to imagine that all I needed was time. Maybe it was that classic undersized-achiever thing: The little guy has to fight for everything he gets. Did I want to be a doctor? No problem. How about a brain surgeon? No question that I could do it — just give me a bit more time.

When I was twenty-three, the penny began to drop. That's when I was cut twice in two weeks, first by Kansas City and then by Tampa Bay. From that experience came the realization that the world wasn't always going to conform to my way of thinking. Now, a decade later, I'm still trying to deal with that fact.

That doesn't mean you can't keep trying to change your own small corner. This stuff is much easier to be involved in than to talk about; you feel as if you're patting yourself on the back. And so you are, in a way. The great American philosopher, Ralph Waldo Emerson said, "No man can sincerely try to help another without helping himself."

That's one of the most beautiful compensations in life. I also like to think that it's a by-product of our efforts, not the reason we should make them in the first place.

I love kids, and I try to help them out whenever I can. In young people I see hope everywhere. We've failed them miserably as leaders, as role models, and all too often as parents. The reason why they're the way they are is that, like most of us, they're an imitation of their parents, the generation that has let them down.

I hope that Rachel and Raven will grow up to be responsible because of Diane's and my leadership in our home, just as my mom led me by example every step of the way. This demands constant vigilance on our part as parents.

Look over in the corner of our living room, and there sits a great big television set. The gulf between what's available on TV today and what was the norm ten years ago is immeasurable. My cable business promotes TV, so by extension I'm part of the problem. That doesn't mean I'm about to throw away our set. Rachel watches programs that Diane and I consider educational; she would be just as happy if we locked it on the music video channel, because she loves to sing and dance. She'd receive a very different education in the process. It's our duty as parents to protect her young mind. Even if we junked the set tomorrow, it wouldn't change the fact that all these influences are here; she'll be exposed to them eventually, one way or another. We know we can't shield her from everything bad or harmful. What we can do is prepare her to confront these things — and, with our guidance, to behave correctly, to make competent decisions.

There's very little difference between kids today and teenagers throughout the ages. We may think there is, but it's one of degree, not kind. Kids have always worried about fads, about how to dress, about their complexions, about who and what are in or out on a given week. There have always been temptations and pitfalls and negative influences; truly there's nothing new under the sun.

Times have changed to this important extent: Today's children are bombarded with a lot more conflicting information — good, bad, and indifferent — much sooner than ever before in history. They have to cope with it, and maybe some of them are ill-equipped to do this, because we've hung them out to dry. If we'd been exposed to the same information that our kids receive, daily and in such frightening quantity, we'd probably have engaged in many of the same activities that they do and that we now point to with a mix of horror and alarm.

As I say, I see hope in every child. I see kids as our greatest asset and us as their biggest problem. The child that everyone else counts out, I count in. Adults fix on the outward rebellion, when the biggest rebel is often the one closest to change. Rebellion is a statement of seeking, of an ambition or drive that can't find an appropriate outlet. When you rebel, you're trying to respond to something. No response equals no hope, no caring, no concern, no emotion at all. That's when you border on danger, ready to give up because you see no point in continuing. If you have no hope, you may be physically alive, while you're actually dead. The very kids that most adults suggest are hopeless are actually full of hope, looking for the right example, seeking a chance, looking for help, even though they may not want to admit it. No matter how weird or mean or cruel some young people may appear to us, they all want the same thing — *love*. Too many of them are not loved; that's the biggest place we adults fall short. They don't find the love and attention that they need from us.

If today's kids are a lost generation — which I dispute, but let's suppose they are — why are they lost? Because we couldn't find it in ourselves to guide them. How is a child's character formed? None of us determines our own character alone. In large part, it's set in accordance with what's happening around us. Kids don't all of a sudden wander off into harmful and self-destructive actions. If there was no such thing as Satanism, do you think kids would dream it up all on their own? If nobody else was involved in drugs, would kids figure out how to make crack cocaine and distribute it to other youth all around the world? These are learned behaviors. Kids have been led in these and other directions, and we're the ones who've led them.

I condemn Satanism. Young people who are so influenced need help. I don't want to condemn young people who use drugs. What they need is help. I call myself a child of God, and the essence of that is my understanding of my own insufficiency. Only the Christ in me makes me sufficient in the face of young people's needs. Everyone is fallible — that's human nature. So when I meet kids, I try only to reach them wherever they are and show them where I'm coming from.

I find that many adults treat kids as if they're alien beings. You know the tune: This and that and the other thing is what they should be doing, but there's probably no point telling them so, because they're so different from what we were. They're different from us only because they've had to wade through so much crap. I know all about broken homes and single-parent familes. Even in two-parent households, kids get far less of mom and dad's time, because society has dictated that both parents have to work. That was fine for a while. The family could have a bigger house, a nicer car. Then everybody followed suit, and the price of housing rose so much that it required two incomes to pay for it. What used to be a choice became a necessity.

That's not the case for every kid, for every parent; we can't generalize. But on the whole, each kid has to handle so much more, and has access to so much less adult direction at the same time. Meanwhile, teachers and other authority figures have been told to be much more passive in their approach to young people. There was a time when teachers, if they saw something wrong, would confer with the parents immediately, or take a more active role, perhaps by exercising discipline themselves. That's taboo now, both inside and outside of the classroom.

When I was growing up in Dunedin, anybody's parent could literally take a hand. If I was up to no good over by Miss Ruthamae Lewis's place, she'd give me a well-deserved whupping. Then she'd call home to my mom. When I got there, rest assured I'd get another whupping from Mom, or at least a scolding that would last me for the next two weeks. That way, we learned to do the right things both with and away from our parents, how to act in different situations. It's different now with my own children, and I'd never dream of scolding a child I saw misbehaving in our neighborhood. Society has told me to steer clear of that; it's somebody else's kid, somebody else's problem.

This is not true. Kids who go off the tracks are everybody's problem. That is painfully clear every night on the news. That's why, three years ago, educators, the police, and I started a program called Tackle Violence in Toronto-area schools. It stemmed from earlier stay-in-school seminars that covered much the same ground. Usually we work with two or three grades at once — say, grade six through grade eight, or grades nine and ten. Everybody troops into the gym, and police officers kick things off with a video that talks about staying out of harm's way. Then we show a highlight reel called *Pinball's Greatest 100-Yard Dashes*, and I come bouncing in to do my thing. I ask the kids if they've ever heard of Alan Page and Carl Eller, stars of the first magnitude when I was growing up, who played with the Minnesota Vikings. They wore purple uniforms, and were known as the Purple People Eaters. They were bad with a capital B; Page would take your head off and mail it to your mom. I ask the kids, Where do you think they are now? Nobody knows. That's the point. So how does each and every kid in the room become a true star, a lasting star that shines to some good purpose and keeps on shining through thick and thin?

Next we take a look at the letters in the word STAR. The "S" stands for Self-control — not control of, or the imposition of your will on, anybody else, but simply taking charge of yourself and what you do. That's maturity; that's adulthood. I show them a picture of Rachel, up on the screen, and everybody ooohs and aaaahs, because she's as cute as pie. Then I tell them that this precious little girl will never see her grandfather, Diane's father, because he was shot and killed by someone who was incapable of exercising self-control. Most kids can relate to emptiness and loss.

The "T" stands for Think ahead, and I ask the kids what that means to them. Back come the answers, variations on "Look before you leap." Good answers, but I take them a little further. Every action has a consequence. If you make smart choices, good things happen; if you make bad decisions, get ready for the flip side. This makes sense to the audience, and the kids are still along for the ride.

The "A" stands for Attitude, which in turn determines Altitude — how high you go in life. Now they get a brief history of Pinball living in The Projects, the idea of stereotypes, of the low expectations that were placed on me and continue to be placed on others who seem to have a strike or two against them. I pick out one kid, and ask him or her to stand up — one of eight in that particular row of seats, 300 children in the gym, 30-odd million people in Canada and 6 billion in the world. How can he or she alone hope to accomplish anything? Every kid in that row is unique and special and significant, capable of making a unique and special and significant contribution to life. Absorb that very simple realization, and a positive attitude can take them anywhere they want to go.

The "R" stands for Respect — self-respect and respect for others as well. Why do you show respect? The obvious answer is, so others will respect you. That's a pretty good answer, too, though it's not the right one. You respect others because you love and respect yourself, because you care about how you present yourself. If you count on their respecting you in turn, what happens when they don't? You're hurt and angry, so you disrespect them back. If you disrespect me, you look bad. If I respond, we both look bad. If I care about myself, I won't let you make me look like a jerk. If you choose to be a jerk, that's your problem, but if I let you make *me* look like a jerk, what does that make me? The kids are on top of this, because they're smarter than we think. I tell them that I want them to get up in the morning, look in the mirror, and say, "I love me." That doesn't mean loving yourself to the point of being full of yourself and conceited. The idea is that, of all those billions of people in the world, nobody else knows what you know, looks like you, walks and talks like you.

I tell them to start thinking of themselves as an artist who signs a painting. He's proud of that; it represents his best work at the time. When he gets better and does another painting, he'll sign that one, too. So I want the kids to put everything they've got into everything they say and do, to put their stamp on it for the whole world to see, to be proud of their work and of themselves as well.

None of which is difficult for my audience to grasp. It's a matter of their doing the right things — because it will benefit *them*, make *them* happy, and give *them* a more complete life. They'll experience more joy, more satisfaction. Things will happen better for them; life will be easier. If they understand that, it's not such a reach for them to start doing right, and doing it their own way.

My message to kids is not an overtly Christian message. We know that love and respect are Christian concepts, Christian attributes. As Tackle Violence takes place in hundreds of different big-city schools, filled with kids of all colors and creeds, these would be the wrong settings for explicit and personal missionary statements; that's not why I'm there. It's not like the Athletes in Action Pro Weeks, where we make a witness that's fitting to the circumstances.

Ecclesiates says there is a time to be silent and a time to speak, and I feel that a part of my calling is to try to leave the most effective message in the most appropriate way. You have to be sensitive to the rules of the establishment you're in, and to your audience. This, too, is still an effective witness, as the kids can see and hear me in a certain way. Later on, they might hear or see me in some other venue, where I'm speaking more plainly about my beliefs. In fact, my beliefs are pretty evident. We used to have question-and-answer sessions after the

Tackle Violence presentations. The kids would come up and say, "You didn't say it directly, but you're a Christian, aren't you?" If asked, I'd talk about my beliefs. But the program as a whole is meant to be non-specific and widely applicable.

Last year we decided last year to take things a little deeper. We began something called MAD, which stands for Making A Difference. This followed a certain number of the Tackle Violence assemblies; individual schools decided whether or not they wanted to participate. The administration would choose about twenty kids who were struggling, who'd been targeted as more or less at risk, the kind of kids the teachers thought would benefit in some way. I dealt with the group I'd been given; no one briefed me beforehand. We'd find a quiet area and get down to work, supposedly for an hour, but most of the time going on two or three times that long. Kevin Guest, a police officer who led the Tackle Violence session, would usually stick around, and sometimes so would guidance counselors and another football player. Doran Major and Lloyd Exeter, partners in Pro Image Marketing, helped me out from time to time.

Of course, MAD is yet another play on words. We'd start by asking the kids what made their blood boil. No problem getting the raw material: Their grades aren't great, they've been labeled dropouts, their parents are on their case, they get hassled by the cops, they're victims of racism, and on and on. We'd write all this stuff on the board, and the same basic themes kept cropping up.

Later on, we'd do a bit of role-playing. They'd be parents, and I'd be the teenager in search of his niche in life. I'd slouch convincingly and talk in monosyllables, if at all. To no one's surprise but theirs, they'd hear themselves sounding exactly like their moms or dads.

We'd begin with straightforward stuff. Someone says, "My mom nags me because I won't take out the garbage." Well, she told you five times to take out the garbage, and you kept on playing Nintendo. Put it on pause, take out the garbage, and then you can play it in peace for the next hour. Someone else says, "My mom is upset because I come home late." Well, how do we work with that? What's wrong with coming home late? Your mom cares about you. She's worried and disappointed because she's set certain rules, and in her eyes they aren't being followed. You aren't being responsible. It's not so much that coming home late is wrong; it's just that she thinks that being on time is right.

Here's an idea: Don't drag home late every time. Fifteen minutes isn't all that important. Why don't you surprise her by coming back early sometimes? That way, you can make a deal. Fifteen minutes early during the week will buy you an hour on Friday night. Your mom will trust you a bit more; you'll have earned a bit more responsibility. What you do with it is up to you, but you'd have to be crazy not to work that exchange.

Kids think that if they straighten up once in a twenty-four-hour period, they'll be applauded, if only for the novelty of it all. Not necessarily. Try doing the right thing often enough, and you'll get to the point where you're doing it just because it's right. Then you'll start to see real change. You'll recognize a practical difference in your life. This doesn't mean the kids will go out and start doing right later that same day, but it makes it easier for them to start conducting themselves properly, and harder for others, like a parent, to dispute the fact or to keep on saying no. So what lengths are they willing to go, to have a voice? I tell them to be there for themselves, to do the things that work best for them, and see what happens.

A lot of this starts with old-fashioned good manners and common courtesy. I ask the kids when they last said "Yes, sir," or "Yes, ma'am." If they go home and try that on, their parents will think they're crazy. Their teachers will think they've lost their minds, too. But if they do it with sincerity, it's going to become a habit. I tell them, "Show respect, and you'll get respect back."

Then the kid says, "Yeah, but my teachers won't listen to me no matter what I say; they've already labeled me." That may be true to a degree; some things we may not be able to change right off the bat. But try it. If you treat your teachers politely, handle things in the proper way in class, do a little more than is expected, I guarantee you'll meet with some success.

I challenge the kids to try me on this, to see whether or not it works. If they get the idea that their decisions directly affect their lives, their quality of living – if they see the cause and effect — then they can build on that knowledge anywhere to get to wherever they want to go.

How much of this sinks in? It's hard to tell. The Tackle Violence sessions are a once-over-lightly; the kids are tagging along with all their friends, the gym is packed, and no one is singled out to speak up. I'm viewed as the lesser of two evils: At least they don't have to be in class. When it comes to getting and holding their attention, I'll use every hook in the book.

They think it must have been tougher for me, growing up in the States, so they tend to give me the benefit of the doubt. They don't say, "He can't understand what we're going through; for him it was so long ago." They say, "Wow, maybe he had it worse than I do."

What really helps is that they don't picture me as being all that much older than they are. Size matters. When I go to a high school, lots of the boys — and girls — tower over me. I don't act like most thirty-plus-year-olds; I come in wearing a sweatsuit and a cap on backwards. I don't sound like most thirty-plus-year-olds, either. I talk their language, though I'm careful here — I'm not one of them, and we all know it. There's nothing like actually *being* seventeen.

The MAD sessions are something else again. They're more in-depth and personal; I have to make a one-on-one connection. These aren't for everybody. If a parent doesn't give permission, or if a kid wants no part of them, I don't press the point. I think two kids have opted out over the course of a year. The one thing I stress is that I'm not trying to usurp a parent's place. I start by saying that the session is optional for me too. I'm not paid to be there. It takes time out of my day, and I have other things to do. I don't raise false hopes or make promises I can't keep. The session lasts a couple of hours. We aren't going to achieve any miracle cures in that time. The kids have to go back to their homes, some of which are pretty grim. What I try to impress on them is that they have to listen to and respect their parents, because parents have earned the right, paid for the right, to expect that whatever they say in their homes goes. If the kids get hurt, I won't visit them in the hospital. I won't be there for them day in and day out. All I try to do is empower them to start taking control, to whatever degree is proper within their family circumstances, because the day will come when a parent won't be there for them, either. Sometimes people they trust, people they think are friends, are going to kick them around and betray them. It all boils down to this: You have to be there for yourself.

During the MAD sessions, I've heard some pretty radical and unsettling things. I try to take these at face value, even though they're sometimes exaggerated. I have to accept that something's going on, or the kids wouldn't be sharing it with me; usually, they don't have anybody else to talk to. I used to ask the group members to introduce themselves, to say what they wanted to be when they grew up, to help them learn to present themselves positively. Some gave goofy or snide answers; they felt they had to show how bad or how cool they were. Maybe they wanted to get a rise out of the middle-aged football player. I deal with this as it comes, depending on the atmosphere. I don't go in expecting that suddenly everybody is going to start telling me the truth.

I have to make contact, establish a rapport. I know right away that some kids aren't serious, so I try to let them know I realize that without calling them liars or by saying, "Get real, punk." But how do I react when girls say they want to be prostitutes?

One kid said he wanted to be an assassin — one of those times I was at a loss to respond. My first reaction was, This kid is too smart for his own good. He's putting me on. Maybe so, but if not, I'd better deal with it. So instead of skirting the issue, I took him seriously, and he began to answer my questions seriously. Pretty soon, it dawned on me that this was something he'd actually contemplate doing. At that moment, he didn't have all that much going for him. Where did he feel most at home? In a gang. What did he do well? He wore his colors. If his gang needed a job done, he did it. I asked him if he'd want to kill my daughter's grandfather, and he said, "It wouldn't be personal, but I'd have to burn him to put money on the table." That was frightening. I could not overlook the honesty of his response.

Is that boy beyond hope? I believe not. If we treat him as a lost cause, as hopeless, then we too lose hope. I firmly disagree that his fate or anybody else's is a foregone conclusion — that the girl who wants to be a prostitute will necessarily wind up on the streets, that this kid will beyond doubt wind up in the cells. Kids are so fragmented; they change so rapidly. The one who behaves so well may be the first to go astray.

I never know, and that's the point: I never know who I'm reaching. If some of the most successful people were to tell their true stories, if they weren't afraid of the skeletons in their closets, we'd be very surprised at what they did on their way up the ladder. Within this group that seems so blameless, we'd find a multitude of sins, a lot of the very actions that make us doom young people to irrevocable fates.

Well, there's something in the Bible about casting the first stone. There's also the fact that people — young people especially — work as hard as they can to fulfill the expectations that are placed upon them. This is the syndrome that I escaped myself, back in Dunedin. There, here, and everywhere, if you're told you'll never amount to much, then where is the will to try to be something better? Sometimes this continues through life, sometimes not. We meet people ten or fifteen years down the line at a class reunion, and see how much their former images were in our memories' eyes only.

Some who were labeled ugly are now striking, and were no less striking at the time. It was a role they played out, a sort of protective coloring. Now the people who used to be cool are cool no longer. Now the geek or the computer nerd is cool; money looks good on him.

It's not that they're different people, it's just that different people reach different points in their lives at different times. If a kid says he wants to be a killer, it's pretty clear that something has to reach that kid in the next little while, or he'll find himself in trouble. Is he any more apt to go wrong than the model student? Yes. Is he any less capable of becoming a success? No, only less *likely* to, because of other burdens that have been placed on him. That cycle can be broken; change can be effected. All of us can change, physically, morally, and spiritually. We don't know when or how change is going to come, or who's going to bring it about. Usually no one person is responsible — a combination of people can reach out to someone and touch him in time.

This isn't altruism on my part. You never know how things are going to come around. Obviously, I don't want an assassin running loose. I don't want drugs in schools, either. I'm a zero-tolerance kind of guy. But they're there, and we've got to face the fact. Can we also face the fact that a kid's dealing drugs puts food on his single parent's table? That might well be the case, and all the just-say-no lectures won't pay the grocery bill.

During MAD sessions, I've had kids admit to me that they smoke drugs, and I've urged them to come with me to see the school principal so that everybody can work together to resolve the problem. According to the kids, and I believe them, they'd be expelled immediately if the school found out. This tends to happen in even the best schools, those that have asked me specifically to come and talk to the students about drugs. It's all very well to talk about zero-tolerance, but if a kid is honestly seeking help, a teacher or administrator must provide it. There's nothing more important than getting a kid off drugs. It can save his life, or your own life, or those of your kids. I don't want to walk into the middle of a drug deal in the parking lot of my apartment building because I turned away from a kid who might have been straightened out. I don't want that kid selling drugs to Rachel in ten years' time, either, when something I could have said or done might have put him on another road.

What I don't know is whether it would be more effective to go back to the same school twenty times with these and other messages, or to give twenty schools a little taste. Years ago, as I've said, we used to do a very rudimentary stay-in-school program, and I was even less sure that anything was sinking in.

Last year, a guy came up to me and said he'd met a young woman in law school who was also going out and speaking to kids, telling them that they could turn their lives around and do great things. That sounded familiar to the man, so he asked her what had started her in this work. She said, "Well, Pinball Clemons came to my class one day, and it sort of changed me." We don't always hear about the results or get the testimony, so we look to Christian parables. We're called as Christians to sow, not to reap. The harvest will eventually come in, although we may not be around to see it.

I'd like to mention a couple more programs that stemmed from MAD and Tackle Violence. Both are in their early stages now. The first, Shining Example, is an attempt to fill a bit of a gap. Too often we pay attention to the extremes, to best- or worst-case scenarios: the promising athlete or the straight-A student, the at-risk kid or the troublemaker. The ordinary kid who just muddles through as best he or she can gets no glory, or even encouragement. Yet plain, normal John and Jane are the kids who'll grow up to make their communities thrive. They're the strength of tomorrow, though they tend to get lost in the shuffle.

So last year, I got together with the *Toronto Sun*, Midas Muffler, and Plain & Simple Sports & Promo Wear, a clothing manufacturer.

The *Sun* solicited nominations from teachers, classmates, or anybody at all who knew of a kid whose efforts had gone unheralded and unrecognized. The winners were written up in the paper and received a whole raft of prizes: we took them to the Playdium at Sega City, to a Toronto Raptors basketball game, and Canada's Wonderland. They were each given a nice jacket, too. Now we're looking at an annual banquet or a grand-prize trip to Disneyworld.

Our idea here is to recognize and reward the stuff that kids are doing quite spontaneously — volunteering their time in hospitals and nursing homes, helping with food drives and charity events, fund raising for all sorts of worthy causes.

This is the lifeblood of our communities, and these young people will continue to do these things when they grow up and assume leadership roles. This is what makes us human, rather than anonymous bean counters. It's the pulse of what we are. We all have difficulties in life, and the best way to handle them is by spreading the responsibility around, encouraging people to take control of their own destinies.

A community is like an insurance policy. A lot of us balk at the idea of paying in; we just want to collect when we're in trouble. The more people who are paying premiums, the better off we'll be.

The last program, Rising Stars, is possibly the most valuable. I'm almost hesitant to talk about it, because I don't want to violate any confidences. It takes place in a suburban neighborhood that's seen more than its share of imposed stereotypes and self-fulfilling prophecies. The idea was brought to me last year by a group of six businessmen. They had roots in this particular area; two of them had lived there when they first came to Canada, and they'd kept up a number of contacts. I'm the token athlete, but not the token black guy; we look like a mini-United Nations walking down the street. They knew they wanted to do something; they just didn't know what. In fact, the whole thing was very vague, and I was initially hesitant about getting involved. I thought that playing ball with the kids wouldn't prove all that much; they could and did play ball by themselves. I didn't know if the businessmen were looking for an athlete to front a fishing expedition for government monies. I've seen that movie before, too, and I'm not a big fan of going cap-in-hand to governments. It always sets a better example if you can fund something yourself; it's literally less taxing. Then as I got to know these men, I decided that they might be on to something I'd want to be a part of. The big difference between this and the other programs is that we're committed to being there in person, on an ongoing basis, long enough to see change if and when it occurs. We'll find out whether bearing down with a smaller group over a far longer period of time proves to be more helpful.

We go in once a month with a mix of teaching and athletic competition. It's a good workout for everybody. Each adult takes half a dozen kids in hand. The majority of them are young guys. We had lengthy discussions as to whether or not we should include girls. We decided that we couldn't turn them away if they showed up. When they did, Diane entered the picture.

The idea is to develop a relationship with each kid — a bit of a reach, when we're only meeting face-to-face every four weeks. In time, we hope to be able to keep in touch on a more regular basis. The initial target age for the kids was nine to thirteen years, because we thought that attitudes wouldn't be as set as they are at sixteen or seventeen. But this raises a problem: Do you graduate from the program when you're thirteen? If so, what about the kid who joins when he's twelve? Do we press on with a tutorial system that will basically have to run itself in our absence? How many tasks can we delegate? Should we monitor what the kids are doing in school, and make continuing in the program contingent on grades and attendance? Do we look toward university, try to lay the groundwork for a series of scholarships? Would this necessarily involve corporate sponsorship? We'll see about these and other issues; as I say, these are early days.

The other men and I agreed right off the top that we might well fail, that the program might dead-end and dwindle away into that great holding tank of good intentions. We knew we might affect nobody or everybody. What we could do was try our best, each in his own way, and believe that we'd reach somebody on some level.

We set up very basic guidelines: first and foremost, to show the kids that we cared. The guys said to me, "Well, *you* have to take the lead. Kids listen to you because you're an athlete." I set them straight on that one. Because I'm an athlete, because I'm Pinball, I could count on holding the kids' attention for about seventy-five seconds. Then, if I was dull and dry and boring and superficial, I'd be history. Kids figure out whether or not you're real at the speed of light. They have a lot of practice at this, because most adults stop caring about them quite as much as they grow older.

Once again, we aren't striving or pretending to be saviors or miracle workers or surrogate parents. Our aim is to let the kids know that there's something beyond what they see every day. We want to take them outside their spheres and expose them to all sorts of different activities, from sporting events to theater to visiting a seniors' home or hospital. In the process, we hope they'll find that going out and doing things and giving something back affects our outlook, our perspective and self-esteem. In time, perhaps the kids will think, "Maybe we're not so bad off after all. We have some things to be thankful for, even though our situation is rough around the edges."

We know we have to be careful here; we can't build them up on the basis of someone else's misfortunes. What we can do is give them more insight into the sum total of life, and show them that their lives can be the better for the experience.

13

LIKE A TURTLE ON A FENCEPOST

So there we have it — one or two of the things I do in what I refer
to as my spare time, which is at a premium these days. Last year, I
was honored to receive the Mayor of Toronto's Celebrity Citizen
Award. I got it at what you might call arm's length. I missed the ceremonies, since I was booked at yet another charity event. The Argos
sent a representative to collect it on my behalf.

The Argos are still my ticket to ride. You could be forgiven for
letting that slip your mind. While it's unusual for an athlete to
receive more recognition for what he does off the field, that seems
to be what's happened in my case. Sometimes I want to say, "Hey!
Remember — I play football too." I'm proud of that, even though
there's the question of whether it's a fit occupation for a grown
man. I earn by far the greater part of my living by running around
wearing a plastic helmet and ungainly padding. I play according
to rules and strategies that are built around the movement of a
leather ball. I'm not real sure what objective value can be placed

on this, or why anybody should listen to me instead of the next guy. I have learned, though, that people do listen to athletes. If this is not true, then a lot of advertisers are throwing away a lot of money.

Given that, should athletes be role models? No more than anyone else, I think. It helps when everybody is functioning as a valuable member of the community, acting as a role model in his or her own way. I don't think every athlete should go out and speak in schools. Some aren't good at it; some don't enjoy it. Personal appearances are another story. If you as an athlete are expected to help sell sports tickets, and this is specified in your contract, then it's a business deal, and you have to live up to your end of the bargain. Theoretically, it shouldn't make any difference whether someone is an athlete, a doctor, or a sanitation worker. In every walk of life there's a cross-section of people who can relate to kids, who should do it if they have the opportunity and the desire.

Not only am I an athlete, I'm an entertainer. Let's say that the proverbial visitor arrives from outer space and asks me what I do to put bread on the table. I say, "I play a game." He, she, or it says, "They pay you money to play a game?" The conversation goes downhill from there.

Any spectator sport is a form of entertainment; people come to the games because they like to watch me and my teammates perform. It's interesting and suspenseful for people to see if, at five feet six, I can survive out there — whether I can keep out of the clutches of men who are much bigger than I am. Perhaps thousands of people are encouraged because I show them I can compete with larger individuals and come out in one piece.

There is a downside to this. People look at me and say, "I can't believe it! You play football?" They think that if I can do it, they can too. I'm fond of saying that I'm a glorified coward — I run away from others for a living. Sometimes I wonder what some people are thinking as they laugh at this, especially the guys who've played on university or high school teams.

Football is an intense, physical game. Despite my nickname, I don't just bounce off those guys who outweigh me by a hundred pounds — or even more. On the field we get hit, we get smashed. We hurt all over. We get so tired that we feel as if we're about to throw up. Sometimes we do throw up, and then we go out and do it all over again. I can work myself into a lather over this for maybe thirty seconds. Then I get self and ego out of the way, and keep on going on.

Then there are the people who come up and say things like "Are you real?" I think this translates as: "Are you too good to be true?" To the world, surely I must have a dark side. Maybe I'm one person when the cameras are rolling, but then I go home and fight with Diane in front of the kids, storm out to bars and try to pick up other women. Frankly, I can't oblige in those departments. If I'm not real, I ought to get another award for the best decade-long performance in a double life.

Which, come to think of it, you could say I lead, if we're talking about Pinball versus Michael Clemons. People often say things along the lines of "Well, you're different." That's nice too, on the face of it — but what do they mean? Sometimes I know what they mean, I think — that I'm like them.

We're none of us free from prejudice, and Canada isn't color blind. There's a far greater degree of tolerance in Toronto and in Canada as a whole, far fewer assumptions made up front, than where I came from. I try to avoid turning minor irritations into race issues. But I have prejudices also; call them preconceptions.

Earlier this year, having failed to settle on a house, Diane and I went to buy a car. It took us ages to attract the sales staff's attention; the salesman's mind seemed to be far away. He tried to steer us toward a sports utility vehicle when we were looking at sedans. We finally left, and Diane said, "Why are we both thinking the same thing?" The people at the car dealership did not believe that a black couple could afford one of their cars.

This sort of thing happens with suspicious regularity. Driving home at night, I've been stopped by the police. I keep on smiling and we get matters sorted out. A driver's license helps: "Oh, hello, Pinball!" To extend this further, if a black man and a white man arrive simultaneously at a store counter, the white will be served first — unless the black is a recognizable person, like a Pinball. This status versus color thing is one more aspect of life to ponder when I have too much time on my hands.

Do I wake up in the middle of the night and start conjuring up "what if" scenarios? Not very often. But here are one or two interesting possibilities. What if I were playing with an NFL team in a major American market, a big city and important media center? Let's suppose that my career has unfolded exactly as it's done. I've been with the same team for nine years. All my statistics, all my awards, are pretty much on par. So are my position and status in the city — I enjoy supporting charities and working with youth and the underprivileged, and I'm respected for that. People like me and they like the team, which, let's say, has just won back-to-back Super Bowls. How much money would I be making a year? Somewhere between US$5 and $10 million.

Now, let's pretend I haven't ever played football. How would my life be different if I'd worn a suit instead of a plastic helmet? There are tons of black football players; I wouldn't have been missed. Somebody else could have taken all the punishment. What if I'd kept my nose in a book at William and Mary? Yes, I graduated, but I don't claim to have had the same passion for my classes that I do for the game. What could I have accomplished? What direction might my life have taken? Suppose I'd worked to polish my debating and communications skills, and become a full-time public speaker. I am renowned for never using one word when five hundred will do. Chances are I'd have given good value on the motivational circuit.

Maybe I'd have gone into the corporate arena. The other day, Paul Phillips and I had an important meeting in connection with our cable business. A roomful of financial wizards had arrived to help us take the business to the next level and continue to grow so that, in five years, we'll become a $15- or $20-million company. They were prepared to loan us money, and wanted to see our projections and plans; we had to know what we were talking about. I hadn't really done a lot with the business the previous little while, but I waded in and was pleased to do more than hold my own. Well, what if I had been there attending to the business every day? Maybe we'd be making money hand over fist, and wouldn't have to borrow any. I could have taken my MBA and looked at a serious corporate role.

What if I'd decided to go to law school and take up the torch for the less fortunate? Or had become a teacher who was able to influence the lives of young men and women, molding them in a positive way? Would that have been more worthwhile? Playing "What if?" is always a futile exercise, but as you can see, I've indulged in it on more than one occasion.

If I lived in that hypothetical American city making millions of dollars in football, could I be assured that when I wanted to get something done for a group, a cause, an idea, I could pick up the phone and be connected with powerful and influential people who'd respond warmly and help me as much as they could? The answer is, there is no assurance. Would I have made the same impact, touched the same number of lives?

I've made all sorts of choices along the line, trying to strike a balance, sometimes failing. I've often used the analogy that I'm like a turtle on a fencepost. If you see a turtle sitting there, you can be assured of one thing: He didn't get there by himself. He had to be put there. So, too, has God put me in this position. God has called me, appointed me to be Michael Clemons, also known as Pinball, a professional athlete, a resident of Toronto, and a soon-to-be Canadian citizen. It's my job to do my best with what He has given me, to be thankful and grateful, and to use my talents to benefit the lives of other people as best I can. I know this is where Diane and the kids and I belong. This is where we're supposed to be, and I've never doubted our decision or experienced a moment's regret.

The thing I have to be extremely careful of is this: While I'm engaged in this mission, I dare not make my own home a mission field. When I'm out trying to use the wealth of the gifts I've been given to benefit the lives of others, I mustn't miss out on what's really important. I don't want friends and family to put in calls to poor Diane with the absent husband; I don't want guidance counselors to step in with Rachel and Raven because their father is too busy elsewhere to invest time in them.

I'm not exactly sure how to do it. There are days when I can't say no to anything, and going the extra mile turns into a marathon. If there's one more call to be made in the evening, I'll make it. Even if I'm out with Diane and the kids, I'll take the phone along with me, rather than say, "My family time can't be interrupted." But I don't want Rachel to learn that there is no private time for us. I want to keep my promises, but I know where ultimately I want to be. Michael Clemons wants to be at home, with his wife and girls, because he's been away too much.

Well, there's an easy answer to this. I've got to just say no, or learn to say it more often. Others do on my behalf. I don't even see most of the requests. There's a screening process — through the Argonauts, through my marketing firm Pro Image, through Diane, through me. And I, in fact, say no infinitely more than I say yes.

It's well known that I've been on many religious programs. Then there's my family — everybody knows about that. Rachel has been on TV and in the newspapers. I've been pictured many times with her and Diane; even Raven has had her moment of fame, wearing an Argos helmet.

Then, I fit into any sort of minority crowd, and this results in a whole lot more requests. Sickle-cell anemia is very prevalent among those of African descent, so there's a walkathon associated with the programs at Camp Jumoke. I've been the master of ceremonies at the Harry Jerome Awards, named for the Olympic sprinter. Strangely, I don't get nearly the number of requests that I might hope for from the black community. I've said that people ask me if I'm real, and I don't want to wonder if I am. Maybe they think they can't get hold of me, that I'm too busy running in so many directions, so there's no use in trying. In fact, I'd go out of my way for them.

Back to the easy answer, which is choose home, do what I can, and don't complain about the opportunity to do all these things. They aren't a burden, they're a blessing — a chance to have so many different experiences and make a difference.

What happens when the person who's done you a favor for something you're working on asks for one in return? What happens when a person who's doing good things calls and is counting on you?

All I know is that three people are definitely counting on me, and I have to be there for them. The thing I have to be careful about is not comparing, not saying, "Well, my dad was never there at all." That's when you become complacent. I'm here, I love Diane, and she knows where I am when I'm off doing things. I provide for the family, I love my kids, I do spend time with them when I'm home, we take extended vacations together, more vacations than people get a chance to take in normal jobs. Is going away on Wednesday night really going to hurt them? Can I make up for that? Everybody's away every once in a while, and it's valuable for the children to learn that.

Making decisions for the good of the family is just as important as the consistencies; you make sacrifices to get from A to B. Even when I'm not directly bringing home a cheque, I'm always meeting people, making contacts. Someone I bump into at a charity event may ask me to address a group for them later on. If I'm in the newspapers, it makes me a valuable commodity because of my visibility. So there are financial considerations, eventual reciprocations involved.

I've prayed for wisdom and guidance in these respects — in time, I believe, all things will become clear. I do believe that praying is important, asking for discernment, asking that His will be done. When I spend time with Him, when I pray and read His word, things come to mind that give me more to choose from, more to decipher. This is one way that I think He enables me to decide what's best. He will point the way that is best for me and for those who depend on me.

Meanwhile, I believe that He intends me to continue as I've been doing as an athlete. My passion and love for football are undiminished; they're why I play. Football requires that I get more out of myself than I know I have, and do it on a consistent basis. It gives me a sense of accomplishment. Every once in a while I get a little bit of confidence and simple satisfaction from the fact that I feel I'm good at what I do.

In the greater scheme of things my being an athlete doesn't amount to a hill of beans as it relates to my salvation or my relationship with God. He accepts me totally despite whether I have a good game or a bad game. To have a loving family, to be needed as a husband, to enjoy a sense of accomplishment and to have self-esteem — the greatest part of these things comes from God. And to be a success in football is just another joy. The Book Of Kings says "Observe what the Lord your God requires: Walk in His ways, so that you may prosper in all you do and wherever you go" (1 Kings 2:3).

Continuing in football will guarantee me a podium. Retiring implies I'll have it, though there's no guarantee. So I try to base my decision each year on several questions: Do I still enjoy the game? Can I still play, or are the Argos keeping me around for old times' sake? Am I fit enough to play a young man's game? The answer so far has been yes to all three. Besides, Diane enjoys watching me play, and I want to please her; it's nice to have a cheering section I can count on.

I doubt that I have anywhere else to go. No other Canadian city appeals to me, as I've made plain. It's true that over the years, there have been expressions of interest from the NFL, but I don't know how serious they were. I never let them reach that stage. At the end of this coming season, I'll still be younger than Flutie when he shuffled off to Buffalo. But if an NFL team phoned me up tomorrow morning, I wouldn't give the prospect a moment's thought. I guess one of the biggest reasons for sticking around is simple loyalty to a team and to a city that took me in, gave me a chance that others didn't. And I have so much to look forward to here. There's been this notion that when I retire I'll make a seamless transition to some sort of CFL ambassadorial role. That sounds promising; Masotti and I will totter around with canes, cutting ribbons and talking about the glory days.

Before we do, we do have unfinished business to attend to. It would be nice to go out on top, because no one wants to see an athlete linger past his prime. When you're thirty-three years old, the assumption is that it's all downhill from here. Maybe what constitutes the top has yet to happen.

Suppose I'd retired after the 1996 season. People would have said, "Good old Pinball! He knew when to hang it up." I'd have been been heralded as a champion with the sense to make a graceful exit at the peak of my form.

Nonsense. What I'd really have done was bow out when I had so much more left in me, as the next season proved. I was able to break all those records because I came back at it again.

I'm not afraid of not succeeding next time around. I don't want to fail, to go out there and perform poorly. Yet I'm also not afraid of striving to do even better. If I do worse, okay. I've had successes and failures. I've had great games, mediocre games, and a few perfectly awful games. Sooner or later I'll have more awful games, and that will be okay, too, as long as I can give my teammates and fans my best.

People say that a 5,000-yard season is unattainable, but people also say that at five feet six and 170 pounds, I can't possibly do what I've done. Logic is on their side (or maybe common sense). But it's happened anyway.

Do I have *better* football left in me? If I get 4,500 yards, does that represent a better season? If I get 2,000 yards, does that mean I've had a bad season? All of these things depend much on chance and opportunity, on the efforts of your fellow players and the caliber of play of your opponents. Statistics may look good on paper and go down in the record books, but they aren't a true measure in terms of the team's performance. It takes an all-out gutsy performance from everybody to get to the Grey Cup, and like the saying goes, giving 110 percent to win it.

I think I have more good football left, maybe just in terms of fortitude, playing as hard as I can, requiring as much of myself as I can. I'll leave any more records to the books.

*   *   *

I'll tell you one thing — it's far less daunting to put on number 31 than it is to tackle writing a book. I weakened only after dragging my heels for as long as humanly possible. I had doubts, because it's not a valediction, not a farewell. At this stage in my life, though, it seemed like a good idea to sit down, put my thoughts into some order, and try to share who I am.

By far the greater part of who I am is a Christian. That I am a Christian is all-important; my faith is my foundation. My relationship with God is a way of life. It's not something I call upon at my convenience, when I'm going through difficulty, when I need or want to do well. Each day, I am reminded that there is a God.

Because I've accepted His way of life, which involves being a follower of, and a believer in, Jesus Christ, I strive diligently to follow and be obedient to His word. Like everyone else, I fall short.

Being a Christian doesn't make you a saint. Nor does it set you apart, or make you special or different from anybody else. I judge what I do according to Him, which keeps me humble. I never feel tempted to say, "Well, I'm doing all these wonderful things, I'm a professional football player, I have a beautiful wife, two beautiful kids, I spend time with charities, I work hard, I'm a good guy." If I did that, I could start to feel pretty high on myself.

The Book of Isaiah says that all our righteous acts are like filthy rags and that we must strive for salvation. But by the same token, I don't beat myself up and think, I can never be like Him. I know He loves me. The reason He sent His son Jesus Christ was to extend His grace, and that grace must be received with a proper mix of humility and pride. I take pride in who I am because I'm a child of God, while I'm humbled because He made me who I am. It doesn't matter what we achieve, what our situation in life may be.

Romans 5:8 says that God's love is evident in that while we are yet sinners, Christ died for us. Whenever I have been in a sorry state, Christ has loved me. His extending that unconditional love to me allows me to forgive when the world says I shouldn't or don't have to. It allows me to show compassion when the world condemns, to smile when the world says I should cry.

So my relationship with God is all-embracing. It's who I am, how I conduct business, how I treat my wife and children, how I treat fans, how I play football. Does that mean I think about God in everything I do and say? Of course not. I fall short. In this relationship, He is the Father and sometimes I'm the erring son, and He has to discipline me. I get the message. He's given me a conscience to know what's right and wrong.

The abilities that I have are God-given. I've honed them through hard work and diligence, but I remember where they came from. So I have the power — again, given by God — to do and achieve certain things. God causes it to rain on the just as well as the unjust. He allows the unjust as well as the just to succeed and prosper, regardless of what you hear about "believe it and it shall be," or "you have not because you ask not" — people take all these verses out of context to prove whatever they want to prove on any given day. When you pray for things within the will of God, that's when your prayer is answered. You pray that His will be done, not for a new car or to win a football game. You won't get one, and it won't happen. When your prayers are answered, it is only because God has allowed things to take place.

God has given us all a witness, a story to tell. But how do we know what we are called to do? If I achieve a goal, or if I fall short of that goal, I'm still called to be obedient to His word. He allows some adverse things to happen to me, and sometimes He uses those things to help me speak for the kingdom. Sometimes he uses them to teach me and others a lesson, though He doesn't need me to do that. If I start thinking that God needs Michael Clemons, I'm thinking too much of myself. I serve a God who asks me to believe in Him not from what I see, but through faith alone. I don't need a sign from God to let me know that He is God.

What happens when people seek the sign and cannot find it; where is their faith then? Yes, He's allowed me to have successes, and now my duty is to use them for His good. I've been able to use my share of failures as well. Yet in all things, I was grateful for His will being done. I have not known what was in store, but I thanked Him anyway.

Sometimes, we get in the habit of thanking Him only for the good things. It is hard to be thankful for the things that hurt us and seem to be unfair. Not long ago, I spoke at the funeral of a fourteen-year-old boy named Danny who died of leukaemia. He was a wonderful person. The other kids loved him, and his tutors and teachers had suffered immensely as they'd watched the disease progress in him. I stood there wondering what to say, and I settled for saying that, at times like these, I wanted to ask God why He had permitted this to happen to Danny. At the same time, that very question was on everyone's mind. I thanked God for allowing Danny to come into our lives, for his short time among us, for his not having to go through any more pain, and for the word we'd been given in Romans 8:28, that "in all things God works for the good of those who love Him, who have been called according to His purpose." Even though we had great difficulty in accepting Danny's death, I had confidence that God works His will for the greater good, and a knowledge that, when we turn to Him in prayer, He will grant us His peace that transcends all understanding.

This is profound to me. We have all sorts of doubts and questions, and we should take them to Him in prayer. He might give us an answer, but if He doesn't, He will give us comfort, and this comfort will transcend any human understanding. There is no explanation that I or anyone else could have offered Danny's family and loved ones.

Certainly the most difficult event of this last year was the passing of Diane's mom in January. She was a great lady and a woman of great faith, who lived her life for God and spoke about Him to everyone she met. She believed that there was something more than the dash that links the dates of a person's birth and death: 1935–1999. Rather than living for that earthly period, she knew that there was something that occurred after the dash that was greater by far.

Her courage was amazing, because she was so sick for so long — legally blind from diabetes, severely asthmatic for many years, and stricken by a heart condition. During the last several months, though, she seemed to know her time was approaching. She told Diane and her sister Betty that she wanted all her children to be there for Christmas because she felt it would be their last one together. Yet she never complained, and someone who didn't know her would never have realized how sick she was. This astounded the doctors who were caring for her. Toward the end, her blood sugar wouldn't register; it was totally off the scale. When that happens, you're usually disoriented if not unconscious, but she was sitting up and talking as if nothing at all was wrong. This illustrated her inner strength and her desire to live. I can't say I understand it, but some people do seem to have that greater will to survive, whereas others give up. She had that will, but when she finally passed it was almost a relief, mingled with bitter disappointment. There were so many things that she didn't get a chance to do. She wanted to see all her grandchildren, but in the last year or two she could not see them clearly. "What if" scenarios are fruitless; whatever happens is God's will. But if it had been my will, I'd have had her do and appreciate a few more things, feel healthy a few more days.

We have some good experiences in this life, but to a large extent it's tough for most of us. Diane's mother had her share of disappointment and loss. She lost her husband brutally and her daughter tragically; both of them were taken from her much too soon. The expression "windblown but not discouraged" applied to her absolutely. When you see someone who lived like that, always with bravery and grace, treating everyone so well, you wish that they could experience more good stuff in life. That was my reaction, and it was heightened because I had the privilege of knowing her. Even though she was my mother-in-law, her wisdom and temperament were almost like a grandmother's. I was encouraged by these qualities, and wanted to assimilate them.

My greatest fear was that when she died, Diane wasn't going to be able to handle it. Her mom was without question her mentor, her hero, the person she looked up to most in life and talked to weekly if not daily, the person she probably considered her best friend in the world. But she exhibited strength I didn't know she had. She handled it so superbly that at one point I thought that the fact hadn't really sunk in. Now, I believe that her mother's passing was to some extent easier than her sister's. It was in a way less tragic, because there was a sense of finality. Mrs. Lee had lived a long life and raised eight kids, all of whom were of age and able to support each other. Now she was tired, and it was time to go home. There was grief among those she left behind, but it was tempered by gratitude for her time among us, and a certainty that she was finally at peace with God.

God calls us to be obedient servants to His will. Too many times, we think this earth is game day, when earth is actually a practice field. Game day is when His son returns. When we're practising down here, we already know we're going to win when game day comes. And unlike practice, game day will last forever. Down here practice is long, and the games are over just like that. But there, practice is short, and the game will continue on and on and never cease; we'll win, we'll be undefeated champions, for God has already given us the victory.

Down here practice can be rough at times. God lets us experience both victory and defeat. Vernette died at age thirty-six; Danny died at fourteen. Loved ones sicken, while love endures; children are taken from us, yet we have more children to love. Just persevere; make it to game day. Sometimes down here you'll be up by a few points, or down by a few. Sometimes you'll be down by a lot. On game day you'll have the victory. That in itself inspires me. God's given us so much in this life. He tells us that He'll never forsake us, never give us more than we can bear.

More than that, He gives us hope, one of the greatest riches we have. I'd rather be poor with infinite hope than rich with no hope any day. There's also a peace that He gives us, a sense of fulfillment that makes our lives complete, and a promise, a wonderful reassurance, that He is a just God. We're all going to get what we deserve, for He has said that we'll receive our just reward in heaven. Knowing this makes losing our loved ones a little easier to bear. It is to me an inexpressible comfort and blessing.

When people ask me about my relationship with God, I tell them what it is not. It's not dogmatic or ritualistic, superficial or rehearsed. It's not concerned with worldly perceptions and convenient labels — what we do on Sunday, what denomination we belong to. It's just me and who I am — what I subscribe to and esteem. When I wake up each morning, I'm making an effort to follow the teachings of Jesus Christ. My relationship with Him is ongoing and maturing — it's falling down and getting back up again. It's what I do every day of my life. I see God every day in everything I do, and when you see me, I hope you see my relationship with God.

14

FAMILY MATTERS

In case you were wondering, I've re-signed for the 1999 season plus an option. This is mainly because of a number of changes that Diane has made to our new house, which we hope will be completed this June. Among these changes are the granite countertop that you can use as a cutting board, which is very much in vogue these days, along with stainless steel appliances for the kitchen and marble in the bath. These two rooms dictate my immediate future.

Delete that paragraph! The real reason is that I don't want to get a real job. Diane and I have learned to live with the pros and cons of the sports lifestyle — the fact that I work six months a year, practise at one o'clock in the afternoon and can be around the house three mornings a week, helping out. There'll come a day when that won't be so easy to accomplish. There's also a degree of flexibility; we can go to Florida to see our families during the winter months. Both of us know that those opportunities may not be as readily available when I'm not playing any more.

Fortunately, it looks as if Diane may be forging a career of her own, and will be able to split the cost of the countertop. She very much wants to pursue singing more seriously than she's done before, with the help of Lloyd Exeter and Doran Major. Gospel music is her great love, and getting into a recording studio is something she enjoys. She's been encouraged in this by many people, and I'm delighted, because (in my unbiased view) she's fantastic. She sang the national anthem at one of our home games, and anybody who can sound good in the Dome has a great future ahead of her. Plus, we won the game. Most important, it's wonderful that she has her own dreams and goals and aspirations.

One reason why we're heading for our new house is that this past September our nephew Demetrious, Diane's sister Vernette's son, came north to stay with us. We very quickly learned that a condominium apartment wasn't the ideal environment for Diane and me, plus a one year old, a four year old, and an eighteen year old — a definite study in contrasts, to be sure.

The first hurdle to overcome was the fact that we'd never enjoyed an intimate and uninterrupted relationship with Demetrious over the years. We hadn't worked out our expectations or defined in our minds his responsibilities. We knew we'd have to face these questions eventually, with Rachel and Raven, but we were out of touch with present-day realities. Nor did we know people with teenagers of their own, who could give us an orientation course.

We don't have all the answers yet, but we've been able to estabish certain guidelines, and stick to them with love. I think that Demetrious understands the motivation behind the instruction, the fact that rules are there to protect, to illustrate authority. We're all learning together, and I for one am finding new humility in the imperfect science of parenting. By my estimation, he's doing great.

By Diane's, he's doing okay. She's a woman of purpose, and change for her doesn't take place nearly as rapidly as it should in any instance. I know that at eighteen he's pretty well molded, and that some things aren't going to change a lot. The majority are good things. The rest, we're working on — but I hope and believe that he understands that regardless of what he does, we love him, and he has nothing to prove. We are in it for the duration. That doesn't mean a year, it means forever.

Has it been easy? No. I have to make it plain to him that I'm not going to let stuff slide because I want to be his friend, or let him let stuff slide because I'm not really his dad. It's been a great challenge, but that's no wonder. Frankie Beverly, my college buddy Reggie Hodnett's favorite musician, used to sing a song titled "Joy in Pain." The lyrics concerned the fact that the source of your pain is the self-same source from which your greatest joys emanate. Certain people are capable of wounding you because you care about them so much. At times, they'll disappoint you, or behave in ways you didn't expect. But sometimes they'll exceed your expectations, and do other things that bring you great delight and satisfaction. That's the way I look at Demetrious. He's required more from us, but at the same time has made our lives more full.

*   *   *

So we'll move on together as a family, ready to get to the next stage in our lives, centered firmly around Toronto as home. We've got two little girls growing up, a young man setting his roots, a new house and a new beginning of sorts. All in all, it promises to be a fascinating time.

As for what I'll be doing to make a living on the football field, Coach Barker always wanted me to take part in the return game; he looked forward to it all season long. We've already had a conversation about this, so even with Eric Blount on the scene, I think I'll be handling a few balls. This will give the team a dual threat, à la the Jimmy Cunningham days. Eric may handle the majority of the punt return duties and I'll augment him on kickoffs. I suppose I see myself returning to the role I played in 1996 and 1997 — the guy who's in the backfield every once in a while rather than most of the time, who catches a lot more passes than he rushes from scrimmage. So in that sense, it looks as if everything old may turn out to be new again.

CAREER STATISTICS

RUSHING

Year	Team	GP	NO	YDS	AVE	LG	TD
1989	Tor.	10	28	134	4.8	23	1
1990abcd	Tor.	16	105	519	4.9	62	4
1991	Tor.	11	64	443	6.9	64	3
1992	Tor.	18	148	572	3.9	20	0
1993a	Tor.	18	89	481	5.4	32	1
1994a	Tor.	16	149	787	5.3	60	3
1995	Tor.	18	181	836	4.6	29	7
1996	Tor.	18	61	286	4.7	23	5
1997ab	Tor.	18	50	315	6.3	47	4
1998	Tor.	16	148	610	4.1	25	3
TOTALS		159	1,023	4,983	4.8	64	31

KICKOFF RETURNS

Year	NO	YDS	AVE	LG	TD
1989	13	356	27.4	45	0
1990	39	831	21.3	51	0
1991	19	216	11.4	23	0
1992	15	295	19.7	38	0
1993	30	604	20.1	41	0
1994	16	317	19.8	40	0
1995	35	706	20.2	63	0
1996	33	883	26.8	72	0
1997	49	1,117	22.8	62	0
1998	8	149	18.7	34	0
TOTALS	257	5,474	20.8	72	0

RECEIVING

Year	NO	YDS	AVE	LG	TD
1989	1	2	2.0	2	0
1990	72	905	12.6	65	8
1991	38	417	11.0	28	2
1992	46	559	12.1	52	5
1993	32	313	9.8	31	3
1994	51	577	11.3	69	2
1995	59	443	7.3	30	4
1996	116	1,268	10.9	52	4
1997	122	1,085	8.9	56	10
1998	93	995	10.7	41	6
TOTALS	630	6,554	10.4	69	44

PUNT RETURNS

Year	NO	YDS	AVE	LG	TD
1989	50	507	10.1	48	1
1990	74	1,045	14.1	92	2
1991	32	440	13.8	94	1
1992	34	279	8.2	32	0
1993	77	716	9.3	79	2
1994	76	671	8.8	90	1
1995	56	470	8.4	44	0
1996	11	145	13.2	49	0
1997	111	1,070	9.6	65	1
1998	10	67	6.7	15	0
TOTALS	531	5,410	10.2	94	8

a – All-East All-Star
b – CFL All-Star, special teams
c – Eastern Division Most Outstanding Player
d – CFL Most Outstanding Player

CLEMONS' ARGONAUT RECORDS
Punt Return Yards (Season) 1,070 in 1997
All-Purpose Yardage (Season) 3,840 in 1997
All-Purpose Yardage (Career) 24,087
Punt Returns (Career) 531
Punt Return Yards (Career) 5,410
Punt Return Touchdowns (Career) 8
Receptions (Season) 122 in 1997
Receptions (Career) 630
Kickoff Returns (Game) 8 at Edm., Aug. 21/91
Kickoff Return Yards (Career) 5,474

CLEMONS' 100-YARD RECEIVING GAMES
114 vs. Edmonton, July 14/90 (10 rec., 1 TD)
107 at Calgary, Aug. 9/90 (10 rec., 1 TD)
100 vs. Calgary, Sept. 20/90 (7 rec.)
130 vs. Hamilton, Sept. 29/90 (6 rec., 2 TD)
112 at B.C., Aug. 11/94 (6 rec., 1 TD)
106 at Saskatchewan, July 26/96 (9 rec.)
126 vs. Ottawa, Aug. 24/96 (10 rec.)
104 at Calgary, Oct. 14/96 (11 rec.)
137 vs. Winnipeg, July 27/97 (10 rec., 1 TD)
118 vs. B.C., Oct 4/97 (15 rec., 2 TD)
112 vs. Calgary, Oct. 18/97 (8 rec., 2 TD)
106 vs. B.C., July 16/98 (6 rec.)
120 vs. Saskatchewan, Oct. 3/ 98 (11 rec.)
106 vs. Montreal, Oct. 12/98 (10 rec.)

CLEMONS' 100-YARD RUSHING GAME
120 at Baltimore, Aug. 20/94 (17 carries, 2 TDs)